Pure Heart, Enlightened Mind

THE LIFE AND LETTERS OF AN IRISH ZEN SAINT

Maura Soshin O'Halloran

EXPANDED WISDOM EDITION

Introduction by Ruth O'Halloran

Illustrations by Beth O'Halloran

WISDOM PUBLICATIONS · BOSTON

Wisdom Publications
199 Elm Street
Somerville, MA 02144 USA
www.wisdompubs.org

Library of Congress Cataloging-in-Publication Data
O'Halloran, Maura, 1955-1982.
  Pure heart, enlightened mind : the life and letters of an Irish Zen saint / by Maura Soshin O'halloran ; introduction by Ruth O'halloran ; illustrations by Beth O'halloran.— Expanded Wisdom ed.
    p. cm.
  ISBN 0-86171-283-8 (pbk. : alk. paper)
  1. O'Halloran, Maura, 1955-1982. 2. Spiritual life—Zen Buddhism. 3. Spiritual biography—Ireland. 4. Spiritual biography—United States. I. Title.
  BQ976.H35A3 2007
  294.3'927092—dc22
  [B]

                                    2007005979

ISBN 0-86171-283-8

11 10 09 08 07
5   4   3   2   1

Wisdom Publications' books are printed on acid-free paper and meet the guidelines for permanence and durability set by the Council of Library Resources.

Cover design by Elizabeth Lawrence. Interior design by Gopa & Ted2, Inc
Lyrics to "Soshin" reprinted by permission of the artist. The song can be heard online at: www.lukabloom.com

Printed in the United States of America

This book was produced with environmental mindfulness. We have elected to print this title on 50% PCW recycled paper. As a result, we have saved the following resources: 44 trees, 31 million BTUs of energy, 3,885 lbs. of greenhouse gases, 16,127 gallons of water, and 2,071 lbs. of solid waste. For more information, please visit our website, www.wisdompubs.org

Contents

Preface

In creating this book, we have struggled to determine how best to present these letters and journals of Maura Soshin O'Halloran. Journals are inherently incomplete things, for the most fundamental issues of a life or an experience are understood by the writer and are often unwritten. Because of this, Maura's journals present us with many questions that remain unanswered—why did she want to study Zen, why did she go to Japan, what elements of her Catholic upbringing led her to Buddhism? We asked Maura's family and the people with whom she studied and, ultimately, the only answers are here in these pages before you. Maura never intended this material to be published. Whatever questions we may have after reading these, her most personal thoughts, are not questions that were most important to Maura. What was important to her was that she become a Zen monk and be able to help other people in some way. This is what mattered to her.

Japanese words are used throughout the text. The first time a Japanese word appears it will be printed in italics with an explanation and placed in the glossary. It will be romanized thereafter.

We wish to acknowledge Ruth O'Halloran's dedication in transcribing her daughter's writings for publication. She was helped by Kate, Jane, Scott, and Beth O'Halloran. I wish to thank Tetsugyu Ban, Tessai-san, and Shiro Tachibana for welcoming me to Kannonji Temple and transmitting to me their love for Maura-san. I am also grateful to Paul

Silverman, Lorette Zirker, and Dai-en Bennage for their insight and editorial guidance.

This book is dedicated to Maura Soshin O'Halloran.

—Michael Kerber

Introduction

BY RUTH O'HALLORAN

In a small Buddhist monastery in northern Japan there stands a statue of a young Irish-American woman who lived there in the early 1980s. During her three years of Zen training in Iwate and Tokyo she was known as Maura-san, or by her monastic name of Soshin-san. She received the transmission of her teacher in 1982 and was killed in a bus accident in Thailand six months later. In 1983, as her mother, I was invited to Japan for the dedication of her Kannon statue, an indication that she had become identified in the minds of local people with the bodhisattva Kannon, the Buddhist saint of compassion.

Her last photo, taken in front of a Japanese temple, shows a tall, blue-eyed, black-robed young woman of twenty-seven, with a radiant smile. How did this daughter of an American mother and an Irish father, educated at convent schools and Trinity College, Dublin, become not only a Zen monk but a Buddhist saint?

Maura O'Halloran was born on May 24, 1955, in Boston, Massachusetts, the eldest of six children. Her father, Fionan Finbarr O'Halloran, was a native of County Kerry, Ireland, and I a native of Maine. When Maura was four years old we moved to Ireland. Her earliest schooling was at Loretto convents in County Dublin. She briefly attended the same school that Mother Teresa had and had hoped to meet her when

Ruth O'Halloran was Maura's mother. She died during the production of this Wisdom edition in 2005 at the age of 77.

she went to India after her travels in Thailand. Maura had expressed an intention of doing work similar to Mother Teresa's, among the poor of Dublin.

We returned to Boston in 1966, living in suburban Waban while my husband did graduate work in civil engineering at M.I.T. He was killed in a road accident in 1969 and the entire family returned to Dublin in 1970.

In her journal, Maura never mentions the fact of her birth and youth in Boston, but her New England background, and especially her grandmother in Maine, contributed as much to her formation as did her fourteen years in Ireland. Her position as the eldest child, flung into the role of second parent to five younger siblings at her father's sudden death, hastened a maturity that few adolescents experience.

After receiving high honors in her Leaving Certificate from her secondary school in Ireland, she gained early acceptance at Trinity College, Dublin, where she matriculated in 1973. In 1975 she received Ireland's highest scholastic award, which provided for all her educational expenses. While in college she did much volunteer social work, especially with drug addicts and the very poor of Dublin. She spent the summer of 1976 at the Rudolph Steiner School in Glencraig, Northern Ireland, where she cared for autistic and developmentally disabled children.

Her highly developed sense of the need for social justice sometimes made her impatient with institutional obstacles to human development. This point of view found an outlet in college protests, volunteer social work, union organizing (she antagonized the management of a restaurant in which she worked in Dublin by attempting to organize the staff into a union), and what I can only call a sort of spontaneous poverty. The latter attitude led to such a detachment from material things, especially fashionable clothing, that she often appeared genuinely shabby (years before the vogue for "shabby chic"). She deliberately limited herself to a very stringent budget.

Over her college vacations she made a series of journeys through Greece, Italy, North Africa, France, and the United Kingdom. In the summer of 1977 she returned to the United States and then went to Toronto, Canada, where she worked at several jobs to earn money for cross-continental travel. She drove with friends across Canada, then worked her way down the west coast until she arrived in San Francisco. There she worked at several jobs simultaneously (waitress, hotel desk clerk, telephone operator, and research assistant). She also studied photography and Spanish to prepare for a major trip through Latin America.

Describing this trip, she says:

Starting in April 1978, I traveled through Mexico, Central America, and most of South America, remaining in Cuzco, Peru, for almost five months where I taught English and improved my Spanish. [She also did volunteer work in Cuzco.] My lifestyle while traveling brought me into contact with people from every social level. I hitchhiked, walked, or traveled second-class, as did the Indians. People, from local campesinos *to wealthy hacienda owners, continually showed me hospitality, bringing me to their homes and talking for long hours about their lives, problems, politics, and ambitions.*

She ventured as far south as Punta da Arenas and flew back from Santiago, Chile, arriving in Maine in the midst of a blizzard on Christmas Day 1978.

After a visit with her family, who had moved back to Maine from Ireland earlier in 1978, she went to Boston where she lived in a studio apartment on Bromfield Street while working at a Cambridge restaurant to finance her proposed trip to the Orient. In Boston she became active in the anti-nuclear movement and continued her study of photography, which culminated in a one-man show of her work in 1979. Her interest in Japan had been aroused by the enthusiasm of the family's old friend and solicitor in Ireland, Frank Sweeney, and by her own long-term interest in meditation. In our Dublin home in the early 1970s one often came upon her in some corner, sitting in the lotus position, calmly centered within herself, oblivious to phone, TV, and family. She had the ability to focus cheerfully and totally on whatever she did, and I have no doubt that this was partly the result of her habit of meditation.

In Boston, where Maura was born, or in Dublin, where she spent her youth and college years, little was known about her experience as a Zen monk until a documentary of her life, *Maura: A Japanese Journey,* was produced for Irish national television in 2002. This film was based principally on the English-language edition, published in 1994, of the journals and letters she wrote during her three-year stay in Japan. The original edition of *Pure Heart, Enlightened Mind,* has been translated into German, Dutch, Italian, French, and Japanese.

Because of continued interest in my daughter, I have, with the help of my family, assembled this new edition containing much material omitted from the original book. Since Maura had no intention of publishing her daily notes, she often used Japanese terms which could be confusing for the reader, so we have included a glossary translating these words. Several additional letters are included in this new edition.

Shortly before she left Japan in 1982, Maura completed the first chapter of a novel based on her own life, only slightly fictionalized. This entertaining account of a young Western woman's introduction to Japanese monastic life supplements her journals and should give readers a vivid insight into daily life in a Zen monastery. A letter from the friends in Bangkok with whom she stayed before boarding the bus to Chiang Mai has also been appended. They describe her last few days in Thailand.

Her last month of living in America was September 1979, which she spent writing, reading, and thinking in her Aunt Anne's lakeside cottage in much-loved Wayne, Maine. After a week spent with friends in San Francisco, she flew to Hawaii and then to Tokyo.

Her journals and letters take the narrative from this point. The following are excerpts from the notebooks and journals kept by Maura O'Halloran during the period of her three years' training in Zen at Toshoji Temple in Tokyo and Kannonji Temple in Iwate Prefecture, Japan, 1979–1982. The roshi of these temples is Tetsugyu Ban.

The Writings of
Maura Soshin O'Halloran

∽

Prelude

NOVEMBER 1979

Dear Family,

Well, the luck of the Irish stayed intact across the international dateline, and I'm doing great. Sure and begorra, let me tell you the tricks.

First off, I arrive in Honolulu at two in the morning and I'm exhausted and bleary-eyed (having, of course, been up with friends in San Francisco most of the night before). So I try to find somewhere to lay my head before trying to track down cousin Ed. I ended up under a palm tree amidst all these bushes, crooking myself in and out of its sinuous roots. Hardly the Hilton, but it does till dawn. Then stumbling and staggering, I phone a million different numbers only to find that cousin Ed is out at sea. At that stage I'd do anything for a bit of sleep, and that's where my next adventure begins.

When you picture me in Hawaii, do you see me in a bikini on Waikiki Beach, sipping piña coladas? Try envisioning me in a sari, at a Hare Krishna temple, explaining how to make Irish potato bread. That's it. In the airport I got chatting with a girl named Nancy, a recent convert who'd do anything for Krishna, including giving shelter to a poor Irish waif. Well, I ended up there for nearly a week, scrubbing pots and cooking in exchange for my keep. And did I learn a lot about the Krishnas! (To get away, I had to pretend I was leaving for one of their other temples.) They dressed me up in a sari and proceeded to try to convert me. We got up every morning at 3:00 A.M. for service and a Bhagavad Gita lesson. This involved singing, dancing, chanting, and making offerings to the deities—all very pretty, but at three in the morning I was less than enthused. Then we go off to chant our rounds before the sunrise, 16 rounds of 109 beads, each one requiring "Hare Krishna, Hare Krishna, Krishna, Krishna, Hare, Hare, Hare Rama, Hare Rama, Rama, Rama, Hare, Hare." Now let me hear you say that fast 1,744 times (before breakfast). I developed the knack of curling up in a little niche in the largest banyan tree in Hawaii and grabbing a bit of a snooze.

They start from the premise that the world is a place of misery, is an illusion—*maya*—a mere unsatisfactory reflection of the real and wonderful world in which Krishna dwells. In order to free themselves from endless reincarnations, they seek to deny themselves any sense of gratification, sublimating all pleasures for the desire to be with Krishna. So if I point out a magnificent sunset sky, I'm told that the color of Krishna's robe is more glorious. I try to smell a flower but I'm stopped as it hasn't yet been offered to Krishna. There they were in a mini-paradise, Hawaii, and couldn't even enjoy it. The air was positively perfumed and soft and warm. The sun was a huge orb and everywhere grew lush tropical plants, flowers, and fruits. They'll never convince me that I'm in misery.

They must have thought me an awful agent of evil and seduction, judging from the things they corrected me on. One poor guy was caught talking to me. That occasioned two lectures as the men in saffron aren't allowed to talk to women. I wore my sari too short (I was afraid it would fall off so I rolled it in well). I shouldn't have let the veil fall off my head while I scrubbed the pots. I was told not to smile when talking to the men! That was modified to an intriguing request not to smile "that way." The funniest of all was when we were sitting down in the temple and I was told to cover my feet. Can you imagine my club feet being so provocative as to cause a devotee one uneasy thought?

My sense of humor became strained, though, when they started the line that women were of a lower order than men. Women should be married or they were like lost sheep unable to fend for themselves. I had a retort or two for that. Yet they were lovely people and kind and good, if a little misguided. And they certainly helped me when I needed it. What was really amusing was dancing out in the streets with them. The reactions were hilarious.

But I got away.

I had been thinking of changing my ticket to Japan and spending time on one of the remoter islands, but when I got to the airport I couldn't be bothered with the hassle. So on I got and a stroke of luck that was, too. When I landed in Tokyo, on an off-chance I tried the number of a friend of a friend from Boston. It was one of those dodgy numbers with a question mark and a smudge. I couldn't believe it when a friendly American voice answered at the other end. She was leaving for the States that afternoon so said I could sleep in her place until Friday when the girl downstairs is leaving and I can have her place until January! Well, I could hardly believe it. If I'd arrived any sooner, there wouldn't have been room at her place. Any later, and I would have missed her.

Her place really is tiny. She shares with another very nice American. It's a doll's house, a two room affair. The sitting-room furniture gets moved at night for the mattresses to be pulled out. Most Japanese really have no room to entertain. The table is interesting. It's about a foot and a half off the ground but has a quilt attached all around with a heater underneath, so your legs keep cozy. And they really do have those Japanese baths; I'm just over a long, luxurious soak.

Yesterday I went walking around Tokyo for about eight hours. At first I was horrified by what I saw. The day was overcast and grey, the air smoggy and raw. I started in the business district. Seas of people in grey and navy surged around me like so many uniformed army ants. Their faces were expressionless, seemingly choked by their tight, skinny ties. The city, gutted during the war, was modern and bleak; the only relief from the grey was the assault of neon. In my best Japanese accent I could only think "Yuck!" I contemplated a speedy packing and exit.

Then, fortunately, I meandered into neighborhoods where rigor mortis had not set in and people were smiling. I had fun going through streets festooned with paper lanterns and streamers, listening, smelling, and watching. It's funny trying to get anyplace. I sympathize with illiterates because you can't even read street signs. It becomes a treasure hunt of clues wrestled from waving arms and broken English. I'm already learning a lot. The girl I'm staying with has been here a year and a half and is giving me loads of insights. She's doing anthropological work here and has a ton of books on Japan and the Japanese that I'm looking forward to delving into. At the weekend we're going to another town filled with temples and more traditional buildings. It should be fun. She's great and is certainly making things a lot more pleasant for me...

Love, Maura

Part I

Arrival

Wednesday, November 18, 1979

I phone Toshoji Temple. Am met at temple by Tessai-san. He guides me through mounds of mandarin oranges, under the paper lanterns, past the vendor plying sweet potatoes. He says, "You came at a good time—tea time." There are four monks like little boys, laughing, innocent, delighted to see me. I meet the master, Go Roshi. When I was told that I could stay there, I felt as if I had come home, very settled and bursting with happiness. There are no other foreigners yet.

Thursday

I see Ueno Park and great museum. Rodin's "Thinker" sits there looking at a bed of cabbage. I have a job interview. They want to hire me.

Friday

I go to Roppongi. Disappointing. I go for a second job interview. The eejit [idiot] blathers for three hours on nothing. He just wants cute young Caucasians—the other three candidates are better qualified than I but I'm offered the job. I turn it down.

Saturday

I go to the temple. The master can't speak English. They give me my room, four *tatami* mats wide. There's a little desk, cushion, and mattress. We go upstairs to chant. The statues look pagan. I've no idea what I'm getting into. Dinner is disastrous. We kneel around benches. There is a precise way to do everything, a million bows. Silence. The damn egg roll is so big and greasy that I can't pick it up. I'm behind the others, gobbling, trying to catch up. The voice of the master shatters the silence. "You eat slowly." I don't know if it's a comment or a command. I take it as the latter and relax and am grateful that the one thing he said was so right.

Sunday

They told me they didn't begin until six on Sundays but they'd already started when I arrived at six. I didn't know what to do. I knelt in the darkness outside Go Roshi's door. As he comes out he smiles and beckons me into the hall. After breakfast, he asks me if I've completed university and how did I know of the temple. He asks me if I'm willing to shave my head, and to beg *[takuhatsu]*. I say okay. He jumps up and springs from the room. I thought he'd gone for the razor but he comes back with robes. I model them and everyone laughs with child-like delight. Tomorrow will be my ceremony. I'll get my new name.

I'm late again. I understand nothing, can only watch. I watch as the sun's broad band creeps slowly across the black, glinting on the ivory, catching each monk, one by one. Taro is always at peace. Tenno won't smile. Takeo holds his stomach, tears pricking his eyes.

We do more cleaning. It seems interminable. I sweep outdoors. My bare feet, pink from cold, look wrong peeping from the wooden sandals. I feel wrong behind the whisking bamboo twigs. I cannot understand or be understood.

The afternoon is better. We chat and laugh a bit. They confer for the right word, tell me they are glad I'm here. I love them.

Monday

My ceremony. I am named Soshin. I like it. It rhymes with Oisin, a name that has always intrigued me. The others had been given names like "iron wolf" or "iron ship," so I was surprised at how beautiful my name was. It was variously translated as "great enlightenment," "simple mind," or "warm/open/frank heart." I'll gladly take any version. I'm to go to Morioka in January to beg. They keep teasing that I'll be famous on TV. I really enjoyed sawing wood. The monks are not at all sexist. I'm totally "one of the lads" in dress, behavior, and treatment. I'd love to be as peaceful and vibrant as Go Roshi. I do wish I could understand him.

Tuesday

My mind wanders so when I do *zazen* [sitting meditation]. A *gaijin* [foreigner] came, named Frederick. He's been traveling around the world but is still very German. At first I really wanted him to stay but then I realized that I am happier surrounded by only these wonderful Japanese. They are good and pure and simple. Eshin's gentle child's face is so unspoiled, totally without guile. He's loading me with lessons. I hope he tires a bit. Frederick made me glad I wasn't on the outside—there's so much distracting nervousness there.

But I was cold. Bare feet on bare boards. The wind rises between the cracks, and it will get worse. For a little while, trying to be with the cold, I enjoyed it, a nice skin-tensing sensation. Brisk. But, oh my feet!

Wednesday

I finally had a really good meditation. For a few moments my mind stopped its incessant chattering and I was down very deep.

In the morning I felt restless with thoughts of how long I should stay, should I go elsewhere, will I be very old before going back to my own world? In the evening there is meditation and service. I feel very high. We had a banquet afterwards, with saké to drink. I look at these men, laughing, enjoying, knowing. Like the old men in pubs at home, they drink through the grey curls of smoke. They are simple men, kneeling long hours on a cushion, leading spartan lives, but they are no Himalayan hermits. They drink and revel. It would be a good and wonderful thing to grow old like these men.

Thursday

An ancient man, a great master, Dai Achukyo Chitana Songi, comes to pay his respects to Go Roshi. Two women help him hobble up the steps. I gasp in awe and reverence, "He's beautiful." Tetsuro repeats my exclamation and another visiting senior motions for me to follow. We sit, the six of us, in Go Roshi's snug reception room. I feel so privileged. I can't understand a word. The others serve us. I can only watch this man, the power, wisdom, and dignity he exudes.

Jiko gives me a present of a gold-colored harp being strummed by a ringleted maiden in an evening gown. "That's you," he says. I'm touched. His name means "sunny." He's always trying out awkward English idioms, like "It's all Greek to me." His face crinkles when he smiles, a Peter Pan. He spends long hours copying chants into *romaji* [Roman characters] for me.

At the service I feel very high, can't stop smiling. At tea-time the Zen Society gathers and I'm briefly questioned about my intentions.

Jiko tells me I'm to be Go Roshi's jewel. I'm elated. About one meditation a day seems to be a good one.

Today I had my first real *dokusan* [interview with Roshi about one's practice]. (I went before but had no interpreter.) Go Roshi gave me the *koan** of *mu*. Nothingness. Only mu. I become filled with mu. ["Mu" literally means "not," from the renowned koan in which the master answers "mu" to the question of whether a dog has Buddha nature. This is often the first or primary koan engaged by Zen students.]

The interpreter and Tetsuro call me to their room. They have both attained enlightenment. They question me about my motives and knowledge. All the time my pulse beats "nothingness, nothingness." Poems have come to me between the beats of mu.

Cathy-san was enlightened in three years, one priest in a year. I need not wait for old age, just follow Go Roshi. I have total faith in him. He can see inside me. He has the strength to kill my ego so that I can be free.

---

*A koan is a verbal puzzle that points to ultimate truth. Many koans have been handed down from teachers in early Chinese Zen Buddhist periods, but all masters in all ages find material at hand for teaching. They are studied in various ways according to the teacher, sometimes during zazen.

"Without fail," he says, "you will attain enlightenment." I can scarcely contain myself. "Nothingness, nothingness." It's like a jungle drum beating through my veins, but I must fight for it. I sleep in a frenzy. I keep awakening hearing "Nothingness, nothingness."

Saturday

I work to mu. I hate the interruption of talking because slowly through the day and its idle chatter, nothingness slips. I meditate three times. My body. Inside and all around is nothing. No thing. No separation. A geyser in a lake appears to be a separate thing but is the lake. In the morning there is question-time. I ask Go Roshi the meaning of enlightenment. He strikes me. Not hard. When you are hit, you feel pain.

Sunday

Ice cubes in a glass seem separate, have form. The sun shines; where have the ice cubes gone? Nothing has been taken away. Their separateness is only form and only apparent, a temporary, illusionary state. Plants have consciousness. If there is reincarnation, and we are reincarnated as plants, our consciousness would be different, i.e., that of a plant. Our present body does not continue. Our consciousness changes with the form. Thus there is nothing left of the ice cube. We are all nothingness.

Another week

I told Takeo-san my answer. He said I was enlightened. Wonderful!

Jiko and I went to the English bookstore. I couldn't contain my joy, looking at the dead people, thinking of nothingness.

I went to dokusan. I was determined not to be tricked into using words. Words give form, apparent substance, to nothingness. Roshi asked me what was mu. I said "nothingness." He hit me. What do I feel? I was about to say pain but due to my resolution to avoid words, I said "nothingness." "Continue," he said. I had reached my answer through logic. He was right. Think only of mu, nothing else. Don't study Japanese or sit in the corridor—only mu.

At the English bookstore, all the conflicting theories of Zen and schools had confused and upset me. I bought a book I already had but then refused to read it. Words. I want to know from inside.

The days went on, full of mu. I avoided the others' company, stopped laughing and only thought of mu. At times it drove me crazy—mu, mu, rattling in my brain, not allowed to think of anything else. I jump up and throw it out, annoyed. Other times I go down, down, down with it, down beneath words where my breath is gentle. Like looking up through the lake and the surface is a sentence and I'm below. Gentle at times. Quiet. A little smile slipping across my face. Sometimes I sit an hour and a half before there's five minutes of calm. At times I'm so happy, other times so vexed with my trivial mind.

Sunday evening

Takeo suggested how I should breathe. I tried and gradually got more and more excited. Mu rose vibrating up my spine, exploded in my head. Everything was simple. I was laughing. Mu was only mu. I felt ecstatic, couldn't contain my joy. I ran out of the hall, kissed the trees, stood in the garden and was the garden, really was it. All through dinner I beamed. Jiko kept staring. The others had described enlightenment. This was so much stronger. I didn't meditate that night, only lay wrapped snug in bed, listening to the rain.

Several of Maura's friends have shared letters that they received from her while she was in Japan. Because she knew her letters home would be read widely by young and old alike, she was quite cirumspect in what she wrote to us. However, writing to her college friends she could be more forthright.
—Ruth O'Halloran

(undated)

Dear Sean [a classmate from Trinity College, Dublin],

Tokyo is hideous, a swarming smear of black and navy. They're worka-holics, living in rabbit warrens. It's a dignified but degrading imitation of the States...So stemming from Golden Gate mushrooms and my con-tempt for contemporary Japan I've ended up in a Zen monastery, a haven of antiquity in this sprawling megalopolis. The monks are lovely, simple men. It's a very different life here, good for the time being, though it's too early to really judge the worth of zazen...

Have a good Christmas, Sean.

Toshoji, Tokyo
December 12, 1979
Dear Family,

...my heart will be with you so think of me at Christmas. There'll be no plum pudding here. Bean cakes are nice, though.

I was settling in nicely to Tokyo life, met a few people and had loads of work opportunities. But I realized I was only meeting gaijin and all the foreigners form a little clique with an occasional Japanese girlfriend or boyfriend. I was speaking no Japanese and wasn't attracted by the cul-ture, so I've taken a leap into real Japan, and ancient Japan at that! I'm living at Toshoji temple and get room and board in exchange for some cleaning every day, and I'm learning zazen. I'm the only woman and only foreigner studying here.

When I arrived at the Togoshi Koen station, I phoned the temple, and they said someone would come down to meet me. I stood up straight, expecting to be greeted by some quiet, dignified old abbot. Next thing, I jump backwards as a bicycle hurtles at me. Billows of black leap and land at my feet as Tetsuro-san straightens his glasses, catches his breath, and welcomes me. At the temple, it's tea-time, and the monks, sitting on the floor, are laughing and smoking and not looking at all austere. They all try out their high-school English and laugh even more. They're lovely, like great big kids, full of fun. I've yet to see one even vaguely vexed. They all chipped together and bought a linguaphone set so that they could talk to me better. So I keep getting "Would you like another glass of soda?" or "Take these suitcases to our room, please."

Each day starts at five o'clock. I wash my face by the light of the moon. I have my own room with four tatami mats and my own little outhouse. The food is good. Our staples are rice and seaweed, but the cook is really talented. Monastery life is certainly a change. I've never done so much bowing in my life. There's a very exact protocol, especially during meals, of bowing and joining hands as if in prayer. They must think I'm very polite because now I just bow at every pause. That way I figure I'm covered.

At times I feel like a cow in labor. You see, my koan is mu, and I'm supposed to bellow this (discreetly, where necessary) at every available opportunity. I scared the wits out of the poor cook, who thought the noise was her cat being brutalized.

So I'm happy, healthy, and out of mischief. Imagine, me in bed by nine every night! And cleaning every day. That's not as bad as I feared. I even clean voluntarily. Can you believe that? They have a wonderful cleaning agent here. We use it on floors, sinks, windows, metal, you name it. Elbow grease. That's it. Not even mops. Everything is done with rags and water.

The place is totally non-sexist. I half expected to be pointed toward the kitchen but I saw wood and move furniture with the best of them. And no condescending "Didn't she do well?" It's just taken for granted. I'm totally "one of the lads," except I'm not bald. Next month we go up to the north of Japan, to Iwate Prefecture, to do begging. That should be an experience, begging in the snow. They say it's very beautiful there. I'm looking forward to seeing some countryside…

Love, M.

Monday morning

Christmas Eve: I go to dokusan. "How have you apprehended mu?" Mu is mu. I'm smiling, happy, not at all nervous, still elated. "Continue!" The bell goes ting-a-ding-ding. I'm dismissed.

I felt crushed. He didn't know. Didn't he know? How could he know? But I knew. Damn. It was Christmas eve. I was cold, and sick of *soji* [temple cleaning], afraid that Tenno thought I wasn't doing enough, so from guilt I was working more. Hating the guilt. Thinking of home and family and how long I'd be stuck doing stupid, menial cleaning and with no enlightenment.

Tears prick my eyes. Juro and Eshin, like mother hens, tend me. I sit in Eshin's tiny, dark, freezing hole, wrapped tight in his wool kimono, listening to music. I try to really listen, to stop words. I don't do any soji and wonder what Tenno thinks. Roshi buys a Christmas cake, the cook buys champagne, and they give me a party. Five monks huddled around wooden benches. When we sing we see our breath. The green plastic holly and frosting tree look odd on the strawberry cream cake. They light the candles. Don't all Western cakes have candles? I wait for them to burn down. They toast me and cheer me. Jiko writes out "The Song of Wandering Aengus" on a subway map. It's not Christmas, but it's the Christmas spirit. They gave me a real lift.

Christmas day, like any other day. Even the post office is open. I decide monastery life is not for me. I love life too much to lock myself away. Maybe six months, a good chance to work on myself. It seems my experience of "enlightenment" was as good as Tetsuro's yet Roshi does not accept it. I remember the book says that Rinzai and Soto [the two main sects of Japanese Zen; Maura trained in Soto] both produce the same effect, so I decide to hell with koans. I'll work on breathing, mental silence, and really being here now. I felt much better. Tetsuro has said several times how hard I work. It's not so, but it relieves my nagging guilt. Zen is very important to me. I think I'll leave by summer but continue to study Zen when I get to Paris.

These men are wonderful. They show me such genuine warmth and love that I'm thriving. At first I took Go Roshi at his word and thought only mu. I wouldn't talk to anyone, dampened myself down. I felt I was going mad. The only variation from day to day was what was on the blue saucer for dinner. Now I'm not so extreme, but maybe it's necessary to go a little crazy to break the ego. Or maybe that's "Zen sickness."

It feels funny to be in my long black robes, darting through the traffic on a sunny bicycle day or waltzing with Jiko in a department store.

Was so still I could feel my heart beat and it was the clock ticking on the wall.

I make it. Making consists of it and me. It and me are one in making.

I tried an experiment to silence my internal chatter, made the running commentary relevant. There is blue, there is smoking, there is sweeping, swish, swish. It made things much richer.

Roshi gave me more clothes. He said my heart was pure. I gave everyone little New Year presents. After dinner, in English, Roshi spoke into the silence. "Very good present, thank you." He bows deeply. I laugh deeply.

New Year's Eve party: These little monks know how to have fun. Here am I, my friends all monks—it seems strange. I sang "Auld Lang Syne." It's the first time I've sung alone in public and not cared. Little by little I'm gaining understanding, though my meditations have been very shallow.

I want to be a Zen master.

Part II

Takuhatsu

(BEGGING) 1980

Kannonji Temple, Iwateken

January 6, 1980

Funny about my age. Go Roshi's son thought I was thirty. I looked in the mirror and I looked thirty. When I came to here to *Kannonji* [country temple in Iwate Prefecture, owned by the roshi], they say I look a teenager. I look in the mirror and I look like a teenager.

Sometimes mu is so beautiful. Kneeling on the bare boards, by the warmth of the wood stove, the day is a grey, snowy twilight. I'm mixing the soup around and around, brown into a foam, around and around. Breathing deeply and softly, a mu, I feel peace.

Five in the morning zazen. *Sutras*, and our breath puffs steam-engine billows of icy vapor. I look at these men, their hard, kind faces, and I love them. I then look at the old woman, bent double, who for the past ten years (since she gave the land on which Kannonji was built) has hobbled over to the temple every morning for *sutra* [the teachings of the Buddha, chanted in temple services]. A bare silhouette in the pre-dawn light, bent over her cane, she shuffles through the snow. And before breakfast we are out shoveling the virgin white, and I don't even mind. Rice and soup, plain and hearty.

Takuhatsu, layer upon layer of clothes, sometimes ten, with our begging bowls and bells we walk slowly through the streets of Morioka, through the snow and sleet, in straw sandals, bells ringing, chanting. The

MAURA BEGGING IN THE SNOW. MORIOKA, JAPAN.

little old women slide open the panel on their doors, drop a coin in a bowl and stand, with bent head and long apron, waiting for a monk's blessing. Sometimes they gasp in surprise when they see me—a woman, a gaijin. When I walk, just walk, chanting, not wondering what time it is or watching the doors, I am very happy.

Riko-san is very hard and very good, a man of precious metal. He walks through the snow storms to get me warm clothes. He teaches me in simple broken English about Buddhism. He is simple and pure and has no doubts. So too is his wife. I love her. A temple woman asked in wonder whether I was a boy or a girl, then brought her child to kneel before me and kept taking my hands to kiss them. I wonder what she was saying.

There's been much fuss since I was interviewed on TV and in the newspaper. Now people point to me, want to put their offerings in my bowl, children follow me on the street. In jest, Taro-san calls me a goddess, Buddha of the caravan. Silly, because the fuss is on account of my being foreign and female.

The devout women of Morioka invite us to lunches. Oh, such food! They never eat with us—probably couldn't afford to—but reverently wait outside the room. With tears in their eyes they thank us for the privilege of serving us. I watch them on their knees bowing and feel weird to be in this role, especially in another culture from my own. At one luncheon it was decided that I had a Japanese face. Of course my face is as Irish as turf but it's all part of their acceptance of me. Several people have said that I don't seem Western. In South America I didn't feel estranged either; they said I seemed Latin. Quién sabe?

The woman in the fish shop served us hot saké and rice. It's warming, after hours in the snow. All around lie the bodies of fish, bodies heaped on bodies, with gaping eyes and mouths. I no longer want to eat fish. I wouldn't catch one myself. Shellfish and eggs I can handle. But then I eat fish for lunch because I eat what's given me.

January 13, 1980
Dear Family,
Happy birthday to my favorite brother in this whole world. Wish I could be with you. You've gone and grown up behind my back. Hope you like school and you're not showing off too much with all A's. An A- here or there would be good for the other kids. Right?

How was the Christmas for yis? I missed you. Christmas Eve was very cold and glum without a sprig of holly or a sniff of turkey. I was feeling decidedly on the wrong side of the Pacific. Word went around the monastery that I was down in the dumps, and they all rallied round. One monk did my chores for me. Another one wrapped me in a big woolen coat (it was freezing), popped headphones on me and played tapes, his prize being hymns from Notre Dame. The abbot went out and bought a "Christmas cake" and the cook bought champagne. They were going to give me a Christmas party. Well, it was the funniest looking Christmas party I ever saw. Five monks and the cook huddled in the cold around four wooden benches. The plastic tree and yule log looked strange sitting on a "Christmas cake" of whipped cream and fresh strawberries. They lit birthday candles on the cake. Don't all western cakes have candles? But they didn't know what to do with them so they turned off the lights and patiently waited for the candles to melt down. Then they played

"Silent Night" in Japanese and took turns singing English songs. Then Tetsuro-san leaps to his feet in full monk's regalia, hips swinging, and in choppy Japanese accent he does his rendition of Elvis Presley. Then there was "Home, home on the lange." Great cheer all around, though you could see everyone's breath as each sang his song. The party ended at 8:00; we all had to be up at 4:30. It wasn't quite Christmas, but it was certainly the Christmas spirit.

All the while there was the build-up to going begging this month. A couple of days before we were to leave for the north, one of the monks came to my room with an armful of bandages.

I asked what they were for. "Your wounds," he replied solemnly. We both consulted our dictionaries to make sure bandages and wounds were the right words. They were. I closed the door and wondered just what I'd let myself in for this time. I felt as if I was going off to war.

I've hit the news again. Aren't you glad it's not a demonstration this time? Everyone was amazed at a girl and a foreigner going begging. It looks hard, walking for hours through the snow in straw sandals (with socks), chanting and ringing a bell. "Severe training for a boy," they say, "but for a girl?" and their slanted eyes widen. So they interviewed me on TV; then the newspaper for this prefecture came around. I don't know what they wrote. The reporter couldn't speak English, so one of the monks told him all about me. Suddenly I had a public. People in buses would wave and point; children followed me in the street; people chased me to put money in my bowl. Today the newspaper came round again. There was such a response that they want another article.

It's funny, the begging isn't bad at all. I wear literally ten layers of clothes and once the fingers and toes are numb, you don't feel a thing. It's nice walking through the streets singing at the top of your lungs. It's like going Christmas caroling every day. Then the little wooden door rattles and slides across and an old woman, bent over, clutching her shawl, shuffles in the snow to drop whatever she can in your bowl, then bends her head reverently waiting for the blessing I can't give.

Most days families from the town invite us to lunch. It's a big occasion for them and they go all out. We wear our ceremonial dress. They put a feast before us. I'm trying all kinds of Japanese delicacies I could never have afforded otherwise. They're on their knees pouring out their thanks to us again and again for coming to their home. If you could see the old women with tears rising to their eyes, holding the abbot's gown and thanking him. It's so strange to be in this respected position. I'm not used to it in my own culture, let alone this one. Fellows my own age passing in the street who normally would try to chat me up instead join their hands as if to pray and bow deeply. All the while I'm trying to keep a straight face.

This amulet that I'm enclosing was especially commissioned by the abbot for you. It is a New Year's blessing to bring health and happiness to the home. On the right is our name, on the left is the temple and the monk that wrote it (the same one that did Elvis on Christmas Eve). They say it should be hung in a special place.

When you mentioned coming to Japan, I must say, selfishly, I'd love you to come over; it'd be great to see you, but in fact if you're going to spend the money you'd get better value anywhere else. Prices are ridiculous. $20.00 for a steak, $13.00 for a melon, $1.50 for a cup of coffee…it's all true. But then you could eat tofu and mandarins and drink green tea instead. Little was left of old Japan after the war; now it's mostly ugly concrete rabbit warrens, but for me it's grand because I'm living in thirteenth-century Japan and it's fascinating. But I must say, of all the countries I've been to, modern Japan would be low on my list of "must come back to's." However, I'd still like to see ya.

Love, M.

Kannonji Temple,
February 1980
It was *daikan* [great cold]. The great, coldest, coldest weeks of the year, coldest prefecture of the country. Go Roshi was delighted that I wasn't used to the cold—better training. I told the temperature by whether the offerings were frozen or not, and often they were. So, wiping a metal cup the cloth would freeze on. Washing in the morning isn't cracking the skin of ice on the basin but taking a blunt instrument and bashing it. Perhaps the hardest part was not the takuhatsu itself but sutras in the morning.

Up and run to the little wood stove in the kitchen. A few minutes respite from the cold, then into *zendo* [meditation hall]. I was first, sitting alone in the predawn dark. The rustling of the robes to the rhythm of running feet, and the bell rings; wood resounds a dull thud. Slowly incense wafts through zendo. I am more asleep than awake, struggling to incarnate, meditations usually frazzled. Tekan-san's cushion always there, so I wonder if he already sat. Tessai, Tessan, and Jiko-san all gurgle, splash, spit toothpaste, then drift in one by one. Tachibana Sensei [the village high school English teacher] and his ten-year-old son. Could I, can I ever do that, lead a layman's life and still attend to my meditations?

From zendo into *hondo* [hall for chanting and teaching] where it's even colder. Sutra clouds of frozen breath. At the end, if I have the control to touch my baby fingers together for obeisances, then I'm glad the day is so warm. Sutra ends and we scurry, run, laughing in the darkness, dashing towards the warmth of the hearth.

Jiko-san, chafing his hands together *"Itai, itai"* ["That hurts!"] through the chattering of his teeth; Katsuko-san, round, cuddly dumpling, smiles sympathetically; Tessai announces the temperature. I squat among the sticks, my long robes flowing carelessly across them, huddled over the stove, warming my hands and watching the red flickering in the slit. Hypnotizes. Soji for breakfast. Soji—we run, bare feet seem to stick, slightly frozen, to the tatami. We sweep out the snow where it has drifted in the cracks, laughing all the while, more to keep warm than from amusement.

Breakfast is hearty. I hold high my rice bowl, blue bears dance across it. The kerosene fire glows warmly in its ceramic reflection. The rice steam curls mu and I am at peace and thankful.

Crossing through the snow in the dawn twilight, I look at the stars. Some days I'm happy, skipping, tingling, other days muttering, promising myself never again, consoling myself—I love you, Maura, you can do it, Maura; it's only X more days—wanting to linger in bed with a cup of coffee, or just once to sleep later than 4:30. I add a couple of sweaters and a kimono, then carry back my takuhatsu gear to the breakfast room. There, with Tekkan-san, I dress, Katsuko-san puttering around, kindly warming damp socks, straightening a belt or fold. Tekkan-san often seems gruff, "Noooo, this way" pulls, pushes, tightens my clothes, pulls my kimono firmly across my chest, just a straightforward arrangement of clothes. Then a few minutes' space before we have to leave, a quiet time. I sit, trying to be empty, to only sit. Sometimes in simple English, with many pauses Tekkan-san would tell me something about Buddha, about life, or read sutra with me. "You must learn to read Buddhist book," he says.

Part III

Tokyo

Toshoji, Tokyo, February 21, 1980

Yesterday I bought books. I read about mu, read that mu is not a mantra, don't just repeat mu but struggle with *What is mu?* I went upstairs to zendo mu. I am mu. I am nothing, nothing, nothingness. I do not exist (though I do). But nothing, absolutely nothing. Something trembled near my eyes. I wept, lay down on the tatami and wept huge, heaving tears. I was nothing, my dreams, my hopes, my conceits were nothing. I cried funeral tears. I was at my own funeral and no one else had come. It was crying and crying and crying and…

Downstairs, it was time to make toast. Tetsuro-san asked what was wrong. I am nothing, and it's very hard and very sad and tears pricked. "*Honto?* ["Really?" / "Is that true?"] You are near enlightenment. You must go to dokusan." I know I'm not near enlightenment but I would like to go to dokusan. I do mu, a deep total mu. Afterwards my vocal cords hurt. Roshi says keep with mu 'til *sesshin* [usually an intensive week of zazen] and then I will attain enlightenment. (As for that "will"—try "may.")

After dinner, Roshi says put an ad in the paper for a new cook. He doesn't like my cooking. The fish was too hard (two weeks old, I scraped off the mold), the salad too hearty. It was true. I wasn't that put out. It was true. Tho' I liked cooking, wished it had been good. I felt too drained to really react, to be really hurt. After all the tears, I had heard the shock of Tekkan-san's possible dismissal by the people of Morioka. There seemed to be an enormous web of conflicting saying and thinking. Morioka people had seemed so warm, generous, and appreciative of Tekkan-san, yet the dear little old ladies deftly stabbed him thru the heart. Roshi dismisses us; the others say they're always hungry but grumble about too much food. I am tired, little sleep, and I am nothing—exhausted, spent. And Jiko-san says, "You are too simple and too honest." And for that time he is right. I can scarcely even feel bewildered, only wash the dishes and go to bed.

You must struggle with a koan, fight with it and for it. My energy in mu is renewed asking, What is it? Getting up in the morning is one of the hardest things for me. So I will get up even earlier and go to hondo and sit.

February 22

> I was not born
> will not die
> for I am
> nothing
> but please do not
> stand on my
> toe.

If mu is mind, consciousness, it is nothing. I am always changing—not a thing. I am not the same person as ten years ago, or a moment ago, yet I am. But then where is I? A fish has the consciousness of a fish. I have the consciousness of a twentieth-century woman and no one before has had my consciousness. Where is rebirth? Consciousness changes. If reborn as a fish, I am a fish, not Maura, but a fish. Consciousness changes. Action and reaction, like a seal stamped on sand. Nothing is transferred but the processes continue. Energy cannot be created or destroyed, only transformed. What is dead and what alive? He said, first and last thoughts. Makes sense. Plants and animals think. Has a stone consciousness? Is it conscious? If consciousness is energy, all form is, not has, consciousness. If we all are not havemind...huh?...what?...hmmm. Are things *mu* [nothing] and *u* [something; existence]? Waves on the ocean are separate but the same. When the wave subsides it doesn't disappear, cease to exist, but does. It is no longer the wave but the ocean which is what it was anyway. Isn't that death? And mu is u and Joshu can say the dog has no Buddha nature.

Dinner was almost a fiasco. Jiko-san, at the last moment, added sauce and soothed my laments.

Does the first thought mean the beginning of a new life because thought is separation?

Roshi asked Jiko-san to place the ad [for a new cook]. He keeps changing his mind. He apologized and asked us to cook for a while, saying it's good to have cultivators in *tenzo* [chief cook of a monastery, a highly respected position], then changes. Jiko and I were sitting eating the brown rice glue that we have dubbed *jiko-mochi* [type of pounded rice dumpling or cake] and I love, I saying the only thing I like more than tenzo is the garden. I didn't look forward to the hours of dusting the clean altars I dusted the day before. Then Tessan-san tells me my new job will be the garden. I can't believe it; I'm overjoyed.

Form is emptiness. It is never the same, always changing, so doesn't exist, is mu, but bang into the wall, of course form is form.

My life force is always being passed into new forms. Each cell born in my body contains my life force and each one that dies is dead. Is it so strange that it passes into a new body? Yet there is no "it." Nothing is transferred. It's the same with cells. I'm having a lot of trouble with this death-rebirth business. It's incredible. Cells divide. Then each one knows what to do. All the minute things, another me, all functioning. Miraculous.

The thing to which I am most attached, can least give up, least admit its transience, is myself.

February 25

I get up and go to zendo at 4:00. Not so hard. Sitting alone, trying the new mu that Jiko-san has taught me. It's more open; I prefer it. I raise and put back my head, saying mu. Someone turns off the light and comes into the room. Perhaps even Roshi. In the darkness I make out the pattern of the doors. It's a warm enveloping dark, a womb, dark, shared with I don't know who. It's peaceful and comforting. I will sit every morning in that stillness.

The figure is Tetsuro-san—Iron Wolf, prowling, always a little unsure, a little outside. His kindness and compassion to me have been enormous, an encouraging and humble word whenever I need it. He is soon to become abbot of a new temple and seems to be anxious. Jiko says he's neurotic. He himself says he imagines people want to get rid of him. He startled me at the sink when he pounced "why were you laughing?" About him, he thought. "Joke, joke," he said. Honest in his weaknesses and nightmares. After all his generosity to me, when I had the chance to get him a takuhatsu hat, I did. It cost 10,000 yen but with my takuhatsu money, it wasn't that much, and money is for such things. He said he worried all night, distraught, asking himself why I had given him such a big present. Issh. He's so funny, so childlike, the way he opens his heart; he's poring over the newspaper.

"Aha," face alight, "Olivia Hussey has married a Japanese."

"Oh, really?" and I add something forgettable about her, not sure of the relevance of the announcement.

"What do you think of international marriages?" I approved.

"So you would marry a Japanese?"

"I'd need to learn Japanese."

Then he throws himself into excited jabbering with Mio-san, the gist being that I wasn't against marrying a Japanese. I love his innocence.

I was sitting up in Zendo and Jiko's words were in my ears, "When you are your mother, when you are Roshi, then you are enlightened." I didn't see how that was possible. If I wasn't myself, I certainly wasn't them. I kept telling myself: you are everything. Hard to conceive of. Then it hit me how totally arbitrarily we have defined our so-called self. I am my body, thoughts, perceptions, personality. So the thought of my mother is me but my mother is not. The real "I" I've defined as not me, and that which is merely the image and not real I have defined as me. Strange. The spit in my mouth is me. The air in my mouth is not. The food I take in isn't, yet somewhere it passes some vague border and becomes me. I myself was so arbitrarily defined—the thought is me, the spit and food is me, but the painting I produced, spawned from my thought, is not me, the tune humming though my head, me—and if I any way reject that definition of self as non-existent, can't I then redefine myself?

And I began. Each noise, sight, movement was me. I was tremendously excited, quivering, smiling. As if there was a statue, my physical body, with a cloth draped over it, hanging close around my body; it was what I defined as self. Now a tack through the head and cloth, someone is raising it and stretching it; it's still attached to my body but covers more and more, and that is me. How can I die or cease to be? I am eternal; I am process and thing. I am my mother. I am Roshi. I left the hondo, a new I; every noise and sight caught my notice, being incorporated into myself.

We went shopping. I cooked dinner and soon my self-conception was back to its usual stifling structure. Does Roshi always feel like that? Before I admired him for having stared at his nothingness in its coffin and still being able to laugh. Now it seemed there was much more. Enormous.

After zazen, Roshi said something about *muji* [the koan of mu] being everything and about the tenzo people (Jiko and I) working from devotion. So maybe it's not because he hates my cooking that he wants a new kitchen helper.

February 29

My relationship with Jiko has been interesting. I always oscillated between being amused at his childlike pranks and being irritated by his childish demands for notice. Constantly praising himself, yet as quick and enthusiastic in his praise of others. I don't believe he has ever criticized another's character—their habits, yes, but not their character. He often seemed to act uppity with me, correcting me on trivial points, straightening a wrinkle, this way, pushing me. It was annoying in a mild way. So I wondered how he'd get on in the kitchen. I can see how I've changed in my reactions. He often flaps around, does nothing, or fiddles with his dictionary while I do all the work. He asked me to do all the lunches since he "sometimes has business." Rubbish. My first reaction was, Hold on, make sure you're really doing more before you accuse, then point out how much you did, etc. Do the lunch and put up with it. Instead, I said no. If he had business I'd do the lunch and he could do it for me the next day.

I asked which day to put out the bins. "Today," he blithely said. "Where do they go?" Starting to resent. "Over…" He began to indicate. Before I would have taken them off, fumed and forgotten it as unimportant. I ordered, "Come on." Not giving him time to take off his slippers at the door, I gruffly commanded, "Take those." He did, obviously meekly and chastened.

In the kitchen I tell him to put things away if I feel put upon. In fact now I can laughingly give him the towel or just shut up when he goes on and on and on and on, asking me to repeat the pronunciation of some word "merry," "merry," "merry," merry." So no tension builds up. The moment it rises, it flickers and so we laugh and joke and love working in tenzo.

He never takes the meals too seriously, which is good for me, though often disaster for the cooking. Every morning he makes *mochi*—a healthful, gluey combination of *komugi* [wheat], beans, *genmai* [brown rice], peanuts or *goma* [sesame seeds] or whatever comes to hand. We sip tea, eat slowly, and listen to his tiny radio. It's a simple, gentle, very great pleasure. He often adds charming touches, like serving on a special plate or with flowers. He does make me laugh so.

For Roshi's son's birthday party, the 27th, we had to prepare a big, sit-down dinner for fourteen. *Okusan* [lady, or wife; here: Go Roshi's wife] wanted two kinds of fish and a meat. I decided to positively avoid getting into a flap…three gas burners, no oven or even a grill. I had my part all ready by 10 o'clock in the morning of the 27th: chicken, fish, each separately marinated. Twice Jiko's rice came out too soft. I was helping him, so there was still a countdown tension but not bad. My chicken was very cold, being in the fridge, so I put it in the rice steamer and the outside went wet. I nearly died. My crispy delicious chicken. I quickly started refrying and all went well.

Dinner—even I must admit—was delicious and beautiful. Roshi's son didn't show up. Roshi, from the other end of the table, beaming said in English "Zank you verly much." He's radiant. "*Do itashimashite*" ["You're welcome"], I muttered, and all oohed. It was a success. Jiko and I hugged, shook hands, laughed, and after cleaning, sat down with flowers and finished the saké. Bejaysus it was grand.

In the afternoon I had time to spare. Tetsuro-san was cutting Tetsubun-san's hair. I shot some pictures and sat lazily in the sun, half in and half out of the big glass window. Playfully flicking the shears, Tetsuro-san teased, "Now, how about you?" I thought for a few minutes. My hair was growing, looking well, would soon be long enough to part in the middle. I had bought a hairbrush, thinking of getting a mirror. "How about you?" The day was warm; my hair was in the way; when would I have the chance to be bald again? "Okay," I said.

"Honto?" "Ii yo." ["Really?" "Yes, definitely."] Tetsuro-san jumped up and jumped down, asked Tetsuban-san, asked Jiko-san, put on his kimono to ask Roshi, then took it off, then put it on and finally shore off my hair.

Surprisingly, it didn't bother me. Of course, with no big mirror I don't see myself. The air and wind feel good on my head. It's a liberating feeling. I remember reading about light affecting some gland corresponding to a third eye in the case of shorn birds. Interesting. The next day it snowed. My bald head was very cold.

After zazen on the 28th, Roshi said it was sad to visit his family. His son took no joy in his birthday. All his family are in education and have no interest in zazen. How sad for him and sad for them. The opportunity they have let slip. I admire his emotional openness with us.

I feel very privileged to be at Toshoji. Roshi is a very great teacher and example. People think the life is hard but I am grateful. Imagine, all my bodily needs taken care of and that which I most want to do—a very self-oriented thing—is not only tolerated but encouraged. Not a care in the world, no worries or regrets, only this enormous opportunity.

I wonder if every living thing doesn't have compassion—Buddha nature. All life has/is (not sure which) consciousness. Plants faint when an egg or shrimp is killed. Is this not compassion at its most basic? It will be argued that many people are bad. I have yet to meet the person whom I could point to and say "he has no compassion." Reflecting on all the goodness shown to me on my travels I can only be humble, goodness far exceeding what I am big enough to repay.

These days I feel very conscious of life. Before, I didn't like eating meat because it was so toxic and I found rather insipid the sentimentality of "poor little things." Now it really saddens me to consume flesh, to see slaughter displayed in the supermarket. "Lashai, Lashai, Lashais," [sounds like *Lashai* but in fact it is *Irashaimasse*] welcome. I feel remorse because of the extra wooden match I use, and though I must serve meat and fish to the others, I wonder where to determine my complicity in the crime. I would not by choice serve meat, but each time that I serve it instead of something else (as I must), must I assume this guilt?

March 1

There was no answer to the ad for a new cook. Yesterday Roshi asked us if we would continue cooking. He said at first he thought we were trying to kill him, hard rice and dinner that smelled like medicine. I have to laugh; I love his frankness, but now he says everything is delicious. He thought we would soon tire of the kitchen, but we are in high spirits and the kitchen is always clean. Jiko said that of course I would rather do the garden, but it's okay. It's still cold for the garden.

This morning, meditating, I couldn't still my mind for a moment. I kept thinking of different things to cook, etc. Was annoyed with myself. After sutra we had the ceremony where each person roars a question and Roshi answers. Tetsuro-san told me to go up.

"I don't know what to say," I whispered, flustered.

"Sit there," he said. So I thought I didn't have to ask a question.

Then Roshi calls, "Soshin-san."

I go up and wait for Tetsuro-san to tell me the Japanese I must say. Nothing. I look at him imploringly. "What do I say?"

"Ask your question." So I ask but my voice is small because of the awe and confusion I feel. "What is Buddha?"

I have so many questions. He waits a long time. I cannot understand the answer. Afterwards Tetsuro-san says, "Roshi said, 'You are silent, but your mind is like thunder.'"

I feel crushed. He's saying my mind is a storm; I have no peace. I think of that morning's scattered meditation, how hard it often is to keep my mind on things. He knows I'm so far from enlightenment, it seems like no use—I'll never calm my mind. I ask Jiko what he meant. "Only an allusion to the weather; never mind." I go again to Tetsuro-san. He says it is a common Zen phrase, no bad meaning, comes from a Chinese poem and is like saying, "the old man is silent but his life is etched in his face." I'm slightly consoled.

Chosan [morning tea at which Roshi discusses important matters]. Roshi has been appointed one of the top teachers in Japan. How could I have been so lucky to stumble upon his temple, decide to stay (under the illusion he spoke English), be accepted, and have to pay nothing?

Roshi said something about when I was silent this morning. The other Roshi who came to announce Ban Roshi's promotion said he admired me coming as a foreigner and doing Zen seriously, that I was simple in my confusion. Jiko fumbles to translate, and Roshi cuts in, saying in English, laughing, "You are wonderful, number one."

March 2

Yesterday I went to inquire about my visa with Tetsuro-san. Watching all the people on the train, they seem lifeless; even Tetsuro-san was slumped into customary subway slumber. People's eyes are blank, or drifting across each other, creating a distance within the crowd by avoiding eye contact. I, too, am good at this. I try to catch the people's staring eyes so I can shatter the game with a smile. No use. They won't let our eyes meet or acknowledge the obvious that we are both there, three hours on the subways. The only one who would communicate with my eyes was a mentally retarded girl on a Saturday group outing. And she's the one defined as out of touch with reality.

Two little boys and their father boarded. They quivered with life and excitement, chattering, laughing, playing, looking at everything with wonder, yo-yos, and curiosity, eyes sparkling. How is it killed, I wondered. They asked their father a question. He ignored them. Another question, a mumbled response as he stares vacantly into space. That is how the crime takes place. And he is a good father; he takes the kids out on Saturdays. Watching them, I want to play—to play tip and tig, hide and seek, pirates, house, red rover, to pretend. Mothers are so annoyed when children return late for tea. How wonderful to be so engrossed, to so enjoy what one is doing that one loses all conception of time. If only mothers could rejoice.

Sunset was beautiful.

This morning Mt. Fuji was clear between the smoke stacks and the railroad tracks. 5:00 A.M. Go Roshi leaves for Iwate. I hope he brings back good news of Tekkan-san.

Everything that happens to me is a mixture of the circumstance and my reaction to it. Nothing can touch me purely without my filtering it, even if the mind is empty. By allowing everything in, I have affected the circumstance. The I-filter is constantly changed, too, by circumstance. "Karma means everything that happens, we directly or indirectly, partly or entirely, set in motion." At least insofar as the circumstance includes the I-filter, this is true, but possibly even the strong case that the quote suggests. You and outside you are not separate. If someone steals all my possessions and I am upset, I say something bad has happened to me. If I do not care, nothing bad has happened, yet it is the same external circumstance.

March 3

Yesterday, sitting, the same question ricocheted round and round my mind. How are we all one? We're all made of the same stuff but that doesn't make us one. Kapleau says Mary hurt in Detroit, Joe feels in Rochester. But I don't. At least not consciously. Then I thought of the plants mourning the egg, excited when many miles away his owner came. I thought of how at Grandpa's death, Aunt Elaine got up in the wee hours of the morning, put on her coat, stumbled through the blizzard, and was with him when he went. Tears came into my eyes. There is knowing between minds. Perhaps (of course) it is usually inaccessible to consciousness. But that it happens at all, and that it is always present in plants, which don't have as complex a consciousness as we do, would seem to mean something.

In the afternoon I was very aware. Without an effort, I was just doing whatever I was doing, without distraction or forcing. Occasionally the thought would pop into my head "Hey, your mind is still." Then even that vanished. Because I was quiet, I was very surprised when Jiko said, "You are in very high spirits."

Today, business and flighty mind as usual.

March 4

Yesterday I went shopping with Jiko. I bought a flash and tripod. I find myself slightly annoyed by his dilly-dallying, pulling and tugging at me, poking me to look at this and that. "*Ii ne, ii, ii*" ["That's good, isn't it? Good! Good!"], on and on even after I answer him. I know we won't have time to do everything, and of course we don't. But I'm more annoyed with myself for lacking a spontaneity. Everything he shows me is marvelous, and we can do the other things another day. We did what was most important, the flash, and saw wonders. I feel perhaps I am being too hard, asking him not to repeat, not to poke me. (Rather, I tell him it's okay for him to repeat but I won't always answer.) When I tell him that and he looks at me with the same expression and intonation as usual "ii" or "oishii" [tasty] and I don't answer or only say "mm," and he persists and persists. He nags until I answer not just "ii" or "oishii," but "ii yo!" or "oishii yo!" and I wonder if he is dense or trying to annoy. I really don't think he has the meanness in him for the latter but hate to conclude the former. And of course it's equally my reaction. If I were more totally immediate, the repetition would not be annoying because each time would be as the first.

Last night I borrowed without permission one of Roshi's books. I felt very guilty and stayed up too late reading. I'm tired and grumpy this morning. Jiko tells me to come over at 9:00 for *omochi* [rice or dumplings]. I'm starving. He fiddles around for an hour and a half with the windows wide open, taking pictures and dropping my batteries. Then I'm freezing and starving. I'm disgruntled and more annoyed with myself than with him. Why should a change from what I had expected be annoying? I decide I'd better rest. The morning is gone.

Back to the kitchen to make lunch. No Jiko. The kitchen's a mess, his breakfast dishes still sitting, ten o'clock tea dishes still sitting. Of course, I had also left the latter. I'd hoped he'd put away the breakfast dishes, since he'd done nothing else afterwards. I can't say I do more work because he spends more time in the kitchen, so though my work time there is more industrious, I have more free time. I'm making lunch. Still no sign of him. Well, the only help he is is to get out a few chopsticks. He had asked me to do lunches, and I virtually do, and don't mind as it's easy. But I didn't want him to take it for granted. I don't really feel over-worked, as there isn't that much to do and usually it was a one-person job. I do what's necessary, and if I feel resentful, I give Jiko a dish towel, usually with a laugh. I'm annoyed at myself for being so petty and decide I'm really tired and should sleep more.

Jiko comes in, all apologies. He'd been in a sound sleep. So he wasn't taking me for granted; it was an accident. I felt much better. Of course it was okay. He started going on and on about how I did much more work—still just fiddling with his dictionary while I worked. I handed him a tea towel and said it was okay. We're a team. There's no need to make comparisons, more or less work; we'll just each do our best. I'm glad the sentiment came from him, and really I don't mind doing more, so long as he does something. I also think he finally got it about the repetitions. We'll see. It is much better for me to be working with Jiko-san than with someone who never annoys me.

Reading that book, I feel so far from enlightenment. Not that it's so important for right now, but I'm on such a gross and sloppy level. Why can I not feel the unity of all?

March 5
Why can I not still my mind? Last night's and this morning's meditations were so scattered.

March 7

The day before yesterday some psychologists came to test our skin potential, resistance, and breathing during meditation. Jiko was first. He came downstairs and told me how twice during meditation he had left his body and the researchers will be very surprised. I thought about my own meditations, how they are often so sloppy. In the afternoon I went up. A wire from my ear, two around my waist, and five in my left arm. I really felt like a laboratory rat. I might have been peevish (as I was a bit for the news interviewer), this "probing a freak" bit, but the researcher does zazen himself so I wanted to cooperate. My meditation was deep. I was one with everyone and everything, including them. I felt strong love for them. At one stage I was their machine and its rotations were my heartbeat. At the beginning and end we just sat naturally. They rechecked the apparatus and kept telling me to just be at ease. I thought I must be nervous and it was showing up.

At the end they came over, extremely excited, *"subarashii, subarashii"* ["splendid, splendid"]. "This is very rare data," they said. "We have tested many monks, 40–60, but this is very rare…Your natural state is thirteen breaths a minute and in meditation three or four a minute; normally a good meditation is three to five." They want to test me again next week. I was very pleased, and it was hard for me not to tell the others everything they said, but I don't want the thing to seem competitive. I needed encouragement and it came. However, the things they are measuring are only by-products; they have nothing to do with my understanding and it is this that I want.

I have been meditating now consistently for three months. (They couldn't believe that—thought it must be a year and three months). I can perceive subtle changes. My posture is different, composure better. I'm more quiet. I remember finding Sean's silences unbearable and needed constant chatter and once had to stop myself from begging him to talk about just anything. I'm no longer compulsive in eating and drinking. If I do something, I like to do it properly and I care less about others' opinions of me. I can even serve a bad dinner, feel sorry that it was bad, but not be upset to the core and watching each expression. I'm much better disciplined, but I don't know how permanent any of these changes are. So I am a bit afraid to go back to the "real world."

Mum sent a letter saying she was sad I had given up the idea of a Ph.D. at the Sorbonne (which of course I haven't) and appealing to me to help her sell her Dublin house in the summer. But I am finally doing what I have wanted and needed to do all my life and am afraid to break. I consider Buddhism my "religion," if it can be called that. On the other hand, I do want to continue with my outside life at some stage and finish the koans. So maybe I should find a suitable temple and get on with it as I'll have to break from here sooner or later. I love, respect, and trust Roshi completely, yet I should not be attached even to him.

Toshoji, Tokyo
March 1980
Dear Mum,
Many thanks for the parcel. Did you realize you had two of my favorite songs on the tape, in addition to "Raglan Road"? I don't know what made you think I'd given up the idea of a Ph.D. at the Sorbonne. For the first time since I left Trinity, I feel I'm making real progress on a would-be original thesis. Things are really clicking, and I'm writing notes all the time. As you know, I got very interested in theories of language, ideology, and the formation of the subject, especially Lacan's work. He is, of course, in Paris. Now learning my first non-Western language and being immersed in Oriental philosophy, many things are falling into place. As I'm sure you're aware, Zen has very different notions of the subject than ours, and grammatically the language is built to facilitate this. Or was it the other way around? Interestingly, most grammar books, in translating, do not make a direct translation, making the different concepts involved more obvious. But they also translate conceptually so that the Westerner hears the Japanese phrase but can still think it in his own terms. Luckily I have found an excellent book written by linguists from Yale that's extremely helpful. My ideas so far stem from Lacan's theories, but I've never seen them applied in such a case. In fact, I can think of a better way of confirming some of his speculations. It's very exciting but difficult, as

I can only proceed at the pace at which I'm learning Japanese. I also need to study Shinto and probably linguistic changes that occurred with the importation of much of the Chinese written language, with Buddhism itself, and at the ideological level, with the attempt to introduce the Chinese political system, and how was all this reconciled with the emperor's god status—all of which occurred at about the same time. This is a huge subject and it's the linguistic end that is most interesting and most original.

But it involves a load of work. I have to learn two more Japanese scripts, one of which is non-syllabic. Nonetheless, if I can pull it off it would put me in an important place in my field, though I'm afraid to get my hopes too high.

As I've said to you before, all this meditation has brought me many benefits, not least of which is much greater concentration and self-discipline. I really don't know if I would have been able to undertake a good thesis three months ago. I was so out of the habit of applying myself to anything seriously. Waitressing 'til three in the morning was not the most conducive thing to academics.

The other day some psychologists from some university came over to do tests on us and psychophysiological changes during zazen. They attached five wires to my arm, hung one from my ear, and put on two respiratory monitors. They hadn't told the others anything about the results of their tests, but I resolved to ask them because I was very curious. But after I finished, they came bounding over, full of non-scientific excitement and saying "wonderful, wonderful" over and over. They said they have tested nearly sixty monks but that my results were extremely rare and apparently I have been having deep meditations that are normally only reached after years of practice. So they want to do a whole bunch more tests on me and are coming back next week. Well, I was very surprised, though I have increasingly noticed changes in myself.

All of which brings me to what is my problem at the moment. This is the first thesis that has really absorbed my interest, that I feel I could put the necessary time and effort into, and that would be worth writing in that it would be a real contribution. At the same time, I want to keep up my Zen. I was fortunate to end up with a really excellent teacher. He is famous (as are his books) throughout Japan and has just been given the highest recognition there is as a "teacher of teachers." But if I pursue the thesis, it would mean at least another year and a half in Japan. That's a heck of a long time.

The other problem is I don't have the books I need and it would be nearly impossible for you to send them, as I'd have to search through bookshops, consult bibliographies, and probably be in touch with Brian Torode and Jim Wickham in Trinity. So I want your advice, i.e., "Mommy, what should I do?" Please try to be as objective as possible about it. I imagine your first reaction might be—two years or two and a half. I suppose I could manage. What do you think, you having been through the "get back to the books and really write" bit? But it is a long time.

Love, M.

March 8

Go Roshi came back from Kannonji yesterday; I really love him.

The day after Jiko slept through lunch, I asked him to put away the breakfast dishes since everything else was done. I came in to find no sign of him. Half-way through lunch and he still hadn't appeared. I thought of someone else's words: "We are one, when a boil appears on your hand, you're not angry at it; you just do something about it." So I did. Jiko was moving rooms when I came in. He, of course, was engrossed in and delighted with the fun of it. I said, "Come and help me make lunch." He said, "Oh," surprised. A while later he came in. I said, "Jiko-san, I asked you to put away the dishes. I cleaned everything else. It's not so much to ask." I didn't like to make the comparison. I repeated myself; it often takes a while for things to sink in. Chastened, he did so. That evening he was all "May I help you? What can I do?" Next day he put away without my asking, but the following day he was back to normal. I hate to always prick his balloon. He is quite marvelous—a child's sense of fun, and what child likes to dry dishes? He is eager to cook new concoctions. "Ah, the joy of creation," says he. He goes to infinite trouble arranging glasses of water to play a tune with the radio. He meticulously cuts a piece of potato into a star, selects the right frying pan as a backdrop—the north star against a midnight sky, then pops it into my mouth. He truly has magic in his heart. I feel like Martha with Mary* when I ask him to clean. I never thought of myself as a Martha. His strength also is admirable. I don't think I could ever fast for twenty-one days.

At last I am intellectually convinced of the indivisibility and nothingness of everything, but to integrate this into consciousness is so difficult.

Babies are never angry. Unhappy and hungry, of course, but not angry. Anger may be a learned emotion.

March 9

Jiko-san asked Roshi if I should go home, as duty would dictate, or stay. He emphatically said, "Stay." He said, for peace in this world Zen is necessary, and he has an idea for me to start a *dojo* [Zen practice place] in Ireland. Hmmm. In the far future it's a possibility.

I felt a bit upset because I didn't in my own mind know what to do. Finally a good solution hit me. I'd stay two years with Roshi but go home in July to help Mum move house, see everyone after three years' absence, then come back to Japan. Seems expensive but a good solution. Mum needs help, and I can explain my ideas better in person. Or better yet, perhaps she can see changes in me. I wrote her a letter stressing the academic things I could do here but also explaining my desire to continue to do zazen. I told her how much I loved her and thanked her. I'll wait for a reaction before I mention meeting her in July.

I've been made "altar boy" now. It's more interesting but hard to remember everything.

Yesterday there was a death ceremony. I tried to put all my energy into awakening the dead spirit and the outpouring was powerful. After the ceremony, Roshi was telling the people the news of Toshoji and praising me. He's very thoughtful.

Jiko-san and I have been having a great deal of telepathy lately. It's almost chilling. I'll think something and he'll say or do it, again and again.

*This is a reference to sisters in the Bible. They were friends of Jesus' but when he visited their house, Martha did all the work and Mary sat with Jesus.

He too was amazed and kept saying, "Who are you? Who are you?" He says many praising things, but I'm really not at all extraordinary, and I don't know what to say. I'm trying to avoid making unnecessary distinctions and having to respond to needless praise doesn't help. I was practicing sometimes not using "I," separating myself from my emotions.

Tessan-san started going on about how Jiko and I must eat the same food as everybody else. We weren't eating meat or fish. I feel peeved. Reminding myself that it wasn't really "I" who was peeved helped, but I'm still very much attached to my ego.

I stood by the open window in the warm spring wind, washing noodles. They were wet, soft, moving between my fingers. The moment was eternal.

Jiko-san said I was an excellent Zen *obosan* [ordained priest or monk follower of Buddha] and I realized it was the first time I had been called an obosan. It was very pleasing. He said he wondered if I was an incarnation of an old Zen master. He sees good in everyone.

Go Roshi said we must lead simple lives. Apparently he said the researchers were bad because they left on the light when they went away. I hope he didn't really say they were bad—they're forgetful maybe.

March 10

My mind these days is so much calmer, still hardly empty, but stiller. The kitchen is such a pleasure. Two years of daily dusting dustless altars would have been impossible drudgery. Ah, but the tenzo—every day different, a creation. Two years would be not only possible, but wonderful.

Such happiness of late. But there's still attachment. That's why there's the fear that if I left here the peace might also leave. When even the peace isn't clutched at, then there'll be peace.

March 11

Holding up my soup *chawan* [bowl; also soup], steam curling, all of us giving thanks, the miracle became apparent, the daily alchemy. This had been life, killed and now made me, made my life. Humble beans and onions passing into me, supporting me, becoming me and I in turn passing into nourishing beans or maybe onions. Endless magical stream, not really of creation and destruction, only a flow.

Funny how in front of seventeen people, most of whom I don't know, I can, as altar boy, make mistakes, be corrected and feel no blush.

The notion of a nation is to a country what ego is to a body.

March 12

Zenkai [also "zazenkai"; a gathering for zazen]. Up late. Didn't want to get up in the morning. Got up. Yesterday the meditations were terrible, hardly there at all.

This morning at chosan, Go Roshi said the kitchen was the best it's ever been, always clean and good food. He said he left the whole business in our hands. He also said he wants Jiko to ascend to the highest level of the Soto sect. Jiko says he's not interested; as an ordinary man he's more free. I think I am still attached enough to ambition that I would at least be pleased and would not refuse. Or maybe not. Who knows? Today Tekkan-san's destiny is decided. I'd prefer him to stay in Kannonji so that I could spend the summer with himself and Kas'ko-san.

It seems that at zenkai last night, Go Roshi was very critical of Japan, of education, of modern, free-loving women. He said the latter will die (but who won't?). I don't know how faithful the translations are of what he says. I'd rather not think of him as being so all-condemning. Surely all is neither good nor bad. But then, maybe that applies also to Go Roshi. Because I love him so much, I want him to be perfect.

March 13

Tekkan-san came. I was very happy to see him and he the same. He kept shaking my hands and smiling and rubbing my bare head, laughing. I wanted to get him a present to bring to Kas'ko-san, but when I returned he'd already left. He must not have been happy with the results of the talk, for he left hurriedly without a good-bye to anyone. Mio-san chased him on a bike. This morning there was no chosan, so we don't know the results.

I mentioned that I might hitch a ride and catch a boat to Korea. Tetsuro-san's eyes grew round with horror and he told me fantastic stories of gangs with knives, who'd pump me with heroin and force me to do strip shows, or they'd throw my dagger-riddled, bleeding body into the sea. Jiko was not so vivid but insisted I'd need fluent Japanese or I'd get lost. They would never be able to really understand me.

Jiko-san is in many ways wise and a wonder. His koan (very awkwardly translated) means something like "everything is okay." When I told him that this sometimes seemed difficult to reconcile with Go Roshi's *"Dame"* ["That's wrong"], he said he didn't have that problem. The koan was okay; Roshi's talks were okay; everything was okay. He's no longer bound by the formal, logical requisite of consistency.

At zenkai last night, Roshi talked about mu. How one must be totally involved with it. Dogen sat for one thousand days with mu and ten minutes of only pure mu is a feat for me. Paradoxical, these ancient masters, because their desire is so strong that their ultimate freedom from desire is total. If I could only be so impassioned.

I got a letter from some librarian who had read about me in the paper. He's going to Ireland in May and wanted me to teach him "Irish."

March 15
Tekkan-san's fate is still not decided. Tessan-san's pre-priest ceremony was held this morning. He may have to replace Tekkan-san. At the ceremony I messed up my part but strangely didn't feel embarrassed. Nor did I mind shouting out my questions in front of everyone at *shosan* [ceremony where all students present questions in front of the assembly], though last night at the end of my introduction, I blushed deeply. I was trying to express the gratitude I felt to everyone, but Jiko didn't even try to translate. Translation can be a problem. At this morning's shosan I asked, "What becomes of dead people?" It was translated "Why do people die?" Go Roshi's answer was rendered as "You study more Buddhism and you will understand that they do not die." He smiled his eyes into my eyes so sweetly but Ho-san told me that that was an inaccurate translation.

A man came from Kyushu. He sits sure and solid as a mountain. His little son came, too. He sat through meals, squirming, wriggling, slurping, watching with a child's wonder-filled eyes. I loved to see the spontaneity.

We "Zennites" seemed self-conscious by comparison, though comparison is not really appropriate. Mio-san corrected him. Each morning of the ten days they stayed he got up brightly, in little shorts, behind a dim flashlight, bobbing in the dark. Exercises and zazen, he does the lot. He sat last night through all of zenkai. Our eyes caught and we were shutting and averting eyes like young lovers. He finally giggled, and I tried not to look. Afterwards, I was in the kitchen washing-up and he came in and we laughed and laughed, though we couldn't speak one word to one another. Children are such noble teachers.

March 16

My moods changed so yesterday. Afternoon, lovely zazen in the sunshine. Evening, distracted, unable to focus. I got frustrated; I'm hopeless, useless. I waited up to give Go Roshi a late dinner. He beamed, really seemed to emit light, and I was elated. He said, *"Saikō" ["The best!"]*, but Tessan-san was outraged. However I made it, he said it tasted like water. Just can't please everyone. All my presents backfired. First the curry for Tessan. Then I wanted to buy him a pastry, but it turned out to be bread with chocolate on top. I wanted to give the child a treat and left it beside him, but he didn't realize it was his.

March 17

Listening to music in Masato's room, I went to another world, my other life. He is a kind of bridge, some thirty years old, long, scraggly hair arranged to cover the incipient baldness. He is gentle and silent, a voice that coos "zazen" with the tranquillity of the wise. Yet he only talks about his stereo and his memories. Perhaps he thinks it's all we have in common. But his peace is real. He hitched across the States and Europe, can understand me, knows the road. The music is American. We drink coffee but sit on the floor. And its very strange. The room is chilly, not cold, just so the skin tenses and tingles. Roshi is out, the music loud. I'm internalizing the music, really am the music, transported, transcending. I can't help smiling. I feel I'm bursting, vibrating up and down my spine.

Mio-san took photos. I looked at mine and was strongly hit by having seen it before. In Masato's room, looking at the albums, I felt I knew all these people well, but couldn't place them. Odd.

March 18
Jiko-san out chanting sutras. I have tenzo to myself, everything fine.

March 19
Again alone in tenzo. I give myself plenty of time to do everything and find the cleanup goes as quickly without Jiko as with him. In the afternoon I read and meditated. I come down to a very calm place. Thoughts aren't fluttering around unbidden and I just do what I'm doing. It's very peaceful not having to talk. Mio-san is the only one who is in. I find I like him very much. He used to seem so intimidating, as if he were looking over my shoulder. I know he accepts and respects me; maybe that's the difference.

Go Roshi brings us each back little cakes. I'm very touched. More than a big present, to have taken the time to think of us and want to give us a little treat, is so very kind. I spend a long, long time ironing his kimono. Could have waited 'til morning but thought he might need it this morning.

Today dawned totally different. I knew when I got up that I'd be grumpy. I felt I hadn't slept enough though it was more than usual. Into tenzo and Jiko wouldn't shut up, spouting nonsense, and I forgot to take Go Roshi the kimono. The marmalade that I knew Mio-san was looking forward to didn't turn out right. I put out the wrong rice, but it was tasty. Jiko ruined it by boiling and boiling it. I washed my hands of it when he wouldn't stop boiling it, but he told everyone it was my fault for doing the wrong rice. I had been proud that when I did the rice it was always good. So I'm annoyed, and still more annoyed at being so petty in giving a damn about rice. Back to sleep for two hours and the world is brighter. Yesterday I was so together, calm, big mind; today so trivial and frazzled.

Keep at it, m'dear.

March 20

For a day that started so awkwardly, yesterday mellowed out nicely. I like working in silence, watching my breathing. Mio-san and I ate lunch in the kitchen. It was much nicer than the cold, dwarfing dining-room. It's hard to talk to him (language), but his good nature shines through.

Yesterday was the first day of spring. Mio-san hung out the flag. Birds sang, and the air was warm and dancing. We opened the windows and I sat with Nakamuro in the sunshine. He is one of the most unselfconscious, wonderful people I have ever met. He's twenty but looks fifteen and knows many different disciplines. Body straight and supple, he bends effortlessly. It's a pleasure to watch him bow. He's always laughing, always helping, but never in a martyrish way, always the kind word, ready smile, and gusty *"ohayo gozaimasu"* ["good morning"]. Goodness is no effort to him, just an expression of his nature. He gave me a book and a painted fan as one gives a conversation.

I wrote "Who am I?" I amn't; I am. In some senses am and amn't. What sense is what? Is there any sense? It's all so confusing. I wish someone could just tell me all the answers. But I don't, really.

Jiko-san came home late, tired, his voice hoarse from all the sutras. The last couple of days I've been rather ignoring him, having enjoyed my days of silence. Last night I listened and chatted enthusiastically, and to see his face light up made me feel ashamed.

I feel timeless, a kind of happiness trembling.

The child came to say goodbye. He reached out his hand, giving me a Western-style handshake, said in English, "Bye, bye."

March 22

Another quiet, peaceful day. It's raining. Twilight in the kitchen. The gentle snugness of warm and dry while the outside drips. Doing the ironing in long, smooth strokes. All day my breath is very slow and very deep, and everything seems to be a meditation.

I sit in the kitchen with my Japanese book. Mio-san comes down from chanting sutra and is poking around. "You are a great woman," he says, *"hai"* ["yes"]. I am very surprised. People have said that before and I can laugh it off. I know they only say it for irrelevant reasons—foreign and female. But he said it not in a flattering way, more like one speaking aloud to himself, not concerned with my reaction. I was so taken aback that I blushed a very deep crimson and could only sincerely say, "Thank you."

Got a letter from Mom. I've been watching the post every day. I had put my involvement here in academic terms and sounded more together than I feel. I will get down to that aspect and must see about books. It made me feel very happy that she understands and is resigned to my being away for a while, though would like if it wasn't so long. Says she was touched by my thanks for her sacrifices. I should have thanked her years ago. Puts me at ease. I think it would be great to go back for Christmas, then come back here 'til after summer. Funny, though, I know if I'd shifted the emphasis of my letter to a more spiritual one, that she probably wouldn't have been so accepting. Yet that's so important.

March 24

The researchers tested me again. They didn't say anything. Just as well.

Jiko and I read sutra at Tetsuburo-san's house. Jiko has such a sense of fun and festival. He decided to turn it into a carnival. We brought all the drums, bangers, and clangers we could find. Bremen musicians. Tetsubun-san loved it. Trying to read sutra, we kept breaking down laughing. Jiko bought saké, and we drank and toasted and watched TV comics. 'Twas a grand night. This morning I whipped into action. During the last week I've gotten used to getting right at the cleaning and getting it done quickly. Jiko was surprised, and it's hard not to just ignore him and take over. He leans against the fridge, "I've forgotten how to do the tenzo jobs. You've gotten stronger; you don't need me." I must not be overbearing. The tenzo is for both of us. But still he only leaned. Everything was done but the putting away, and I hoped he'd just do it. I began the laundry and the rice and finally asked him to put away the dishes. It makes me feel like a sergeant. I don't like that role; it would be terrible to get used to it. Working with Jiko is good for me. I can learn much from him, and he brings out in me many tendencies that I don't like but then I can work on them.

Tessan-san suggested that I go to Kannonji as kitchen helper with him. I would love it. I couldn't possibly be happier if I tried. He said to tell Roshi, asked Jiko to tell him. He didn't seem enthusiastic, maybe afraid of how it would alter his situation. Fingers crossed, but either way is okay.

Chosan this morning for the first time in a week. Wonderful to watch Roshi again.

March 25

Last night we catered for a party of twenty. It went off grand. Tessai-san came. I was very glad to see him. Strange. He only criticized. Not like him. Hope nothing is bothering him.

I had a great time with Jiko. I used to think he is the variable factor. He is the only one who annoys me, therefore it's his fault. But in some of my moods he annoys me, and in some he doesn't. So I'm the variable factor. Thus I'm at least as much to blame and a lot easier to try and deal with.

Go Roshi left for Kannonji. When he got to the end of the road, he turned round and waved his hat like a young boy going on a holiday.

March 26

At nine in the morning Tetso-san says, "Do you want to go to Kamakura?" Okay. And we're off, and a wonderful day it was. The sun shone. We went to see the big Buddha. There we were—in Buddha. I was very happy and excited, the blossoms' sweetness blending with incense. I felt a great yearning, a child calling his mother into the emptiness, hearing only the silence of his own voice. Oh, how I was aching for *satori* [enlightenment experience]. If only I could be a child and hear the silence of my own voice. Walking, there was only sunshine and fun. We were the only obosans, but their evidence was everywhere in perfectly swept paths. Bowing, they let us into the temples—free. Two excited giggling schoolgirls tried their English on me and asked for an autograph. We came back late.

Part IV

Korea

I packed my bag for my trip to Korea and went to bed, but slept little and got up early for zazen. Jiko-san very thoughtfully made me genmai. Tetso-san rose from his bed (after a hard night's drinking) and drove me to the highway. He asked several drivers until he got me a lift to a stopover. There I'd scarcely put out my thumb when a family stopped. The father spoke English graciously and took me about 200 kilometers down the road. Though I knew it would be more practical to look for a long ride from a truck driver (the family kept making stops), I liked them and decided just to go with my feelings. He was interesting, a leftist who told me about Japanese politics and education. He had tried the monastic life thirty years ago but got too hungry. I was surprised at the imperialistic wave of desire to convert him, but I resisted it. The little girl, who never looked me in the eyes, practiced her high school English. On the Tomei expressway, we discussed the relative attractiveness of the Beatles. She was glad to speak English. They fed me, then drove me to a stopover to find me a lift. They invited me to stay with them in Sendai.

The next lift was with three guys, little English but much laughter. We stopped at a café, and they said there'd be few rides to Shimonoseki so maybe I should take the boat from Kobe. But I want to hitch, so they take me to a stopover near Kobe. There are no cars for Kyushu, so I agree, it's the ferry. While one buys me juice the others secretly get my ferry ticket. They write a note in Japanese to show people for directions, then ask the steward and my neighbors to take care of me. Tears prick my eyes. Sunset is beautiful.

After I arrive at Kyushu, I cross to the mainland, hitching. The driver drops off his load, then makes a special trip with me to the ferry. The kind man at the ticket office does mine specially; then I watched the sea 'til time to go. I talked to a gorgeous Swede (does acupuncture) but felt silly as his girlfriend was there. A Frenchman takes lots of pictures of me with sunset, etc. but his movements are sharp and desperate, and there seemed to be a terrible rage in him. He kept following me around and there was something about him I didn't trust. I didn't want him to attach himself to me, but wasn't one obliged to help a desperate man? I didn't know what to do, so I left to do zazen.

Everyone in my section was kind, talking to me, feeding me. I fell asleep early but was wakened by the New Yorker on my left talking to the Londoner on my right. Larry was talking about women and wondering aloud if Buddhist monks were celibate. I didn't really want to talk to them but somehow, late in the night, I did, and found they were grand. Poor Larry is lovely, but lonely. They're going to Seoul. I couldn't believe it when Jack said he'd lived in Morioka two years, knows Richard-san.

When I arrived Saturday morning, it's raining and the visa office won't open 'til Monday, so I tried to decide whether or not to go to Seoul. Then I schemed, thinking that if I went to Seoul I could probably stay with Larry and Jack, but they didn't invite me. They talked about people I should meet but only recommended a cheap place to stay. I'm surprised and then glad, because I had been scheming. It's better that a scheme should fail and that I should succeed innocently in something else. Anyway, I was sure that good things would happen. They offered to pay my train fare, but I wouldn't let them. However, I carried a camera through customs for them. The customs inspectors, of course, only bowed and waved me on, delighted with the gaijin monk. The money changers, too, were charming. With robes and a shaved head is the only way to travel. In the waiting room all the foreigners are clustered. By this time we are all friends, exchanging addresses and hugs. The Swede lives in Kyoto. I liked his girlfriend but he was inattentive to her. I decided to catch the cheap military train. Jack and Larry insist on paying for the taxi.

After a ride through magnificent countryside, we arrive in Seoul. A thin man with the eyes of a child asked me if I'm a Buddhist monk. When I say "Yes," he asks where I'm going, then weaving in and out of the crowd he beckons me, leading me I know not where. I follow him to a bus stop. Then from his briefcase he draws a slender black book, gold lettering, obviously often tenderly held. He writes in it, thrusts it into my protesting hands, and bundles me on to the bus. The girl lets me off as he directed, but I'm lost.

Spying a gaijin face, I ask him, does he know of Hillside House? He does and smiles a faint, impish smile. "Are you going to speak there tonight?" "No," says I, quite surprised. "I sometimes do," he says. He works for the U.S. Army. Another one, think I, a bit patronizingly. He soon dispels that, humbling me. It seems that he takes in street kids. (Makes me think of my street kids in Cuzco.) He spends $1500 a month of his own money on them. He makes them work or go to school.

I go home with him. The house is bursting at the seams with slightly scruffy, smiling lads. He tells me their stories, of street fights and prostitutes, pimps and gangs. They look like such innocent children. He chides them in English. They love the excuse to mock wrestle with him. A girl sits in the corner, a bouquet of flowers on her lap. They published an article in the paper about him, and he got a wad of proposals. This girl insists they're made for each other and keeps popping around with flowers. He ignores her. He tells me about professional matchmakers and how society is strictly hierarchical (status and age). One uses different word endings depending upon one's relative position.

He gets one of the kids to take me on the bus to Hillside House, but first he phones to make sure there's room for "a priest he's sending over." The divil! He didn't mention that I was female and Buddhist. Mrs. Francis looked openly horrified when she opened the door to me. No room at the inn. I offered to pitch my bag in any old corner. Then she relented.

Hillside House is just for Army people and Christians. Well, you can't win 'em all.

That night, Saturday, was Bible night. There were a bunch of straight middle-Americans and fervent Korean converts. Debby sat opposite me, kept staring at my hair (or lack of it). "Well, I suppose it's easy to take care of, but how could you shave your hair off?" she kept stammering, shuddering, gaping, aghast at my bristles.

After dinner was religious discussion. The subjects were naïve and kept returning to the threat of Communism. The Koreans, though very ardent, obviously knew very little about Christianity. Afterwards they gathered around me, especially the Koreans, fascinated, bombarding me with questions. Of most pressing concern to them was not why I was Buddhist instead of Christian, but why was I a Japanese Buddhist instead of a Korean one. They repeated, resentfully, that they had had 36 years of Japanese occupation.

On Palm Sunday morning they invited me to a full gospel service with the largest congregation in the world. I'd never been to one, so I was game. Didn't the people ever stare! And the service was frightening. Thousands of people swaying, sighing. It made me think of a Paisley or Hitler performance. The sermon was interesting, making the promise best suited to an oppressed people, the promise of future rewards. "The Lord wants men with dreams," that is, men with desire. Forget this real world and dream. Be good and get yourself a reward—always "self." But the scale was awesome, simultaneous video and translation. Clean-scrubbed Pastor Malone, with piercing eyes and a limp handshake, approached us afterwards with offers of coffee. Downstairs in the coffee bar, the pastor who had been most stirring was surrounded by buzzing followers. She had risen at the end to exhort the congregation into a frenzied praise of the Lord. Catching sight of me, she knifed through the crowd around her. "Buddha, Buddha, Buddhist devil," she shrieked, "out, devil, out!" banging me on the head, the back, the chest. Laughing, I assured her I was no devil. She'd recover herself, then flail at me again, tugging at my *rakusu* [bib-like abbreviated monk's robes, also worn by lay practitioners], looking imploringly for someone to confirm her urge to rip it from my neck.

The Francises and Pastor Malone shooshed me out, embarrassed. They then took me to lunch at the base, that little oasis of imperialism.

Coming back in the afternoon, Miss Kim of the previous night was waiting for me to take me to see some temples. We went way up a mountain. (The bus driver wouldn't let me pay). The setting was magnificent, in a niche between two jagged peaks, nestled among wispy clouds, a waterfall coursing down the mountainside. The temple itself is painted in many bright colors contrasting with the simple grey robes of the monks.

I was very surprised to see so many women, mostly old. It seems that if they are divorced or deserted, this is a refuge for them. Good idea.

They have a custom of bowing before the Buddha; the extent of devotion is indicated by the number of bows but marathons don't interest me. If I was a Buddhist devil in the morning, in the afternoon I couldn't have been more welcome than the Buddha himself. They laid before me a vegetarian feast of Korean delicacies and invited me to stay. I declined but these *bodhisattvas* [Buddhist enlightened beings committed to helping all beings awaken] were wonderful, their hearts so warm I could almost physically feel heat. Bowing, smiling, radiating good natures, they drew me into their room, urging me to put on socks. (A marvelous system of underground heating makes socks unnecessary. The cold is really the only thing that gets to me in temple life…)

There were two older-looking gaijins meditating there. I was intrigued. The man wore a Mexican jacket, his long white hair swept back, the air of an artist. The woman immobile in a subtle camel coat, silver hair in a tight knot. I thought they were leaving and rose. His eyes, startling blue, caught mine and we smiled at one another. When they came out they told me that she was a Swiss swami who had studied yoga in India for 20 years. She was amazed that I had been accepted into a male temple with no fuss. She'd read that it is difficult. They offered to drive us down to the town, then offered that I should stay with them. When we were leaving the temple, the moon hung full and luminous. Mists curled around the temple spires. Over a loudspeaker we heard chanting, the echoes reverberating. The cliffs seemed to call to the forests, chanting in reply.

Virajananda and Jimmy (she called him "the dreadful druid") took me to their immaculate apartment, tasteful but not lavish. There were Persian cats, a balcony, azaleas, and a lemon tree. She was a truly ecumenical spirit—a blossom lay beneath a picture of her guru with palms beside it from Palm Sunday mass. They were overwhelmingly generous, wouldn't let me pay for anything, kept trying to give me taxi money, lunch money, bought me vitamins and a T-shirt and wanted to buy more. She was a real inspiration, meditates four hours a day. She gave me many warnings and exhortations. We felt uncannily close. (She's sure we've been involved in a past life). People used to take Jimmy for Irish because he was so droll. He also likes to drink, and I felt a great urge to join him in a bottle but under Viraja's purer influence, I refrained. The Indians are really into renunciation, unnecessary as a permanent way but good training.

When I went for my visa (I had forgotten my passport!) I ran into many people I knew from the boat. One man came up to me, smiling a timid, Japanese smile, said, "I saw you on the boat; hope you're well." An American agitator leaps from the doorway saying, "You must be one of the people I read about." (Some foreigners in a Korean temple). Next thing he's telling me all about strikes, wages, working conditions in Korea. Interesting.

The visa people were charming, didn't even charge me. I even met an Irish bloke there.

Miss Kim and I met for lunch. The visa people had pulled apart the folded paper that Go Roshi gave me at my initiation. Underneath a lineage from the Buddha, Go Roshi had written something that neither Miss Kim nor her Buddhist father could decipher. Then the owner of the restaurant introduced herself as a Buddhist of some high rank, and she translated the words into Korean. Miss Kim's friend explained it to me in French, and I tried an English interpretation. Who knows how close my version is? It seems that Go Roshi chose the following phrases from Buddhist texts just for me: "The person who follows Buddha's precepts and laws will attain great enlightenment." Well, that could hold for anyone but still there was a feeling of being in touch with something ancient, secret, almost magical.

I then bought a few gifts to bring back, got good and lost but saw a lot of Seoul.

Jimmy came home from work, and we had a warm evening, sitting, chatting, drinking Campari. Reclining in luxury on the black leather sofa, we talked about austerity—a delightful way to do it. They filled me with determination. Viraja, by hand, strung beads which were seeds from the Bodhi tree where the Buddha was enlightened. She laid them on a vial of Ganges water and other holy things (whose significance I didn't know), packed me a lunch and other treats. She tried to give me $20, which I refused but later found in my sleeve. We embraced. "We'll meet again; we have before," she said. She was soothing while I cried. "You have it," she said. I couldn't believe her heart. As I was leaving, she stood behind the bars of her iron gates, hands joined, eyes lowered, chanting a mantra for me.

How can I ever repay the world the goodness that has so guilelessly been extended to me? Surely there is no bad person in the world and so many with loving hearts. My eyes were watering. I was sad, but somehow not sad, as if I wasn't leaving and had always been there, and as if all the kind spirits in my life have been one, weaving in and out, so they were never far apart. Viraja is a wonderful woman with a deep and daily spirituality, a part of her every act. Yet somewhere she seems to feel something lacking, as if there was something she hadn't burst or a peak from which she had lowered. I thought, what if I'd gone with Larry and Jack? I'd probably have enjoyed it, but what happened was so much more important.

Viraja and Jimmy advised me to catch the train; that seems best as I don't want to miss the ferry. Again, like a spirit, a little old man appears and takes me where I need to go, then disappears. In Pusan I get on the wrong road and lose lots of time, but I finally get a lift. It was a truck driver, a simple man. We had to wait ages for his cargo, while he kept talking about how I can sleep in his bed tonight. This makes me wary, but he's okay, takes a beautiful mountain road. It reminds me that Japan isn't all concrete and wire. It's exciting to be back on the road again, but I have no regrets about returning to Toshoji. At 6 o'clock, with still a way to go and drizzle starting, I knew he'd let me out soon. I didn't worry. I knew from experience that something would work out.

He drops me at a terrible hitching spot, by traffic lights and nearly in town on the wrong road, but two women actually do a U-turn to pick me up. At the station the older one, who is from *Eiheiji* [the Soto sect's main temple], buys me an express ticket and presses 1000 yen into my hand for something to eat. The train is about to go, but again I have tears in my eyes. How are people so kind? I feel almost humbled before such generosity. I don't know if I'm capable of it myself.

I arrive at Toshoji at a respectable hour, not too tired. There's someone in my room, a new dormitory student, but this one is a woman, Mayumi-san. They put her into the kitchen for training with the idea that she is to go to Kannonji as cook. I'm also to go there, at least for the summer. Mayumi-san is tall and timid, often quivering like a startled rabbit. She's hard-working, quick to laugh, and a joy to have in the kitchen. But Toshoji isn't what she had in mind. She wanted time for zazen but instead is thrust into the kitchen. At first I too resented all the time not spent on the mat, considered it time wasted, but it really is only a greater challenge. Her hopes are pinned on Kannonji. The first few days she couldn't eat in silence; it scared her. She'd giggle and leave half her food. Now it's okay. It seems funny—she knows she's getting married in the autumn but not to whom. Go Roshi tried to fix her up, but she'd have none of it. I think she'd like to marry an obosan. She's 27 years old, has never had a job, was groomed only for marriage, i.e., cooking, sewing, flower arranging, and the tea ceremony. Eeyuk! I wonder what's behind her interest in Zen. Good on her for trying.

Jiko-san was to go to Tokyo, so Tessai-san's wife arrived to take his place in the kitchen. She had been kitchen helper for three years and anything different from her style was "dame" right down to the way I'd sit. Still, I had to admire her energy and orientation. She was basically right and not bitchy but only strong-minded and rough in asserting herself. At the same time, Yugi-san seemed too intent on corrections. She'd say the rice was too hard, he that it was too soft, and both would nit-pick about trifles. At times I could let it run right off me, but at other times I was definitely niggled. It's easy to see how little control I have and how firmly entrenched my ego is. These things couldn't have affected me but for the idea of "I." It helped to try distancing myself and to look at the conditions which caused each to be so critical. This is a point which I definitely need to work on.

I had great energy when I came back from Korea. I needed drastically less sleep. However, my meditations were very flighty, and I'd want to get up from them. I got a terrible pain in my left eye, and Jiko-san went to great trouble to find me a chiropractor and to bring me to her. She is excellent, and my posture already feels different. She's a spiritual person, though looking coolly efficient in her medical gown. Seeing my sewing in a plastic bag, she gave me a homemade purse for it.

Part V

Spring

1980, end of April

Last night after washing up and a very distracted zazen, we called on Tetso-san. Suddenly he says, "Let's go to Ginza." So we're off, himself, myself, and Jiko-san, cruising through the flashing lights, priests of the night. On to Roppongi, where we go to a bar, the Berni Inn. I haven't been in a bar since I lived in San Francisco. I feel I'm encased by this red wallpaper, English crockery, dart board, and the sound of "old boys" English interspersed with the clickety-clack of Japanese. Too subdued for a pub, it had supermarket music and more sherry than beer. *"Namu myo ho renge kyo"* ["Homage to the Lotus Sutra," chanted as its main practice by the Nichiren sect], said someone as we passed—a strange sight, I suppose. Two Japanese approached us, bought us Irish whiskeys. Jiko-san was getting definitely looser, laughing, boasting of how wonderful Ireland was. Very comical. He was in his element, with whiskey and an audience. I enjoyed myself thoroughly, laughed and laughed. Tetso-san was quiet, seemed somehow out of things. He was drinking juice (was driver) but it wasn't only that. Jiko-san was a riot. Often as I've cursed the old devil, I actually miss him now that he's in Kyoto. When I was responding to circumstances with my ego, feeling put out by criticism or when

Takeo-san would lose his temper over nothing, I'd think of Jiko-san. *"Ii yo, nandemo ii yo"* ["It's OK! Anything's OK!"]. Totally unflappable.

This morning Takeo-san blew up at Mayumi-san because she was slow at making tea. At Chosan she cried and cried. I could empathize but could also realize how ridiculous it is to be put out by one of his explosions. He's worried about his new temple and says himself that he's neurotic. Watching his face, I thought how truly wolf-like he looks when he pushes his mouth out like a muzzle. When he raises and knots his brow, adjusting his glasses, his eyes become small and beady. They're close together like the eyes of a wild animal, and he jumps up and runs like a wolf. I went out of my way to be decent to him so that I wouldn't feel resentment over what I knew was my stupid "self-notion." It worked incredibly well. When they are barking at me, they are victims of causes and conditions, but when I am gentle and kind, they respond accordingly. Then they, too, are *yasashii hito* [gentle people] and it's impossible to bear a grudge. It's true that if you love your enemy you have killed him for he ceases to exist.

I thought I noticed changes since beginning Zen. It seems as if I'm laughing all the time, but I can't really remember how I was before. I think I've always laughed, but I don't remember laughing this much. Looking in my tiny, grease-stained mirror, I can never see all my face at once, but I think lines on my forehead have smoothed out. My hunchback posture has become straight. I was very surprised, though, when the chiropractor said, "You have an abnormal spine—it's perfectly straight."

Eshin-san said last night, "Your face is completely different from when you first came to Toshoji."

Takeo-san agreed and I thought, "Well, of course, I'm bloody well bald."

Then he said, "Your face is shining; it is an enlightened face. Your friends will be surprised."

I'm still trying to work out the best way to deal with correction and criticism. At first I thought, "Well, at Kannonji it will be okay because there'll be no one over me. That was one of the attractions. Or, if I have my own dojo, then I can do as I like, etc. Well, I realized I simply can't always be boss, so I'd better figure out how to deal with it.

Then we were folding covers for the monthly newsletter and I folded a huge stack in half, which was wrong, and I had nearly finished redoing them when they told me I was folding them too wide. I had to start the whole stack again. Eshin-san said, "Even Soshin-san makes mistakes, even excellent lady." Well, that seemed so funny compared to my own self-image (where I'm constantly making mistakes and being corrected by myself or others) that I started laughing and laughing. It really seemed hilarious. Then poof, all tension was released. Doing the stack all over again didn't bother me. And it didn't smart when Eshin-san said "Soshin-san is good with her head but not with her hands." All was well with the world. If I can divorce myself from my ego enough to laugh at my mistakes, then I think this will be the most effective response. Now I'm eager for criticism so I can try it out.

While I was waiting at a subway station in a seedy part of Tokyo, I was looking at the daytime-dead neon light, the sleeping seaminess, waiting for night. It's an attractive world because it's earthy and grubby, alive, real yet totally false without the pretense of reality. Vibrant throbbing music and bodies. I thought about the alternatives that confronted me when I first came to Japan last November—the usual job as an English teacher didn't interest me. Either monastic renunciation or sensory wallowing drew me. A soul seeking surrender? It was either accident or providence that the former happened first. Either way was a search for liberation—freedom from inhibition, from other people's values, from their suffocating puritan ethic born from the delusion of a retributory hereafter. Or else the other option, spiritual liberation, but from what? This one was hazier. Those who suffer want liberation from suffering, but I seldom suffer. My life has been wonderful, blessed. Who could enslave me? I did as I wished when I wished. Now I feel gratitude that this Zen way took me, because I consciously, fervently, could not be said to have taken it. Now I feel there is no turning back.

I've been reading an excellent book that draws the distinction between positive and negative *samadhi* [intense effortless concentration]. This makes many things clearer. I understand the Go Roshi of dokusans and sutras, the Go Roshi of chosan and daily life. I understand why soji is so important and have slipped naturally into positive samadhi in the kitchen.

Someone said that we must take care of things simply because they exist. This occurred to me as I was sweeping the floor. In the dust pile there were 16 grains of rice and two tiny crawling things that didn't need to die. It felt neither good nor bad.

I look at the clock. It is two o'clock. A long time later I look at the clock and it is only two o'clock. It is always two o'clock. I feel a great peace.

Preparations are almost finished for Eshin-san's ceremony. Tomorrow he will be a priest. The ceremony is very simple and thrilling. Outside hondo the monks bow, then we file slowly in. Takeo-san beats the hell out of the drum in a heart-pounding chase intensity. I clack two pieces of wood. Eshin-san holds a fan. Ping bell, clack wood, bong deep resonant drum. Everyone bows. Eshin-san does various bows, receives the stick from Jiko-san and holds *mondo* ["Dharma combat" ceremony with Zen questions and responses]. Each of us in turn shouts *"Shakusha wa"* ["Oh Teacher"], and then each strides up, kneels before him, and addresses some Zen query. Then bowing, retreating, we roar *"chincho"* [Literally, "How valuable" or "Thank you for your answer"]. The loudness of my voice startled everyone, especially me. I enjoy bellowing out. My questions are, "What is emptiness?" "What is Buddha nature?" "What is man before he is born?" After having them answered, I'm afraid I'm still not much clearer in my mind…Then more bowing. We each in turn offer our congratulations. Pronouncement from Go Roshi. We bow, and it's over.

Nakamuro-san sits with his fan, all athletic tension. Takeo-san once said that I was like a mirror, reflecting back impartially whatever was in front of me. But I didn't really know what he was getting at until, while watching Nakamuro-san, it became clear. He is beautiful. Sitting like that, he must be in deep samadhi. He's always happy and helpful, vibrant with energy while there so profoundly tranquil.

I was physically born in 1955. Can I die and be born this month of *Showa*
55 [1979–80, the 55th year of the reigning Showa emperor, Hirohito]?

Kannonji, Iwateken
May 2
The second day of the fifth month of 1980. Twenty-two days before I cel-
ebrate a quarter century.

Sesshin has begun.

Dokusan. I did mu with all my heart and all my soul and all my being.
Everything was squeezed out until my head touched the floor.

"Is it your mind or your heart or your body saying mu?"

"I don't know." Tears are flowing without reason; I laugh without
reason.

"What is the difference between I don't know and mu?"

"No difference." Go Roshi whacks me.

"Ouch!"

"Who feels pain?"

"I do."

Then, when I'm not looking, he jumps up, embraces me. *"Bikkuri
shita!"* ["You surprised me!"] I tumble backwards, laughing. He holds
my hand tightly, my thumb.

"This is I don't know."

"I know."

"You must see mu in everything." I leave dokusan, crying and laughing, with Tachibana Sensei apologizing for his English translation. That's
okay. He encourages me.

I go to dokusan with Kobai-san.

"Where does mu come from?"

"I don't know—how can it come from somewhere? It doesn't have a
place."

Kobai-san is very fish-like, cold comfort.

"We've all struggled with the problem."

"It comes from me," I told her.

"If that's your answer, go to dokusan."

In we go again. Go Roshi says, *"zenzen wakaranai"* ["You don't under-stand at all"].

I'm crushed, devastated. Roshi says, "Next time, come alone."

After lunch we rest. I'm crying, feel wretched, forlorn. I can't do it. Tessan-san has such strength in his mu; the fellow in white has such per-sistence. I couldn't keep on like him (I take big pauses between mu's). He thumps his head like little Sandra [the most troubled child at Rudolph Steiner School in Glencraig, Northern Ireland, where Maura worked for a summer], bleating and beating. I lie down, weeping and mu-ing and half sleeping. I resolve not to go to bed that night or any night until *ken-sho* [flash of enlightenment; experience of "seeing [Buddha] nature"].

Going into zendo, I hear Go Roshi say something about Soshin (prob-ably saying "I was wrong; she's hopeless"). I'm called to dokusan. I feel so dejected, empty-minded. It doesn't even occur to me to wonder why Go Roshi wants me to come alone.

"Mu-dō?" ["How is your mu?"]

I mu for him with all my strength, raising myself high and squeezing every bit of breath into mu until my head touches the floor.

"Once more again," he says in English. (He doesn't speak English but I don't register surprise).

I do so.

Then "Once more again."

My first and only thought was "He may make me do this for ages." Then he jumped at me, grabbed me—"This body is muji, this head, eyes, ears."

Suddenly I'm laughing and crying muji. I don't even realize "Now I am muji," but I simply was muji and everything around me.

And he hits different parts of my body. "This is muji." Count 20 in muji—20 parts of me, 20 muji in Kannonji, all around me. We're hold-ing on to each other, laughing and laughing. "Heart muji," he says, thumping me. "And Go Roshi's heart muji," I say, belting him back. We're embracing.

"Kensho shita" ["You have realized your Buddha nature"], says he.

I'm surprised. I was too self-conscious even to know that it was kensho.

Only when I got outside and was looking at everything and really seeing mu did I finally know. Suddenly I understood why we must take care of things just because they exist; we are of no greater and of no lesser value.

At dinner the only words spoken aloud rang in my ears, *"Mora-san go kensho itashimashita"* ["Maura has seen into her Buddha nature"].

At first I was so exhausted I felt neither joy nor sorrow, just relief. The next day I was ecstatic, couldn't stop smiling. Then all was as before—or at least, so it seems. Everyone tells me I look different. It's hard to be sure. I can't be bothered looking for big changes. I began the koans and flew through about twelve. Maybe they came easily because of my reading. I don't know.

After the kensho itself, a wonderful thing happened. That morning I had been fed from the strength of Tessan-san's and the others' mu's. Now that I had been "passed," as it were, I felt the desperation in their calling and I put all my strength into mu. With each breath in I thought, "Tessan-san is—" the huge breath out was "MU!" I called and I called to him. He went to dokusan and had kensho. There was still work to be done. Tessan-san and I cried and cried to the other monk. He answered, wailing. In harmony we shouted, trying to urge him harder and harder. I lost myself completely. I was him, Tessan-san, mu, all dissolved. But he didn't have kensho. I resolved that if he stayed up late, I wouldn't sleep but would urge him on. He didn't stay up. I was exhausted. Everything was expended. My throat was raw. I lost my voice, couldn't speak for two days. Still I tried calling to him the next day. The other head priest thought it strange and asked me to stop.

Mid-May

I wonder if Go Roshi judges by the right answer or how it's done. Probably both. I hope I'm not cheating myself by knowing some of the answers, but am afraid that I am. Koans were great fun. Go Roshi and I dissolving into laughter, he jumping up, careening around the room, hiking up his kimono to take a dive into a fictitious sea. It was so much innocent play. Yet I felt I wasn't going deep enough.

At the end of sesshin was Go Roshi's *teisho* [formal Dharma talk]. He spoke about me, said of the 20-odd foreigners that he'd helped, I was the purest. He felt me to be like his child and wanted me by his side until he died. He said his plan was to make Kannonji an International Zen Center for me. He turned to me beaming, "*Wakaru?*" ["Do you understand?"] (He never addresses the audience in teisho.)

"*Wakaranai*" ["I don't understand"]. I had to reply. I love that man so dearly that I almost cried when Tessan-san told me what he said. Still, I can't see myself living always in Japan, being an obosan. Though it would be a good life for me, I'm just not that pure.

Go Roshi left and we began to settle into a routine. Tekkan-san and Kas'ko-san were still here. I fixed myself a room in the loft of a storage hut. I love it. Up high I feel myself to be a bird in my nest. All around the eaves birds wing and poke, calling. Two huge windows and sliding door give good light and ventilation. It smells so wonderfully of wood and now of tatami. Of course they all thought I was quite mad but Tessan-san now says it's the best room. I climb in and out a window, commuting from the main temple.

One afternoon, on a whim, Tekkan-san took us up the mountains looking at blossoms. We picked many wild plants, brought them home for cooking. Gathering our dinner in the sunshine from nature's abundance somehow all seemed to be as it should be. Tekkan-san can be so gentle and always totally immediate and involved in what he's doing. This makes him brutally honest and when angered he is totally angered. It really annoyed me, though, to hear everyone putting him down, bitching behind his back. Not a soul stood by him—only Kas'ko-san, who could hardly be said to be a separate soul.

Tachibana Sensei took us (Tessan-san and me) on a grand outing. We went to another temple. It's much older and much more beautiful than Kannonji, but really made me appreciate Kannonji more. We're very free here, plenty of time for zazen. They do little zazen, only maintenance. We saw some very beautiful sites. I felt possessed, no longer human (or extremely human); an incredible energy was surging through me, sparking, flashing, a pure joy. He is an extraordinarily good and kind man.

Last night after dinner Tessan-san played the guitar. Me sitting on the floor, drab grey kimono, bare head, bare feet, doing my embroidery. He singing from the depths of a world of memories and dreams, his journey and love of life. Yet there was only that moment, rich and vivid. He made up a crazy song about Soshin-san cooking delicious pumpkin even if it was a little old and hard. We laughed like drunkards who can hardly remember why. He's so Japanese, yet a dropout (as he says)—two years traveling, playing his music, yet his ideal is the little woman on whose pretty face he can gaze as they both sit sipping tea. The dear little woman for whom he will fight all day so that he may relax, bathing in her innocence by night. Doesn't he need some education!

Women really are repressed here, forced into the mold of a giggling innocent. At first I rather enjoyed the surprise and admiration with which I was treated. Now I feel its oppressiveness, for its only because I'm female. My heart went out to Kobai-san. She wished she could sit as freely and naturally as I, but couldn't. Such a simple thing. Always raised to sit like a lady, she was too self-conscious to be merely comfortable. It's odd, though, that she too said I look Japanese. I don't understand how so many people can say that. My eyes are distinctly round and colored; if I had any more freckles I'd have a suntan.

The only change I can put my finger on since kensho is in reading *ookyo* [the sutras]. Now I love to shout in a big booming voice. Previously I simply could not. It's such a relief to really shout those sutras, lose oneself (I could even sing at Tekkan-san's party). I finally realize the value of ookyo, but it must be done loudly, then the breathing is very beneficial. The "screamers" in Ireland possibly did catch on to something effective, although they seem to lack the integrative benefits of a 2,500-year tradition. I can see shades of many therapies in Zen. I've started chanting *"Kanzeon, namubutsu, yobutsu u in..."* [beginning of the Kannon Sutra for Protecting Life] while I'm working. It regulates my breathing, and I can work with less distracting thoughts and a greater sense of oneness with the work.

I planted veggies, built a compost retainer, am preparing new beds. I feel such a peace puttering around in the dirt with all the wiggly, slimy, ugly little creatures. The creatures digging and fertilizing the garden and worth no more or less than I. I'm careful about them now; try not to disturb them, carry them to appropriate homes when they take over indoors. At first I was put out that Kobai-san was doing the kitchen, but it's worked out perfectly. I'm learning more about Japanese cookery and get to work in the garden. I'm very, very, very happy.

I stood in the rain for the longest time without getting wet. Nobody knew. It was my koan. The rain noises were on cement, on stone, on my plastic mac. The bird in the apple blossoms shook the moisture from its feathers and sang. I, in sympathy, shook in my mac and was silent.

To become is not to annihilate. To become the quarrel does not really stop it. It both stops and continues it. Wet and not wet. Is and is not.

How can one be Buddhist and not be socialist? How accept and allow the perpetration of a system based on desire? A system that functions as trigger and effect of the desire for money and commodities. A system that, to feed itself, must resort to crass commercialism and ever spiraling desire.

I wonder sometimes about Kobai-san's relationship to her own sexuality. She is staying with us until a husband can be found for her. She's apparently not worried about facing her future as the servant of a total stranger and has no idea at all of marrying for love. At first I thought perhaps she had come looking for a husband. She seemed to know nothing about Zen but talked incessantly about how hard it would be to marry someone without any hair. Tessan-san, she says, is her favorite but she told him that she didn't like men, that she was afraid of them. Often she would avert her eyes from me, or put a book in front of her face, laughing, saying my looks were too seductive. One night she said something to Tessan-san, using a word normally only used between lovers or close friends. He was furious, railed at her without letting up for fully an hour and a half. Banging the table with his fist, spilling the soup, stubbornly refusing to eat, threatened to call Go Roshi and said she was welcome to leave. Kobai-san barely spoke. She sat meekly, eyes down, fiddling and folding a crease in her apron. She seemed neither particularly cowed nor perturbed. I, of course, couldn't understand and couldn't possibly imagine what could provoke such a reaction. Tessan-san's entire face was transfigured, almost unrecogniz-able, fascinating. His eyes burned into her. He seemed not to blink, every muscle in his body tensed, knuckles turning white as he gripped the table. It was all that seemed to support or restrain him. The following day she apologized and no tension seemed to linger on either side.

Yesterday Tachibana Sensei brought me to a jazz coffee shop. Good feeling to it. The waitress said, "*Maura-san desu ka?*" ["Are you Maura-san?"] I was shocked. How did she know my name? It turned out that she is a friend of the editor of the local newspaper, who apparently spoke highly of my English. The result is that she, her sister, and a friend will come every Sunday to Kannonji for English lessons.

It seems that many American jazz singers come and she wants to be able to talk to them. She was delightful and I think we may be similar souls—rare enough around here. She gave us free cheesecake and promised to take me to big concerts in Tokyo and anywhere I wanted in the area.

Funny...I thought of ringing Richard-san; then I met him. I wrote a letter to Jiko-san and found his waiting for me. Then a couple of coinci-dences with Kobai-san. Now Kobai-san is convinced I can read people's minds. The telepathy between Jiko-san and me was often extraordinary but I have certainly no special powers. Kobai-san asks me if I chant ookyo only for myself. Of course, for whom else? But she is trying to invest me with some kind of mysterious character.

May 24

My birthday: Working in the garden, sure that today would be like every other day, but not particularly bothered. "*Gomen kudasai*" [words that one calls instead of knocking]. I went to the door. A telegram. For me. I've never had one in my life before. In inscrutable *katakana* [Japanese phonetic script used for foreign words] it said "Good Morning, Happy 25th birthday," addressed to Soshin O'Halloran *Sama* [an honorific title of high respect], from some woman in Tokyo—I have no idea who! How did she know my address, age, Buddhist name? Who could she be? Pos-sibly the chiropractor...

I made banana pudding. Tessan-san said, "What, no cake?" I pointed out the absence of an oven. The closest we could come was "hot cakey mix." He made a huge plate of plump, delicious, greasy donuts. He brought the stereo into the kitchen. There was great fun and love in the air as we prepared. Me in my long ceremonial gown dancing to Steely Dan on the tatami. We split one beer three ways. Tachibana Sensei remembered the date and brought me a radio. What a man! "Do you like jazz?" said Tessan-san. "Yes," said I, while thinking to myself, I'd like Phoebe Snow. Phoebe Snow it uncannily was. Often, with very simple things like that, I think of something I want and it just comes. Strange.

Sitting around the table we whipped a candle from an altar, balanced it in an ashtray. Tessan-san played the guitar. I sat crosslegged in my robes, smoking a cigar and laughing at it all. A grand birthday.

May 25

The next morning, Monday, Tessan-san and I had our first disagreement. On Sunday we had gone to the hot springs with Tachibana Sensei. I had, as usual, bought a little something for his kids. Tessan-san muttered "Oh, I must get him something, too." Next morning he launched into a lecture on why it was bad for priests to give presents. They were only supposed to say "thank you" and take. I was furious. The cheapskate, trying to twist things around. He said priests don't have money except what is presented to them to spend on their needs. I have very few needs, and I would damn well give presents until I really did have no money, instead of not doing so because I shouldn't have money. I shouted and argued, tripping over myself with rage. Then he rambled on and on without connection about various things, never outright attacking me, but saying, "You will get sterner with yourself," implying but not saying that I wasn't stern enough. He divided and separated us by saying, "You still have your foreign ways" and "I hate to have these discussions with a woman." I was so angry I knew that if I spoke I would cry and corroborate the "woman" bit. So I glared, bored into him with every iota of anger I could muster. I shredded him with my eyes. Merciless.

Finally I had to start cleaning but couldn't stop mulling the whole thing over. Why had I become so terribly angry? It was really a small thing. I've seen him now, arguing with everyone, and Tetsuro-san had warned me about his "new priest that knows it all" ways, so it was easy to foist the blame on to him. But my reaction was exaggerated. I needed release. He was on his way out to school. It was the wrong time but I called him anyway. "I was very angry with you. I'm sorry. Sometimes you act as if you know everything and nobody else knows anything." I don't know if he caught the latter. "Your face was terrible," he said, "your eyes—" We laughed. It was okay. We're human. Since then I've purposely discussed Tachibana Sensei's present. Thankfully, no reaction.

I have so little control really. The day before, I was bursting with joy. Every twitch of the breeze, ripple on the mountain, whine of machinery, everything delighted me. Then, boom, I explode at poor Tessan-san.

Dear Sean:

…Things are going extremely well here. I'm living in the country, me and another monk; we're running this temple. It's a good life for the moment. The zazen is great but I feel like Freud must have felt when he discovered hypnosis. It has so many implications for theories of the unconscious and language. I really want to do some reading—peace and quiet and no distractions.

…Both Margy and Kate are getting married. Can you believe it?…So in the summer I'll be going to the States and Ireland, then back to Japan. When I'm in the States I want to buy enough books to keep me going for the next year or so. Would you be a pet and give me a reading list so I can finally come to terms with language and associated issues…

I have to dash, Sean. Me and the other monk have a ceremony this afternoon; we have to bless some geezer's new car. Did I ever think I'd be chanting Japanese sutras over a Subaru? People ask us the funniest things, like to drive out ghosts. It's so totally contrary to the spirit of Zen, which is refreshingly iconoclastic.

Take care.
Love, M.

May 26

Kobai-san has been having a heavy dose of *makyo* [distorted perceptions occurring in zazen]. She hears footsteps, sees many priests, sees herself as a young girl in a red skirt among the flowers. Hears ookyo and our voices. Seems to have a fixation around ookyo. She can't do it loudly in the morning but since the onset of makyo does it loudly each evening. The obosons may have to do with her fear of them, as in Toshoji she feels there are people behind her.

Once she realized it was in her mind, she felt better. I slept beside her for a couple of nights. Zazen really does change consciousness. Just as consciousness-changing drugs may prod hallucinations, so may zazen. I'd love to understand the whole thing.

May 28

Kobai-san seems better now. Though I can't talk to her, I'm very fond of her. She is so honest and candid—inhibited but not too inhibited to admit it. She wants to touch us, but can't. I try to make light of it, chase her around the room, threatening to tickle her. She doesn't know what to do. She says I have many faces: beautiful, pretty, angry, child-like, frightening. People react to me differently of late. It's strange sometimes, my face is too bright, like glaring sunshine. The child said I look totally different and now look Japanese. The foreigners came and were fascinated, stared too long—perhaps it's the shaved hair. No, it's really odd. I look in the mirror and don't know. I don't know how I looked then and how I look now. It'll be interesting when I go home for Margy's wedding—hope that little sister of mine is doing the right thing.

May 30

I had my first zazen "student," Richard-san's English student. He came to meet me. Tessan-san invited him to my Sunday morning classes. It was a fiasco. His English is too good. I said I had no time. He asked if I had time to talk about zazen each day. That was my duty. I said there wasn't much to say; it was a question of doing, but I'd give him time before soji. He wanted to know all about English manners and customs. He came the next day. I talked Zen at him. He didn't seem interested. I felt tricked. He only wants free daily English conversation lessons. I'd give him a few more days and then get tough. Next day he asked me to teach him how to sit. I did. He was so enthusiastic, so hopeful, it gave me real pleasure. Then he stopped coming. I truly mustn't be a bodhisattva, for I felt a little relieved. Then he came again. I'm glad.

(undated)
Maureen [Carroll, a college friend], m'dear,…
Here life goes grand. I'm feeling very healthy and happy—doing all those sensible things like brown rice, early to bed, early to rise, hard work, Protestant ethics turned Oriental. Well, fortunately, not quite. The similarities are superficial. Ah, but it's lovely to be in the country. I'm sitting here, drinking a cup of tea, watching the afternoon turn into twilight. Crows, cuckoos…

Now I'm going wild doing all the cooking for the retreat, sleeping 2–3 hours a night and busy…I'll just summarize it—i.e., life is great and I'm coming home in the autumn. Hope you're doing brilliantly and even tho' I never write I still love you, so mind yourself and meet ya for a pint soon. Happy Birthday.

Very much love, hugs, kisses & best wishes, M

June 1
For Tachibana Sensei's birthday I pushed my exhausted self, spent quite a bit on food and presents, cooked and cooked, decorated the sitting room. He phoned.

"Happy Birthday," I said.

"But it's not my birthday."

"Ha, ha, you can't fool me; I remember you said May 31st, a week after mine."

"A mistake. I meant March."

What a laugh! So he went along with it and we had a smashing party. Then off to the jazz café. The atmosphere was of the wee hours of the morning, snug, not quite asleep, a warm cradling sensation.

The wasp and ladybug invasion taught me plenty. *Busshari-to* [Hall of Buddha Relics, where relics of the cremated are enshrined, usually including family ancestors of the congregation] was overrun with them. Tessan-san sprayed. I brought up the Hoover, but it seemed wrong to vacuum up the live ones and have them suffocate in its dusty bowels. What to do? One by one I picked them up on the shovel and put them outside. It took ages. Each time I cleaned Busshari-to it was the same. It was annoying but I had to. Yet somehow, in an ever so slight shift of focus, it brought home to me that I am no more and no less than, and not separate from, a fading lady-bug or a dying wasp. Respect life, not because it's right or good or moral but because it is. It's a nuisance to pick up the sesame seeds one by one when everyone has finished eating *goma sembei* [sesame crackers], to eat the potato peels that the others don't like, to chase and rescue even a single grain of rice. That the single grain of rice is all rice is all things, is nothing, is valueless, that there is no value and not-value great or small; only is. As I swept up the corpses in Busshari-to I realized I was distinguishing life from death.

Each day in the garden I explain to the weeds that they do not really die; they change form as they are doing anyway. Yet I distinguished. I didn't want to pick up the cadavers with my fingers. Clean-dirty, dead-alive, even plant-animal (for handling dead flowers caused me no qualms). So for training I made myself pick up all the dead flies, spiders, moths, and bugs that crossed my sweeping path. Not really so bad after all though I'm still more inclined to use the broom. Have several times just forgotten and picked the thing up.

I love getting filthy in the garden. The others get disgusted. I had an interesting dream. Rushing to work in a place like Dunster [restaurant in Cambridge, Mass., where she worked in 1979], I jump off a bridge-like thing and land on a table where a nun is selling potato cakes. My filthy shoes first, then I sit on them. I begin to eat the ones I've destroyed; she gets almost hysterical, "You can't eat them; you stood on them, yuck, dirty." I'm in a hurry to work, trying to eat and explain that I dirtied them so I must eat them; no one else will, so they mustn't be wasted. She's in a flap. Finally she calls Reverend Mother who is also upset but acquiesces.

I, thinking, how stupid, wolf the cakes, dash to work. I explain to the cook why I'm late. He laughs. Obvious dream elements—Buddhist/Catholic contradiction; the potato skins I made myself eat; Tessan-san saying my feet were dirty, the endless waste that revolted me at Dunster.

Sesshin Toki [time for intensive zazen]. Someone made a mistake on the announcements and hardly anyone came. Go Roshi was not perturbed but changed sesshin into zenkai, so fewer sitings of zazen. Pity.

It was a pleasure to see him again, an inspiration to watch him peeling an orange; he was deeply involved in the tearing of each vein. How many oranges had he peeled in his life, yet still enthralled! Watching TV. When I first came to Tokyo I heard the TV from his room. I thought "How insensitive his wife is," felt somehow superior to this soap-opera-addicted woman. She moved out and still the TV blared incessantly. Roshi himself watched it. "Oh, well," thought I, not really knowing what to think. Now I could watch him watch. He is so totally engrossed, a child pulled right into the screen. Beautiful. I remember how the Ryans [Ruth's best friends and former next-door neighbors] used to invite Scott to watch TV so they could watch him. Go Roshi was the same.

During the zenkai I was given a koan about a man digging a hole and not getting to the other side. Tetsuro-san's translation left out the fact that the question was "Why couldn't he get through after having dug the hole?"

Go Roshi said my answer was that of an unenlightened person. I was crushed. It tore open all my insecurities about whether I really had kensho or not. Later I gave a similar answer—that when digging there was only now, no after digging, therefore no through, only in the tunnel and digging. Roshi said that was the answer to a different kind of koan and explained that the man was universal and greater than any of his creations, therefore greater than the hole. Still, all my self-doubts were triggered.

He said the koans would get more difficult (a warning, perhaps) and he hopes I run away to Ireland (laughing). He asked me to stay ten years.

"I don't know," sez I.

"Nine," he bargained. "Eight and a half," I offered.

He offered me his room at Kannonji instead of my loft.

"*Yuck, iranai*" ["I don't need it"] I said and he laughed. Always laughing. What could possibly disturb him?

During teisho, he said that I alone could become the greatest woman priest. (However, the competition is not exactly overwhelming.)

The final day of sesshin/zenkai, the TV people came to film me. They were fascinated and alarmed at my room. "Aren't you afraid of ghosts?" is the universal reaction. Even educated Japanese seem to be obsessed by ghosts. They eeked and ooed and generally fussed outrageously as they lugged the camera and lights up the ladder to my loft. They were funny. I liked them but felt silly talking about myself.

"Why did you do Zen?"

I told her the story about Ciaran [an old friend who became a Buddhist monk in England]. Afterwards, thinking about the question, it seemed like something I never decided to do but something deep inside that I knew I was going to do, not with a sense of determination but in the same way that I know Monday comes after Sunday. Inevitable.

Kobai-san was funny after seeing the documentary thing. She started calling me *Kannon-sama* [Kannon, the much beloved Bodhisattva of Compassion, who hears and attends to the cries of the world]; she loves idols.

Go Roshi's 70th birthday-cum-book publishing-event was at a hot springs hotel. I barely finished my present for Go Roshi in the lobby below. Many masters had gathered for the occasion. They were beautiful men, radiant. Each gave a speech. At my turn I fumbled and blushed; how could I put into words what I felt? Lear's youngest daughter. Tessai-san's wife told me to give my present. I didn't want to in front of everybody but I did while she blithered on about it taking three and a half months and me finishing while everyone slept. I was crimson. He passed it around.

The roshis were amazing, on the stage fooling around, as innocent as babes. Those knowing sages, knowing it all, were leaving all knowing behind and just doing. There sure as hell is something in that Zen. Go Roshi, cancer-ridden, celebrating his 70th birthday. The night before he chose his gravestone; tonight they hurl his tiny frame in the air, catching him three times. He laughs good naturedly. I went to pour him a drink.

He grabbed my hand, pumping it vigorously (they love an excuse to shake hands), saying "Thank you, thank you." in English. I was crying.

I had to take my turn on the stage. Amazing—it didn't faze me to have to sing a song. I didn't use the mike but boomed around the hall with all the strength the ookyo had freed. I bobbed around making a fool of myself with the Japanese dancers. Okay.

Kannonji, Iwateken
June 1980
Dear Mum, Margy, Scott, and Beth,
Phew! Am I exhausted! We had a sesshin where a bunch of people came to the temple. It culminated in a memorial celebration of Roshi's 70th birthday, so there was a ton of work before and after the whole thing. The actual celebration was at a hot springs. So very Japanese, with the women all taking baths together and the men likewise. Then there was a big spread upstairs. Although I hadn't realized it, Roshi is very famous, and great Zen masters from all over Japan came for the occasion. (As usual, I was the only foreigner and the only woman monk. Only recently I learned how unusual my experience is when I heard of a German woman who bullied her way into a man's temple but was never allowed to wear robes or to be a monk. Interesting. Most temples won't allow men and women to study together.) Anyway, they're marvelous men, these old monks. They're like children, joking and playing. One old fellow gets up on the stage, a revered and respected Zen master, hikes up his robes, straps a pillow on his back and dances a strange dance about a "babe" on his back. Roshi just had a huge definitive book published, so that was also being celebrated and we were each given a copy. (Much of it is written in the script I've learned so I'm struggling to read it.) They all took turns singing and of course I had to do an Irish solo. (Blush, blush.) Luckily they didn't know how the tune was supposed to sound.

The ladies were all swaddled in pastel kimonos. Several of them did one of their abstract (to me) Japanese dances. Then I was dragged up to join them. I tried to imitate them but they resembled fluttering butterflies, while

I looked like someone shoveling snow. The difference was much more than a pastel kimono.

There was no doubt that it was a Zen party when, at the end, we went around from guest to guest graciously putting their left-overs into our boxes. We're already sick to death of them after only one day.

It's nice to be back at Kannonji again and to be living in the country. Although we're near the highway at the front, out back rice paddies spread to the mountains, punctuated by bamboo groves. Less romantically, the buildings are full of creepy, crawly creatures.

In the midst of the preparations for Roshi's ceremony, we had an entire day of interviewing and filming for television. They came again this morning to film my room at the top of one of the wood sheds. It's really just a platform, and the women from the TV studio were terrified they'd fall over, so they clung to the wall. They kept mumbling that they were sure living in such a room was good for my ascetic practice. In August I've been asked to give three talks about Ireland and about my life, during a three day UNESCO conference...

Love, M.

Dear Sean...

I'm afraid I'm in a lazy mood at the moment, so you'll just have to bear with my ramblings. I just woke up on a sunny summer afternoon with rainy season expectant, heaviness in the air. Last night I didn't go to bed at all but stayed up doing zazen all night—alone with the moon, the midnight breeze, and my mind. It's fascinating, Sean, to play these little games with the consciousness. And sometimes frightening. I've seen people have the strangest *makyo*—hallucinations, wild megalomaniacal fantasies that one finds hard to distinguish from the deepest states of supposed enlightenment.

There was a girl here of puritanical background, aching with the frustration of twenty-seven years of enforced virginity and an infinite future of the same yawning before her...So whether it was this energy or whether zazen in tampering with the unconscious somehow shifts a dream-reality filter, I don't know, but she began to see many monks that weren't there, hear footsteps, hear me chanting sutra. She couldn't tell herself from me, herself from carrots, herself from Buddha—which is very deep or very crazy. It coincided perfectly with full and half moon. Female hysteria?

There was another fellow, similarly sexually obsessed and repressed, with many morbid and ghoulish fantasies. This so-called "makyo" is quite a common feature of people in the early stages of practice. Anyway, I'm quite sane, or as sane as ever, whichever you prefer...

Thanks for the reading list. It all sounds heavy, I must say, but I really need a bit of theory...

Margy gets married on August 29th; then we go to Ireland September 1st and start getting in gear for Kate's wedding...It's coincidental that eleven years ago this summer my father died; suddenly both Kate and Margy are tying themselves to permanent male-type figures—and I end up with a teacher who always calls me his true daughter...

[Your trip to] Morocco sounded great—I like the place but hate the macho. [Maura briefly visited Morocco in 1972.] Maybe it would be different now; don't think I'd feel as threatened...

I don't know how long I'll stay here; sometimes I think another year will do me fine; sometimes I feel ten years would barely scratch the surface. It doesn't matter anyway. I'll leave when I leave...Waa, the air is getting hotter and stickier; don't know where the ants are getting the energy to crawl all over me, or if I can maintain the energy to keep writing this. Interruption. A little old lady just came in bearing sweet rice cakes and cold barley tea. She's funny. A couple of weeks ago they did a short documentary piece about me on television. Since then she's convinced I need some family and keeps popping around with little treats or seedlings for my garden. People here are really very kind. It's hard to believe sometimes...The old Japan is really appealing. I wear a kimono, heat the bath with a wood fire, and ignore the 20th century. I'm sure it will go away...

Sean, do you think I'll be able to get most of those books in Boston, or should I try to order them first? If you have any good lecture notes next year, or interesting essays, I'd really appreciate a copy, especially with relevance to language and conception of self and other. Playing with both using a completely different language and philosophical structure, I need some theoretical perspective.

Anyway, Sean, the sweat is gathering, drops poised to form trickling rivulets. It tickles. I'm hot & signing off. Take care.

Love, M.

July 1980

My eye kept causing me trouble. Takehiko-san put in needles and electrified me, but the eye is as bad as ever. I went to an Occidental doctor, who gave me some drugs to mask the pain. I won't take them. I bought a massager. Maybe by loosening the shoulders I can help the eye.

Kannonji, Iwateken

July 20, 1980

Dear Family,

...glad to get the invitation to Margy's wedding. It looks so official. Things must be hectic there. It's been that way here, too. We had daisesshin, the biggest sesshin of the year. However, the usual kitchen helper was called to Toshoji beforehand, and the other monk was busy learning to drive, so alone I did all the cooking, cleaning, weeding, flower arrangements, and sesshin preparation throughout this big temple. After all that build-up I was exhausted, then did five days and four nights of zazen. But strangely, after the second day of sesshin when I was most tired, I broke through a block and got a sudden, huge, unexplainable surge of energy, which took me right through sesshin, not tired at all. Now I'll take it easy for a couple of days before going off to the coast for this UNESCO conference. And soon after that I'll be heading off to Maine for the wedding. I leave Tokyo August 17th, so see you soon.

Last night, for a complete change of pace, some friends took me to a country festival. One of the mothers dressed me up in a kimono, binding my waist so tight I was sure my ribs were crushed. It was great fun, with all the little girls decked out in kimonos, beautiful origami chains festooning the streets. But it was so different from South American festivals, where everyone would get roaring drunk while they banged out the same tune on whatever would serve as an instrument, stumbling and stomping insanely 'til dawn. The Japanese version was much more restrained, prettier, understated, much bowing and fanning. Lovely, but I think there's a bit of the Latin in me.

After the festival the same friends took me to a jazz club in Morioka. The group had finished playing and were sitting quietly getting drunk by candle-light under the dark wooden beams of what could have been a Breton grenier. One of them was American and hadn't had a chance to speak English with a native in a month. When the gaijin in the yellow kimono with the punk haircut came in, he felt he had to invite us to join him. So we wined and chatted into the wee hours. We must have squeezed in an hour and a half of sleep before getting up for zazen and sutra. I'm writing this after breakfast as we await the arrival of thirty school kids coming to learn zazen. Should be funny. Anyway, must iron my kimono, change the flowers, and whip up to the shops on the old temple bike. See you soon…

Love, M.

July

My kid sisters, Kate and Margy, are both getting married! I can't believe it. I feel much too young to get married. Lately, I've been thinking of staying ten years to become a master. Then I wonder if I'll miss out on some love-type relationship. I'd be 34. But, really, I don't think it will be a problem. I feel that there'll always be men.

I worked hard on my koan and had a few really good sittings. I was wooden Buddha and flame. All must change, but nothing really changes, as it is always changing. As nothing really exists, how can it cease to exist? The flame is no more permanent and powerful than the Buddha. They are all muji. There is always change, change we perceive and that which we don't. We perceive change in relation to fixed ideas, but it's really not fixed, thus not a change. Words tricky, but inside it's crystal clear. A little breeze became a raging gale; it's changed yet not really; both are only particles of air in motion.

I did four nights of all night zazen, starting June 22nd, the longest day of the year and my longest night. It was incredible. The first night I kept thinking all beings are Buddha, could feel it. I felt totally purged, riding some high crest. The second night I kept thinking no separation. The next day, pulling weeds, they were part of me but different, like the back and front of my hand are different but not separate. Taking a break, I drank a cup of coffee. It was like no other cup of coffee. It was me, like sucking my own blood, but more intense as its familiarity was shocking. The third night "there is only here and now" reverberated in the corridors of my mind. The fourth night was bad; I kept nodding off. I love doing all night zazen. (I lie down for about an hour.) My eye went gammy on me. I want to do very hard cultivation. Already after only two days I've lost intensity and am as spiritually gross as ever (though I had a nice little samadhi this morning). I keep thinking that ordinary effort gives ordinary results. Before, I was looking forward to going home, but now it seems like an interruption.

I've been having some cases of telepathy. I got a beautiful letter from Jiko-san, full of Buddha and very supportive of me. He's going soon to his temple—Buddha and he are waiting for me—he underlined. The temple was meant for us, etc. He really is very pure, very good but I wouldn't be into it at all.

Go Roshi came up for sesshin. I had been slaving. Tessan-san had most conspicuously not been. There were too many weeds. We were scolded. I couldn't stretch myself any thinner and resented Tessan-san, resented when I had to do all the work. All Kobai-san's and the little he had, was left undone until I did it. While he smoked, listened to music, I ceaselessly scrubbed, cooked, pickled, and did zazen, then hated myself for resenting him. If I was truly involved in my work, I wouldn't be looking to see what he was or wasn't doing, wouldn't be measuring and comparing.

Go Roshi asked if I could hammer. I said I could. Together we went out to nail up the donor plates. I did the top row, he handing me each one in turn. I was rather proud of how I handled a hammer. When we came to the bottom row, he did one. He licked the nail, and with two blows of the hammer it was firmly affixed. So we continued, I doing the top row—tap, tap, tap—he the bottom, strictly, smoothly. We laughed and giggled at my clumsiness. Each board seems funnier, our heads coming together like conspirators in laughter. Tessan-san came back from driving-school. He took the hammer from me.

"Man's work," perhaps he thought. He did it better than I, so I relented but the fun dissolved. Roshi returned to his room.

I decided to do a really good sesshin and stayed up each night doing zazen. During the days Tachibana Sensei had to go to school, so no one could translate my koans. Sometimes I went to dokusan alone. One time Roshi asked me about my sisters' weddings and then when was I getting married and to whom.

The second night of sesshin, the young priest seemed near to kensho. He went to Busshari-to. I was doing zazen above him and came down to take a break. He and Nakanagi-san had joined one another in *Jizo-sama's room* [The hall dedicated to Jizo Bodhisattva, with an enshrined image. Jizo (Earth Storehouse) especially looks after deceased children and prisoners, along with all those roaming in the afterlife and any people in hellish situations]. As I gulped my coffee I felt a sense of mission. I'd help them that night. Going back in, their mu's were flagging. I started crying with them. All night we roared. When Nakanagi-san began to doze I shook him, crying into his ear, holding him, guiding him to the window, anything that he might continue. The young priest kept going of his own accord. I had to stay strong, when we were all fading, had to bellow a mu that would resurge us. Mu seemed to throb in my *hara* [belly], seemed to be a pump surging up and down. I became them, them me, all only mu. It was deeper than anything that happened to me before kensho, first time I'd done mu 'til morning.

Nakanagi-san had kensho next day, but the young priest finished sesshin without it.

Part VI

Resuming

Kannonji, Iwateken, November 1980

After a long absence, I resume. Ireland over, weddings, ups and downs. Margie's not so good but Kate's was a laugh—parties, singsongs with Chris, the best man. Me playing the spoons, all of us battering, rejoicing into the night. Cooking for weeks ahead. Orange ambrosia and mushroom soup forced on all who entered. I'm extremely happy about Geoff [husband of Maura's sister Kate]. I couldn't stop smiling throughout the ceremony. Many flirtations and reunions. Comforting to know that men are still falling in love with me and friends are still close. But it was hard to walk home alone by the canals after the last pint, the last bus, past the strolling couples, their greasy late night chips steaming from yesterday's newspaper. I had a lost feeling, wistful, not knowing for whom or what, for my practice that's not as good as it should be, for the lover, so wonderful, that I've yet to meet? Or was it just the whiskey and the damp? Who knows?

And who cares, for as time went on I felt less frantic, less constrained to live all that I was going to live in those six weeks. There was much love, deep warm womb love, coming from those I was afraid had forgotten me. It took a little time to bridge the gap, the missing years and sharing, but it was all there still. Much to do. They wanted me to give a talk on Zen; some wanted to train; the politics pulled me. So many places to extend myself, but first I must train myself, and rigorously.

MAURA IN IRELAND FOR
HER SISTER KATE'S WEDDING.
OCTOBER 1980.

Back at Kannonji, I was surprised to find that Eshin-san had run away. The stories…In a way I was relieved. My training would improve and their terrible pressure to marry me off in May would be gone. Apparently in my absence this plan was even more formalized. Tessan-san is kind but severe, teaching me ookyo, screaming at me. I can't understand the Japanese, don't know what I'm doing wrong. Tears come but they are like sweat, an excretion. Inside I'm not really affected. I don't dislike him (though he shouldn't take pleasure in his role), am not angry or really upset. This is the first very definite progress I can see. I'm grateful.

Kannonji, Iwateken
Nov. 12, 1980
Dear Mum, Scott, and Beth,
Phew! Back in Japan at last! You must be back in Maine by now, Mum. Hope your trip was less eventful than mine. I got to London with no trouble except for the ton weight of baggage. Then going out to Gatwick I made every mistake in the book and ended up on a train that sailed gaily through Gatwick, hurtling out into the countryside as my plane prepared for take-off. Arriving at the desk in the airport, I asked the attendant what was the next one I could catch. "Sorry," says she. "This is an Apex fare, good for one flight only. Your ticket is now worthless." I nearly died. She

must have seen my face falling nearly into my runners because she took mercy and said she'd pretend I'd rung up beforehand to cancel. That way she would only charge me the cancellation fee. But that was still £37.75, and sterling at that. I guess my face didn't rise much because she finally took pity. "Don't tell anyone or I'll lose my job, but I'll reissue your ticket." What a relief!

Had a stopover in Saudi Arabia. I only saw the airport but it was odd to see the men in the lounge in full desert gear and the women hidden in their long, black tents. Our next stop was Hong Kong. I had a whole day there, time enough to wander around and be glad to be getting away from it. It's a huge, hot, teeming city, totally Asian in feeling despite the Western-style skyscrapers. I thought I was beyond feeling squeamish at marketplace sights after a year in South America, but I have never seen so many slimy things writhing, wriggling, being slashed, scraped, and gutted, in any such a tiny area. Everyone seemed to be involved in some kind of carnage, but the day of sunshine did me good.

When I arrived at Tokyo, it was the middle of the night. I knew the gates would be locked at Toshoji, so I decided to snooze in the station until it was time for the early morning train north to Morioka. I found myself a bench and settled in. I suppose every self-respecting Japanese has a home to go to, so my fellow bench-mates seemed to be mostly down-and-outs and drunks. Just as I started to doze, one rather inebriated character decided he had to welcome me to Japan and to practice his English.

I can guess what his contact with the tourist industry must have been since all he knew was "Hello," "No, thanks," and "Get lost." Then one of the better dressed ones, who was a mute, set himself up as my protector; he wouldn't let any of the other curious or friendly bums within yards of me. The shock came at one A.M. when the train station closed down. All the subways had stopped and all at Toshoji were asleep. Using signs, gesticulations, and little drawings, my mute got it through to me that there was an all-night café nearby. There, for the price of one expensive cup of coffee, you could try sleeping to the thump of Japanese rock music. That seemed to be what all the clientele had in mind as they sprawled across tables or hunched in their chairs. At four A.M., when the station re-opened, my escort accompanied me back, ascertained my train, and sat patiently for another two and a half hours until he saw me on to the train. I was so touched by his kindness—and we couldn't even talk to one another.

When I got back to Kannonji, I was amazed to find that the monk who'd been here when I left in August had run away. (They always seem to run away rather than give notice). Another fellow has been sent, at least temporarily. In Tokyo this one always seemed surly and very bossy, so I wasn't exactly thrilled. But I just do what he tells me. He works like a wild thing, which is great. Luckily my Japanese is still terrible, because there was talk of giving me a crash course in ceremonies and leaving me to run the whole thing! So we'll see what happens with this fellow. He doesn't know any English at all but so far we're getting on fine. But facing into this eternal winter, it crosses my mind that I must be crazy or masochistic or something. Oh, well—it sure as hell is good training. The Army couldn't be much tougher. Anyway, m'dears, I must go gather wood for the bath fire. Think of me when you turn on the central heating (I'll try not to think of you at such a time…)

Love, M.

December 1980

December 3rd was the first anniversary of my arrival in Japan.

Shimo-san has been sick. Exaggerating. Looked like a pig peering from under the lurid pink blanket.

I went to dokusan. There was much questioning about letters and return dates. It seems that Go Roshi had a premonition I'd return before Kate's wedding. So much for premonitions.

I passed the koan of the big and little mountains. Now am free from desires, ambitions, and attachments, can do real action, not just reactions, being led by the nose. No longer does he accept blindly but is free to accept or act because he can accept. It's real because it's the action of the real man.

The snow has started. It's still novel enough to be beautiful. It lies a white cushion across the mountain and rice fields. Somehow the world seems new, an infant, untainted, quiet, sounds absorbed by the snow. The mountains echo a deep silence pierced only by the occasional cry of a crow.

December 9

Hondo—dust, shoji, and sweep; *Ue* [upper levels]—feather-dust & sweep; *A-Genkan* [entrance where footgear is left]—sweep; H-wind *Roca* [hallway]; Zendo—dust, shoji, and sweep; kitchen, roca, and *dai-genkan* ["Great," main entrance hall to the temple]—sweep, *renshu* ["practice" or "exercise," as in practicing music, or a foreign language].

December 10

Busshari-to 2, 3, and 4: Vacuum and do stairs, damp towel but not take down, dust walls.

Shimo-san has gone to Tokyo for 10 days. Whether he is here or not is equally okay. I'm amazed. In Toshoji he was the one spoiling influence for me. I didn't want to be stuck here for the winter, didn't want to be with him, didn't want to do takuhatsu. I wasted much valuable time and energy pondering how to avoid doing these things. Now I've asked to do takuhatsu—even alone. (I'm sure there'll be times I'll regret that.) Life with Shimo-san and winter are fine. He was sick for a few days and rather repulsive. The combination of his expression and Asiatic features gave him a distinctly Down's syndrome appearance. After he recovered from his sniffle he was marvelous, always laughing, writing me little songs, helping me at every turn. I have to admire his hard-working nature and generous heart.

Tachibana Sensei had me over at his house on Sunday. We sat under the kotatsu watching an old black-and-white English movie. It was bliss. Cream cakes, apples, and brandy. There was no more in the world to ask for.

These last two days, alone, I slept later than usual. The first day I forgave myself. "It's merely conditions; you'll get down to it." Today I was disgusted with myself. My zazen is not good or strong enough for nonsense like missing a sitting. In fact my zazen seems very bad. I know that is only a thing of my own creation—"good zazen/bad zazen"—but it reflects where I'm at, which is a pretty unadvanced state. Nuts. Get down to it!

Kannonji, Iwateken
Dec. 11, 1980
Dear Mum, Scott, & Beth,

...Back here the picture is still unclear but will undoubtedly sort itself out. The new monk here has a bit of a chip on his shoulder, as he's been a Zen student for five years but hasn't managed to have *kensho* yet (the initial breakthrough). So he feels that all the younger trainees who've had kensho have to be shown that they're not as great as they think they are. At Toshoji all he did was argue, so I decided to make things easier for myself up here by doing things his way from the start. The first few days he pampered a cold, sat all day beneath a pink blanket, looking for attention. I'm afraid I was less than sympathetic and Florence Nightingalish. However, he recuperated and attacked the wood-chopping with admirable vigor. Soon my attitude towards him completely changed. I did as I was told, so there were no arguments. We actually had great fun in broken Japanese. Then this monk had to go back to Tokyo on business, and I was left here on my own. I was managing morning and evensong in dubious Japanese. (The lengthening or shortening of a syllable can change the whole meaning so who knows what I was saying?)

Last night, just as I was finishing dinner, a shout came at the door. A monk had arrived from Tokyo to keep me company for the next ten days. He's a bit of a character. I remember that last summer he asked to become a priest and Go Roshi threw him out on his ear. I wonder what happened in the meantime. He talks to himself and grunts a lot and does everything the opposite way from the other monk and insists he is right. I wish there were some definitive authority on the subject. It's confusing changing everything around with every new face. Next month will be the begging, so there'll be a bit of a gang here. Maybe by then they'll have found someone else.

The weather has turned quite cold, but I wear my Goodwill duds under my kimono and scarcely feel it. I look a big lump, but who cares? Tachibana Sensei takes good care of me. Last Sunday I went to his home. We watched an old Gary Cooper movie, ate cream cakes, and drank brandy. I was in my element, loved being with a family on a Sunday afternoon. Of course nowhere nearly as good as my family, but still very warm and kind…Happy, happy, happy Christmas!

December 11

I finished dinner and was reflecting on the fact that it was one year to the day since I became an obosan. Led to the inevitable pointless analysis of change, progress, etc., getting nowhere fast. Then a shout came at the door. Go Roshi had sent help! This bloke is a right character. He does everything differently from the way Shimo-san does them and insists he's right. He was here last summer, asking to be an obosan. Go Roshi got rid of him—yet here he is and apparently knowing it all. He's obsessed by food, continually grunting, groaning, smoking, and talking to himself. His breathing is really quite strange. I was sitting in the kitchen doing zazen, basking in the warmth of the wood stove. He was inside, laughing away good-o to himself. "In this Zen, it's marvelous," thinks I, "anywhere else he'd be thought quite mad." Ah, well. His smile is great and he's good about soji. Either way, it's only ten days.

December 13

Shimo's really quite a character, still snorting and adamant over tiny details. He's advanced a lot in koans and I can see why. He has the talent of losing himself totally in what he's doing. He still has a very sharp ego but that only proves to me how much of an ego I still have. If I didn't, I wouldn't be bothered protesting when he insists I do something I know is unorthodox. However…

I could have punched him out last night when we went to Sasaki-san's. That dear old woman is always giving us food and help, so much so that I'm embarrassed to go down with him. He goes down (she's busy, but he plunks us there anyway), and the first thing he says is "Obachan, there are no flowers in Kannonji," with a big peal of laughter from him. She is mortified, apologizing, explaining the price of flowers, the price of the train, wringing her hands, telling him to ask Jakuda-san, not her. She keeps bringing up the subject, obviously disturbed. She tries to tell him some story about the temple; he's only laughing insanely, she shrieking "Listen to me, listen to me." In desperation she tells me the tale. I pretend to understand. She gets out her precious goek instruments, is playing us a tune. It's beautiful, the expression on her face, mellow, intent, holy. He laughs, halfway through, "We have no more time; must go." For a fraction of a second she looks crestfallen, quickly recovers, finishes her tune through his departure noises, and then she mutters on again about the flowers.

December 14

For the last two days I've been able to enter a shallow samadhi. The exciting part is that I have some measure of control over it. As Sekida [in *Zen Training*] has pointed out, it's fundamentally connected with breathing and posture, though his exact methods don't work for me.

Today I feel rotten. For the first time I feel like quitting. Other times I've felt like leaving, but always in the future at a definite date. Now, because the future has no definite date, I just feel like leaving. I won't, of course. I know it's only a mood, and it's quite obvious what's brought this mood to a head. Last night Tessan-san was to phone for takuhatsu information. I left the information and went to *onsen* [hot springs] with

Tachibana Sensei. It happened so quickly I hadn't a chance to think, but about two miles down the road I regretted going. Sure enough, Tessan-san was annoyed that I wasn't there. Knowing that threw me into a kind of wretched mood—totally stupid, the kind of thing I thought I had gotten over. I thought things no longer disturbed me, or at least, only affected me on the outside. Nonsense, another disillusionment. Every time I think I've progressed, I seem to mess it up again.

I volunteered for, insisted on, takuhatsu. Now it seems so ominous. They predict this year to be very severe weather; this time no gloves. It's been nice sleeping in the living room while Shimo's gone. When I'm feeling down, I try to cheer myself up with little perks like that. It would be nice to have someone I could talk with. I don't actually feel lonely but do enjoy company betimes. Before, I always used to console myself with the thought "ah, well, it's good for me." And it is—yet I feel I could live a more natural life in the West and still continue training. Bah, I know this is just a mood. It's infuriating to be such a victim to moods.

December 15
Such a day as yesterday I wouldn't like to go through again in a hurry. My mind was in such a whirl and confusion it's hard even to recollect my thoughts.

I hated him for a thousand little, insignificant things. The fact that they were trivial and insignificant made me hate myself. One year of ascetic practice and I seem to have got nowhere. I sliced through my finger, through the nail; the tip was held on by a sinew. He grudgingly bandaged it, asked nothing about how it felt, only grumbled about my not watching the fire. I felt vaguely hysterical. Did I need stitches? Would I be fingertip-less? Hating him was only a projection of my mind. What blackness was there in my mind. I lay on the floor, cold, tired, still pumping blood, the room so smoky my eyes stung, and I cried. For a long time.

Tachibana Sensei phoned; he was alarmed to hear my voice. He took me to Morioka. The poor man didn't know quite what to do with the sobbing female but was wonderful. Just to unburden myself, to have someone, anyone, to talk to. We drank coffee between philodendrons, his eyes heavy with concern. "There, there, it only proves you're human. Human relations are important." It was a combination, I guess, hating Shimo and his bossiness made me unduly upset at having angered Tessan-san (by missing his call), my finger, the oppressive greyness of the weather, shoveling snow…I felt trapped for months in the cold, and was secretly dreading takuhatsu.

December 20

On the 15th I looked at the calendar and could scarcely imagine lasting the five days until he left; the first five had seemed eternal. He even spoiled the thought of returning to Toshoji for there I would be with him again. I comforted myself, trying to see the bright side—like the fact that I could sleep in the living room. Big thrill.

But he left yesterday and by then all had changed. I knew it was my mind's projection. We talked; he drank saké, his face turning red by the fire. He never offered me, the guest, any, but it didn't matter. I couldn't understand most of what he said but that didn't matter either. The warmth was there between us. He said I seemed an extraordinarily happy person. That made me laugh and laugh, having tormented myself so over the last few days. He was earthy. He showed me innocently how to work, to throw oneself wholeheartedly into one's work. (I'm practicing doku-san with some minor successes). More than any dokusan koan, he was a living koan, singing and hearty.

Me and my day of sobbing was all only mood. Now it's gone, released. The pressure of the resentment I felt towards him was checked from anger, so flowed down in tears. Yet it was so encompassing—my very being. All the while I knew it was my own creation, that I was free to rid myself of it, but I couldn't. I, me, my ego-self, was the mood; now it's over and that self is over. The "I" constantly mutates. It has no "essence." Yesterday, alone, I felt very happy, very at peace. "What is it that I lack?" Nothing, absolutely nothing. But that is equally a mood. Because it is more pleasant, I would like to see it as somehow more real, truer, always there behind, but in the same way it will come and go.

Things are resolving themselves nicely. I wanted eggs—expensive, I won't. Then Chiba-san brought them. Tessan-san told me to buy *geta* [wooden platform sandals]; Chiba-san says that for a New Year's present she wants to give me geta. I dreaded no longer sleeping in the living room when Shimo comes back, but realized that if I sleep in the little room I can easily warm it. That was a real weight off my mind, one of my greatest sufferings (amn't I weak?). So I feel sure that takuhatsu will be grand. The dread is gone. The trapped-by-winter feeling is gone. I don't mind at all doing all the work by myself. I'm surprised. Soji just doesn't bother me any more and I feel no urge to skip or shortcut. I have things organized now; there's time for the temple and for me.

Eshin-san wrote again, a beautiful letter. His love is so pure, sincere, and loyal, much truer than I deserve. In my reply I told him about Killian [an Irish boyfriend]. It only seemed right. Not that Killian is by any means "the man," but I still do not feel committed.

Dec. 22, 1980

Still alone and happy. Winter is very much here. In the mornings, getting up at 3:25, it's extremely cold. During the first few days and leading up to the 14th, I strongly resisted the idea of winter. I felt trapped, fed myself lines like "this is the last winter," "Tekkan-san and Kas'ko-san managed," "only four months," etc. None particularly helpful. Now, strangely, it's changed (not through any heroic efforts of mine.)

In the morning delivering *buppan* [little rice offerings placed before Buddha statues] at 4:30, I warm my feet on the cooker afterwards, hands like clubs; the same during ookyo. It stings to touch the metal door handles; the buppan are frozen. But these days I feel cold, but that's all. There's no comment; my self isn't resisting it nor having to persuade it. Like the koan about not getting wet, I'm cold; of course I'm cold, but not really cold. Takuhatsu will be fine and I've wasted so much energy worrying about winter.

Kannonji, Iwateken

Dec. 26, 1980

Dear Mum, Scott, Beth, and Jane,

Hard to imagine that you're basking now in Florida sunshine as I look at the falling snow. How was your Christmas this year—beaches and coconuts? Probably as different from our Park Avenue [the O'Hallorans' home, next door to the Ryan family referred to previously] ones as my one was. (Somehow Park Avenue always seems like it was really Christmas.) I have been minding the temple alone of late until the beginning of next month, when a bunch arrive up from Tokyo to beg. The first couple of days seemed a bit lonely, but when I felt a little lonesome I made myself go do some cleaning, and then I was fine. Now I really like having the place to myself—perfect peace and quiet, no one bossing me around, I can do things at my own pace.

Christmas Eve we had a small blizzard. At the start of the blizzard, I took off into the woods, not to be daunted from my celebration, and lopped off the top of a little pine tree. Between the prints of two celestially borne Buddhas, on top of the telephone table, I set up my tree. Trimmed it with old bits of ribbon and some "things" I cooked. No oven of course, so I deep fried and frosted some things with a texture reminiscent of doughnuts and a shape like Christmas balls. (I tried stars, it took all my trigonometry to cut out a pattern for one, but I guess I never got far enough in physics, 'cos damned if they'd keep their shape. So much for Christmas and higher education.)

Meanwhile, the snow got more insistent. I was doing evensong—the introduction *Dai hi shin dharani* [Great Heart of Compassion Dharani, an incantation chanted daily, usually at evening service] is followed by an impressive drum crashing. Right on cue as I thumped the drum, the power failed. I finished evensong squinting in the twilight, then whipped a candle off the altar and hightailed it back to the kitchen.

I stoked up my fire, sat down to watch the snow fall by candlelight. It was very quiet and peaceful. It had the "peace on earth, good will to all" quality that Christmas should have. All that was missing was you guys, but you were in my mind. Not able to read or do much of anything, with no light I settled down to meditate for a while.

Hardly had I tucked up into a *lotus* [Cross-legged sitting position: full lotus has both legs up on opposite thighs, half-lotus has one leg up], when Tachibana Sensei burst in like Santa himself, bearing a bag of goodies. Behind him his two sons, like Santa's little elves, came bumbling in ready to tuck into a feast. Tachibana Sensei, bless his heart, brought not only crackers and sweets but a little naggin of whiskey (for the cold, of course) and a Gateaux "Molly O'Rourke" fruitcake. I was stupefied, made right in Dublin. Someone had given it to him five years ago and he'd never touched it. (Must have known a Dubliner would be around for Christmas sooner or later.) I was a bit wary of it; Gateaux cakes at their freshest can often taste like they're five years old. Didn't know how this would be, but time cures all ills (or something). It wasn't just good but the best fruitcake I've ever had. Must have been the whiskey. Cake with a vintage!

So we sat round the stove in the winking candlelight, chatting and laughing. The kids were delighted at the Christmas tree; it looked better in the low lighting of a one-watt candle.

Christmas morning after breakfast I sat down (with another slice of fruitcake) to open my presies. Thank you. Bethie, I opened yours first, as I could guess what it was, and I played it while opening the rest. A very nice choice of music, it made me feel like I was back at home. I was dying to dive right into the book, Mum, looks great, not only Rome, D.C., and Korea, but the hero spent part of his childhood in Dublin. I've heard it's very good and someone else said I really should read it. Thanks. I hadn't the chance to sit down for a good read, as I had people coming for a ceremony and a heck of a lot of Christmas Eve blizzard to remove before that. It was the first ceremony I've done alone, but it went well. Christmas was a spectacularly gorgeous day—blue skies, virgin snow, and that savage piercing winter sun that transforms everything to crystal.

Last night I was exhausted and ready to call it a day early. Didn't feel much like cooking, so my Christmas dinner was a simple rice gruel and piece of tofu. At least no worries about Christmas calories! (Actually it was very tasty.) Did you have all kinds of tropical treats? I suppose you ate out, hope it was good. Takes all the work out of Christmas, leaving all the fun bits, I hope.

Later

Well got in my Western Christmas-cheer bit after all. A bunch of the Morioka gaijins got together for some traditional fun. Had a bonfire, sung carols in the snow (snowballs and all). For dinner everyone brought a dish. We were American, Irish, English, Afghani, Iranian, and Indian (no Japanese at all!), so the dinner, far from turkey and ham, was very exotic, but finished by mince pies. We all regressed, as we reverted back to childhood memories and party games—even pin the nose on Santa. Great fun altogether.

I'm dying to hear about your Florida festivities. My love to the Sweeneys [very close family friends] when you see them. It'll be great having a holiday with them. Richard, who gave last night's party, says he'll make some tapes for me. Thanks for the blanks and the vitamins, they'll be good to keep me fit for begging. I've been holding onto this, hoping to hear from you, but no news. Hope that means you're having an excellent time. I'll pop this off (and probably hear from you immediately).

Love you all dearly, M.

P.S. to Scott and Beth, my heartiest congratulations on your report cards. Those were excellent grades, but even more important than the grades themselves was how they pleased Nana. She wrote telling me how proud of you she was. Making her happy is even better than being top of the class. Anyway I'm proud of you both, too (but don't get swelled heads or I'll bash 'em down). Love yis.

Dec. 27, 1980

I told Tachibana Sensei about Eshin-san's proposal. His reaction was shocking. It almost frightens me, the suddenness and depth of emotion with which the Japanese can respond. You feel you're always sitting on a potential explosion. He talked non-stop for two hours, carried away, repeating himself, then recovering himself. Eshin-san shouldn't be allowed back. The *hara-kiri* [ritual suicide by disembowelment] mentality—he explained he was of the old school, but…I was a bit shocked at the end of the session. I was afraid ever to have anything to do with Eshin. Mentally I prepared to write him a letter of rejection. The next evening he phoned.

He declared his love, sounded as if he were reading lines from a play, though I'm sure he's sincere. When he hung up, tears came into my eyes. Why? After talking to Tachibana Sensei, I'm worried about his coming back.

Christmas Eve I was a little lonely at the edges, so I packed myself off to do soji. It worked. Then I lopped off the top of a pine tree during the blizzard and covered it with colored ribbon, then deep-fried over-iced "things." The electric power failed. Dinner was by candlelight—gruel and cabbage. Watching the snow fall, so soft and firm like a mother patting her baby to sleep, by the gentle glow of a single candle, I felt quite still and at one, in peace with the world. No Christmas Eve celebrations, and it didn't matter. The lights were out, so I settled down to meditate by the wood stove. Tachibana Sensei burst in like Santa, bearing a bag of goodies. Behind him, his boys tumbled in like elves. He brought a naggin of whiskey and the best fruit cake I've ever had, made right in dear dirty Dublin and enjoyed in Japan. Looking out the window, the candle seemed to glow inside me, but the wood fire seemed to crackle from inside, too. Felt so happy, so simple.

Christmas Day saw loads of snow to shovel and a little unwrapping ceremony while I had my fruitcake breakfast. It made it seem as if the family were here. The day was too sparklingly, spectacularly beautiful to feel homesick or lonely. The sun, dazzling on the virgin white, was elating. In the morning I did my first ceremony alone; it went well. The rest of the day no one came around. Christmas dinner was tofu and rice gruel. Very delicious. No complaints.

Being alone these days, I can work at my own pace. The division between work and rest seems not as sharp and, interestingly, I get flashes wherein time actually feels subjectively different—where it is now totally, not overshadowed by other. Never realized before how very "not-now" my ordinary consciousness is.

Two gaijins are coming for the takuhatsu and Tessan-san will do tenzo. Wasn't I daft to have been worrying? And isn't life grand?

Jan. 6, 1981
Takuhatsu has begun. I'm tired, but it's okay. Last year I could only survive by promising myself never again. Now it hurts just as much, but it's as if it doesn't matter. I feel I could go on and on. I'm working hard. In the morning I do buppan or *chokka (ino)* [morning service], walk for three hours, rest a half hour, then soji, practice ookyo at 3, at 3:30 collect buppan, at 4:00 do *banka* [service with chanting, usually in late afternoon], then every second day I cook. Up in the morning at 3:30 for zazen; evening, too.

Shozan-san has left. Tessan tortured him. He was slow, slow of wit and body, but quick to laugh and share a biscuit. He was always apologizing, grovelling, smiling. He used to be a taxi driver; it shows in his servile manner. Tessan grew impatient, wanted to teach him, and the only way he knew how was by shouting. He picked him up on any little thing, roaring, swiping, even throwing a soup bowl at his head. He left, driven away. Then a poor innocent came who'd never done zazen. He wanted to stay a while. Each took turns exercising ego at his expense. He lasted a night and a day. It was interesting to see how Tessan's relationship with us depended so much on having a release. Shozan-san was his fall guy, and we were marvelous. Shozan left and he laid into us. Shimo-san came, and the foreigners became excellent, whereas Shimo was crazy. But he'd hold his own in a fight. The first night they roared at each other (the night the innocent newcomer came for his first taste of the monastic ideal). Tessan-san seemed pleased—an ally in his camp. Together they bitched about Tessan, and it provided release, but Tessan-san missed Paul and Galli-san. "At least they were normal," said he.

We did have fun with them here. The Western youth in me that lies dormant so much of the time in this male, Oriental temple life, came out. Galli-san whipped tuneless, heartfilled songs from the guitar; I played the spoons. (Paul composed one about Maura of the mountains and a great one about "I hate takuhatsu, I hate the snow, going back to Tokyo.") After Shimo came, Tess' reaction was to go mute, hang his head, and be as surly as possible. At first he maintained his pleasant disposition towards me, but after a while, during the day, that disappeared too. He wouldn't answer my greetings, made huge fusses about nothing. There were periods, then, when he had to take out his frustrations on me and he'd blow his top over trivia, especially if I did something like give Tess a cup of tea at an inappropriate time (i.e., anytime). But at least I could understand that it wasn't really me, that he just needed a release. Usually it was grand, though at times I, too, needed a release and cried. It was all so obvious, one bouncing off the other, none of us with real control, a series of moods, pressures, and repercussions squeezing back and forth in a box. (But at night he usually became charming again.)

Tess did carry *kanshugyo* [practice in the cold] to extremes at times. He wasn't doing it himself, admitted he disliked it. (One of his favorite lines to me when anybody made a mistake but I was to be blamed was "You wanted to do takuhatsu; you wanted to." Although I had never complained, it seemed a fixation to him.) Food would be hidden away. He'd stop me from cooking anything vaguely interesting. Tessai-san was suffering from acute war pains but would sit freezing in his room rather than come in to Tessan's company. I really had to beg Tessan and use all my influence to get him to let Tessai-san use a heater (paying for the oil himself). Meanwhile, Tessan slept in the warmest room in the house, snuggled into the kotatsu.

As for us taking turns at tenzo, he did take advantage. His errands were always on my days off, and several times he just plain told me to do his turn. I didn't really mind, though. It's better training the more I have to do. (Bed by 9:30, up at 3:30 to do zazen.) But although I didn't mind the work, at times his bitching got to me, and I must admit that when the backbiting started, while I didn't really join in, I also didn't try to bring about reconciliation. That was wrong of me. I feel it strongly. Ultimately, in a situation, it all doesn't matter. Whether we criticize or praise, it all passes, it's all empty, all phenomenal, so I might as well try to make peace in those situations. I, too, was just reacting to situations—or rather the tentative "I" is merely a reaction to different events. All during kanshugyo I was very aware of the passing, phenomenality of circumstances and people. It was so obvious and made everything easy.

Truly this takuhatsu seemed to go fast and was not hard, yet my frost-bite was terrible, bleeding and oozing pus. (Though I could have worn gloves, I only did so on a couple of excruciating occasions.) My room was freezing (no heat). Paul came in and was really shocked by its size and temperature. (What with my head in the closet and my feet at the door…) Working most of the time, just no problem.

Last year, however, I suffered more. Trying, subjectively, to recall, it seems as if I had more highs off takuhatsu last year. This time it was just something I did and got on with it. There were some lovely moments, though. Sometimes you could actually feel an energy of givingness and purity from the people, and I'd feed off it, it surging through me, my voice becoming loud and untiring. Sometimes after *tenjin* [a refreshment after takuhatsu], sitting by the altar, soft candles glow and warm welcoming home, having done *choka* [morning service] before dawn and walked, roaring, all morning, then offering ookyo again, a wonderful peace seemed to pervade. I was not only here and now, but the whole universe was, and stopped. Everything was very, very still. (Often in the distance, especially when we'd come home, I'd hear sutra-chanting—usually "*Namu ki e butsu*" ["I take refuge in the Buddha"]—strange, as we weren't chanting that. And one time I heard the Kanzeon Sutra with Paul's voice; mild hallucinations.)

Then, on several occasions during our breaks, people gave us tea and senbei, toast, okashi, or pastries. Oh, but they tasted good! Incredible. I wished I could always appreciate each bite, each sip, with such relish. At times I felt guilty—all these people giving, giving. Little old ladies running after us in the snow, people stopping their cars, young children on their way to school, workers on the upper stories throwing money out the windows, giggling. And why? So we can live. They'll never come here, never be refreshed by the peace of Kannonji, by a good sitting in a quiet zendo. They're all so unselfishly giving only so that I can carry on my practice. I owe them a debt, the debt of my self-orientated (though there is no self!) practice. It's a huge debt, one I'm inclined to shirk.

I got a cat, Gion-chan. At first I felt like a new father being handed twins, awkwardly holding them—"Now what?" But she's lovely. She rides on my shoulder while I cook and keeps me warm at night. Sometimes she's obnoxious.

Tetsugen-san wrote me three letters and sent two parcels. He comes on the 8th. I think it will be good. One of the ladies said my complexion has changed. Tachibana Sensei says I look younger and seem stronger. I think I only look plumper from eating loads of sweet mochi rice cakes. Tessai-san, because of his dislike of Tessan, was inclined to exaggerate the extent to which I've been working, so now everyone thinks I virtually carried takuhatsu. But it's not so. I worked, but not very much more than usual. It just was no problem.

January 5

I realize how easily people are fooled in spiritual affairs. They want to believe people have attained depths and to feel associated with the extraordinary. At Jakuda-san's, after dokusan, a new woman was seated with us on the floor around the kerosene stove. They were all devout old women, religion the most important issue in their lives. Transposing cultures, if I were with these same kind of women in my own Ireland, I'd represent the antithesis of all they devote their lives to. Here, in a culture totally foreign to my old one, I not only sympathize with them but am even more involved (fanatical?) than they. Strange…The new woman asked questions about me and they began talking about me, not telling untruths, but the things they selected to point out made me seem special, deep—even the shine in my eyes. The woman seemed almost infatuated, holding my hand, gazing into my eyes, saying how glad she was to meet me. It made me wonder if there are hundreds of unscrupulous people with as little insight and understanding as me, masquerading as being in some way developed and capable of teaching. Irresponsible.

During takuhatsu I got a letter from Jean-Luc [a French man with whom Maura had had a relationship]. The first time. I hadn't heard from him in almost a year. I dreamt he came to Kate's wedding; the next day this letter arrived. I was thinking how I'd made a bit of a fool of myself writing five postcards but with so little response. I sent him a Christmas card; he didn't answer. Then next day, this letter. Lovely. He's very interested in Zen, wants to be my student in Zen. He signed beautifully in English, Spanish, and French. I allowed myself the luxury of daydreaming about him a bit. He's spending next month with his girlfriend.

Many times during the past year I wondered if I wasn't somehow missing out, vaguely feeling that by the time I re-entered my old world everyone would have settled into couples. Those feelings aren't there anymore, partly from having gone home when I did, partly from feeling there will always be men, and partly from not caring whether there are or not. It just doesn't seem to occupy my mind. I suppose now that I've said that, it will become an obsession. It seems as soon as I recognize any change or progress, its opposite makes itself apparent.

January 10

Tetsugen-san arrived and seems gentle and undemanding, helpful and appreciative. He has a quiet nature that is at times tinged with sadness but he is usually smiling. His kidney has been removed, and twice a week all his blood has to be cleaned by machine. He has been practicing for ten years and seems to me to be much more of a true priest than Tessan or Shimo. He has no need to assert himself egotistically. In fact he is perhaps too humble, saying that he's disappointed with his progress so far.

I didn't realize quite how basic Tessan-san's and my life here were until Tetsugen-san came. Even in the depths of the northern winter, we didn't use a heater and only lit the wood stove a couple of hours a day. I was used to doing breakfast and buppan with numb fingers in temperatures of -9°C. I couldn't believe it when he offered me a stove for my room. (However, I refused.) He even buys food. For months now we've been surviving on a basic diet of *daikon* [Japanese radish], cabbage, and rice. Tessan-san didn't want to use even brown rice because it took an extra five minutes of gas to cook and that was a waste. There are little things, like the fact that now we don't have to keep boiling the same tea leaves all day, so they were only bitter. I used nearly to blind my eyes trying to make out the tiny *hiragana* [phonetic Japanese syllabary letters] in the morning dimness; now we can use a light. Yet Tessan-san provided a good training, for now I really don't care one way or the other about such things.

January 12
I feel very glad to be young, not just mentally (as I sometimes feel) but physically. After shoveling snow in the sunshine my body felt strong, straight, and young. It was wonderful striding through the snow, shovel on my shoulder, breeze in my hair.

January 15
Buddha's *inaku naru* day [the day Buddha entered Parinirvana, leaving this world]. I tried doing zazen all night. Very cold. Not very good.

Jan. 16, 1981
Dear Maureen,
I write your name and a host of pleasant memories spring to mind. Happy Christmas and New Year's and every other day. It was great to hear from you and see you feeling as open as ever about the future. Lately all the news I get seems to be about people getting married or having kids. Of course there's nothing wrong with that, but from this distance I sometimes get a sinking feeling—like I'll go back and find no one has anything to talk about but decent nursery schools and cheap therapy training, travel—let me know what you decide...

The monk I've been here with has been in and out of hospital lately and is in at the moment so I'm puttering around alone here and enjoying it immensely. I was just outside shoveling snow. The air is pure, the sun is glorious. Everything sparkles. The roads haven't been cleared so there's an unearthly silence and a few noisy crows. Maybe the composition of air is different after the snow, but it filled me up and made me feel so exhilarated I thought I'd surely burst. It felt so totally magic that I thought "God, I'd like to write to Maureen now." What I really meant was wish you were here to feel it...Maureen not only understands magic but weaves it.

Back at the monastery (as they say) things are going grand. My monk had a brush with death and swears the point to life is to do good. So I'm hoping he'll be practical about it when he comes back...I was down at Tokyo for a retreat, there a week ago, did the cooking for 27. Traditional, temple vegetarian cookery. It's finicky and takes a fair bit of time but I really enjoyed it. It was one of the best retreats yet. Maybe because my teacher's due to die soon and figures I'd better push on with my training—I don't know—but stuff that normally he wouldn't explain, but says himself that he usually gives a student months to work on, he was just shooting out like ping-pong balls—ping-pong balls with the force of bowling balls. I could hardly digest it all. Am still mulling everything over & totally impressed by the depth of his understanding. Phew. Impressed and all, however, I'm still planning to come home to the ould sod towards the end of next year. Tho' I'm seriously thinking of returning to Japan again.

By the way, I don't know where your idea of my Japanese proficiency came from. I'm hopeless and that's not being modest. But it's an incredibly beautiful language. Not in the sound, but in the subtlety. At first I thought it so cold the way they never touch each other but now am finally figuring out that it's all in the nuances of their speech...Anyway, not much more space so if you do set off wandering, remember that Japan's not as far as it looks and there's a little town in the North where a monk I know will make you Irish stew or sukiyaki or whatever you like.

Love ya, M.

January 16, 1981

I'm amazingly untired. All day and when I'm falling asleep a voice resounds in my head, "I am empty, I am impermanent." There's a peace about this voice; it keeps other noisy thoughts from entering.

After his trip to the hospital, Tetsugen's arm always hurts, though he says that otherwise it's not really painful. When he comes back he looks weak and drained. Often he looks grey. His eyes are close together, so from the side they're scarcely visible. He stares into space and seems colorless, eyeless, lifeless. Other times he's full of energy but talks little. He's very good to Gion-chan, who lately has been driving me bats. She's been bringing out the worst in me, so I imagine what it would be like to be reborn as a cat and try to treat Gion as I'd want to be treated.

We're having a spring thaw. Beautiful—a black old man pushing a black barrow, etched against the wintry fields. The mountains breathing greys, blacks, whites in mists of *sumi-e* [ink brush] paintings. Coming home in the dusk from the onsen, I wanted never to stop...

Kannonji, Iawateken
January 26, 1981
Dear Mum, Scott, and Beth,
Glad to hear you enjoyed your holiday. Lucky divils. Sounds like you finally got the Christmas you've been wanting, Mum. Scott, how was your birthday? What did you do to celebrate? If you took any pictures, I'd love copies. Any more good ones of the weddings? I thought the photos in the paper were good, though not Geoff's best angle. Beth, how are your rabbits? I got a new kitty; she's all black and full of mischief, and I'm mad about her (she's sitting on my lap right now trying to capture my pen). She keeps me lovely and warm at night. I gave Mu-chan your letter, Wiggs [Beth]. She was very pleased, but it took her three days with a dictionary to read it. She promised that she'll answer you, but she may be slow. She wants to go to school in Ireland and wishes you'd come to Japan so that she could meet you.

Back here, begging has started, and the temple's been like a 3-ring circus. Of the people who came for begging, two have run away completely from monastic life, and two returned early to Tokyo. That leaves me with three very strong-willed monks that don't get along with one another. It can be like treading on eggshells. Each one takes turns being wonderful to me as I am the neutral party—or should I say "referee." But so much tension builds up that at times I get my head blown off for no reason, so I keep a low profile. It's pretty comical, really, and at times it's hard to keep a straight face. After all my worrying about the cold when begging, it turned out quite grand this year. The clothes are a big help, but even at that I must be more used to it or something, because my hands are still bare and frostbitten yet the whole thing doesn't take anything out of me this time…a pleasant surprise and relief. I've been on television again, three times, local and national. Mum, I'm sure you were disappointed by the videotape of the program that I sent you, but they shot for a day and a half and from that cut out all except the image they wanted to create. They chose to edit out everything about you guys, my studies at Trinity, of my "bourgeois" background. They had an idea of the poor little monk that they wanted to push, hence the shots of my room and my tatty sandals…There have been quite a few lunches out during begging. The local people put on these wonderful spreads. This time I've been taking notes and asking for recipes, so next time I see you guys I'll make a big Japanese feast. Meals here at the temple are mostly cabbage, daikon, and rice. Any good recipes?

Much love, M.

Kannonji, Iwateken
February 12, 1981
Dear Nana,
Happy Valentine's Day and happy spring. I hope the winter so far hasn't been too harsh for you. Here we're just finishing *daikan,* the great cold. Yesterday we had *mamemaki,* something akin to Hallowe'en in so far as it is a day for driving out evil spirits. Everyone throws beans and peanuts, shouting to scare out whatever evil may lie in store for the new year. Then we had a big party. Go Roshi, the teacher, was up from Tokyo and all his students came. It was great fun as everyone helped out—but we'll be eating leftover seaweed rolls for weeks! There is a new monk coming to stay here next week. He has been training in the temple on this card [Sojiji— one of the two headquarters of the Soto sect with Eiheiji] for four years. Seems amiable. All my best wishes. Be careful of the flu.

Love, Maura

Kannonji, Iwateken
March 1981
Dear Mum,
…They say the most pleasant months to visit Japan are May and December. May would probably be too soon for you. August isn't nice and June rains a lot. I'm presuming I can get free time. As soon as you're definite, I'll ask. Except for sesshin times (about 5 days a month in summer) I should be able to get some time off, if I know in advance. I may be here at Kannonji for some time yet. As I guess I told you, the present monk really can't manage alone. They're looking for a wife for him. It's so business-like here. Until then, I've been asked to stay and help here. I gladly accepted. Spring and summer are so much nicer here than in muggy, big city Tokyo. Our normal quiet work routine was disrupted for the past ten days when Galli-san, a hilarious Italian who lives in the dormitory section of Toshoji came to visit. He's vivacious and animated, also a big help. The poor little mute monk here didn't know what to make of him but had to giggle. So the temple mood was decidedly different. Things are always happening here. That was fun, but this peace is also wonderful. The only sounds are the birds calling and the dripping of the melting snow (though actually we can usually hear the nearby highway). Next month we'll have the first sesshin of the year. I'm looking forward to it. They're like a transfusion and I can make progress on my koans. Now that you're reading so much about Zen, these terms probably make sense. Have you heard of the *Mumonkan* ["Gateless Gate"] collection of koans? I'm beginning those now…

Lots of love, M.

March 7
Galli-san has come and gone. He was meant to stay two or three days but gradually it extended to about two weeks. We had fun—sheer, innocent, can't-stop-laughing-over-nothing, really funny fun. He said that in Tokyo he had been very angry and upset.

We talked a bit about muji. He was suffering the same way I had from not really understanding what he was trying to do with it and there was no one he could talk to about it. I told him just to lose himself in his work, to throw himself into it, and he is muji expressing itself. This idea he seemed to grasp for the first time and thus totally. He did a commendable practice, diving in with energy and enthusiasm. Having spoken with him and seeing his efforts, I was re-inspired to heed my own words. Our *gaijin ookyo* [foreigners' sutras] in the morning strained at the rafters. So we did muji yuki kaki, muji soji, muji dancing [jocular references to doing all things with complete presence of mind]—all the while laughing and throwing snow balls and sipping *umeboshi* [plum] tea. At times we felt sorry for Tetsugen-san. He went through a dark period for a few days when he scarcely spoke or even answered the most mundane of greetings; meanwhile, we could scarcely restrain our spontaneous mirth. At times it infected even Tetsugen-san, and he giggled. Up on the roofs, we abandoned ourselves to shoveling snow in the sunshine, conquering each new piece of ice, slipping, catching, victoriously detached slides, down, down…Back on the ground, pulling the waste from the outhouse, carrying it in reeking bucketsful to the fields, or building a snowman, walking singing to the post office. He was very Italian, emotional, easy to bring up. Poor Jiko-san would watch his hands, waving a mile a minute, like a dizzy puppy or a kitten waiting to spring.

Jim gave a party and we went. Galli threw himself into dancing with the same vigor. He was taking muji very seriously.

He danced on, oblivious to the small clutch of females now gathering around him, subtly dancing for him. I left the room and found another scene—people sitting on the floor, playing guitars, less frenetic, very warm. It only occurs to me now that the same thing happened to me as happened to Galli; a little group of inebriated admirers gathered, fawning. We danced and sang 'til very nearly zazen time. I grabbed a couple of hours sleep but scarcely felt tired.

Jim came to begin my sculpture. We were standing in the chilly corridor, my hands turning shades of blue and purple. He was shocked and insisted on bringing me to the hospital. I was embarrassed—they seemed so much better. The infection had gone inside and was erupting in mounds of pus. I remembered all the mornings when I (like the little match girl!) clawed at the twigs, my hands red and oozing, trying to shake off the snow from the sticks so that they'd light. I realized I must have been carrying an infection for two months. They gave me an antibiotic, and it's nearly gone in just a week.

I went to dokusan. I had to repeat the koan about "All this universal law is like a dream, a vision, foam, shadow, dew, thunder. This you must realize" [a key verse from the Diamond Sutra]. I did a mirage; he didn't understand. For my foam, Go Roshi burst into laughter as I blew it. For shadow, he loped around, trying to kill his shadow. (I had merely sat still, one hand following another.) For dew, he hiked up his robes, stalked through the fields, heaved a heavy stone to find himself drenched. (My dew had disappeared with the sun. I'm still too intellectual.) For thunder, he banged and tumbled to the ground. For "this you must realize," he said I must roar it, thumping my leg. He asked for the meaning. Originally, I had explained that it was all my daily activities but I thought he felt this was wrong. So this time I said I was empty and impermanent. Tachibana Sensei, trying to translate this, looked puzzled. I explained I meant myself and all things. Go Roshi said it was my everyday activities.

He asked me to stay at Kannonji until Tetsugen-san married. (He used to laugh at that possibility.) And then he'd have me come to Toshoji. Either way is fine with me.

I thought, one day, of my father. I loved him. He lived 43 years, died, and is no more. It made me sad. He was such a wonderful man. No one knows him any more, loves him any more. He can no longer touch any one, move people. Lived, died, and gone like so many hundreds of millions. As I will. Galli-san says he loves my father; for that I love Galli-san. He really had a feeling for him, kept asking about him, reminding me to give him his photo.

"I want to meet your father," he said.

"You can't," I said, "He's dead."

"I will. You will be my father."

Perhaps the reason that I love Galli-san's love of Dad is not so much from my love of him as of my own frail, human shunning of my own mortality. Yet, I do not exist. There is nothing to lose.

March 11

Coincidence—I was thinking of how I no longer have to teach English and was glad. Then I was thinking about how Chiba-san wanted to learn English once. Just such silly light thoughts. Then Chiba-san came and asked me to resume the English lessons.

My zazen is rotten. I read in Dogen Zenji's piece that if your mind is contemplating Buddhahood and Bodhisattvas, the deep meaning of the sutras, etc., it's no good. But as soon as I sit down to meditate, I'm filled with thoughts of what to cook for dinner. Before my koan comes to mind, it's thoughts of soup. I know good samadhi concentration is really important, and I don't seem to be able to concentrate at all.

March 13

Yesterday I spent the day sewing at Sasaki-san's. She's an incredible woman, 70 years old but simply bursting with vitality. She ascribes it to hard work and going to the temple for ookyo at 5:30 each morning. Even through fresh snow she wends her way to Kannonji, bent double across her walking stick from years in the rice paddies. She's always talking excitedly, breathlessly, hands animated, gesticulating, bouncing on her worn legs, cocking her dyed black head flirtatiously—70 years old and irrepressible. While sewing and cutting, she can't suppress the smile flowing from her joy in life. Too frank to play games, she freely "praises herself and chastises others" [a reversal of the Seventh Precept], all the while laughing and working. The sun streamed in. We sat on the floor, stitching, her wrinkled hands as nimble at the needle as in speech. She wears a thimble like a wedding band. In and out, in and out, in perfect rhythm, every stitch straight and of equal length. She piles me with goodies, says "hurry back," and I scarper through her little oriental garden of pools and rocks and tapered shrubs. I half walk, half skip (she's infectious) past the snow-covered apple orchard with its single black crow on a naked bough, then back to make the lunch and to stretch out with a cup of tea. The mountains look higher, more nebulous. Life is wonderful. Truly, what is it I lack? Nothing. It's so simple.

March 15

Jim came. He asked me many questions about Zen and consciousness, etc. I felt reluctant to answer. I knew my explanations could only be shallow and his approach only intellectual. So we talked. It was hard to explain on a level he'd appreciate which means, of course, that I was intellectualizing, too. He's forming a little *benkyo'o-kai* [study group] for reading and discussion. As he was leaving he kept saying that he really hoped I'd be able to come. He had obviously found our discussion stimulating.

So, shortly afterwards, as I was walking down the hall where he'd been sculpting, with buppan in my hands, the thought flickered across my mind: "Jim thinks I'm interesting." Then, CRASH, I hit the door with the tray, spilling water (nothing broke) and I suddenly woke up and felt very ashamed. Humiliated. He thought I was interesting because of what I was saying about Zen—bandying about "no-mind" and "emptiness" and the like, and here I was, not only thinking and intellectualizing, but being vain, too. Am so ashamed.

Then there's the cat. She really had been bold of late, dirtying my bed, stealing food, climbing where she knows she not supposed to. We figured we'd have to train her while she's young but we just seem to be punishing her too often. She ducks if you move your hands suddenly. She doesn't drive me crazy any more. (I've got used to her shrieking and pouncing on my shoulder when I'm concentrating.) I only punish her when she deserves it—which I still think may be too much. But Tetsugen-san upsets me a bit, because he punishes her cruelly, unnecessarily. He is always jumping at her, teasing and tormenting her, shouting, locking her out. He used to be kind to her, kinder than I. Now she's afraid of him.

Perhaps he feels guilty. He had a dream in which I took her away because he was always getting angry at her. I feel awful. She's here because I like cats, yet she must feel miserable. It's my responsibility.

March 17

I'm disgusted with myself. I'm dawdling in my practice. I'm resolved to get up in the morning promptly, eat less, do four hours of zazen daily, and not stop until I reach complete enlightenment. No more fooling around. I'm trying to work with "What is this mind?" It's teasing and frustrating.

I've been thinking about Dominique [an English girl, teaching in Morioka]. I feel a sense of responsibility towards her. She really wanted to do zazen but has never gotten around to coming. I've told her the bus but never gave her the extra little push of offering to meet her or arranging a time. She was so excited at the possibility. I must arrange a definite time.

Kannonji, Iwateken
March 17, 1981
Dear Mum,
Happy St. Patrick's Day. Your card arrived today and I wouldn't have known the day but for Beth's nice decoration…Go Roshi gave me a surprise a while ago. You recall my telling you the plan for his daughter, Mariko-san, to marry a priest from Kyushu and then inherit this temple by way of dowry. Temples are passed on in that way. Well, I guess poor Mariko-san didn't like the monk; anyway she refused. So Go Roshi stripped her of the dowry and in dokusan suddenly floors me by saying that if I marry a good Zen man, he'll give me the temple as a wedding present with which to build an international Zen dojo. I was very touched by the offer, after I got over my shock, but had to turn him down. They're so matter-of-fact about marriage here. People are obviously beginning to worry that I'm getting long in the tooth, and they really find it hard to credit that I don't want to get married! By the way, you came into the master plan, Mum, you and any of the kids would be brought here to live and would be taken care of!…

Winter is jerkily giving way to spring—can't believe it went so fast. Life has settled to a lovely pace and a peaceful routine. Plenty to do, but not too busy, and things seem so quiet. The air is fresh and pure off the mountains, smelling of pine trees and spring thaw. The birds are returning and chirping away.

After I go to sesshin in Tokyo, I'll be going to my first ever Japanese wedding. The second Tessan-san who was here (can you keep track of all the names?) is getting married. The whole thing still is hard for me to conceive of. They've met once. He wasn't even all that impressed, but she wasn't bad, and he liked the temple that came with her and he really wanted to get married. So the date was set. As business-like as that. One puts more effort into buying a new car. Strange, then, how well many of these marriages turn out. Perhaps they're not going into them with all sorts of illusions and expectations. Glad to hear that Kate and Geoff sound so happy and are working hard on the new house.

Mum, you said you've been reading about Zen and Japan. What have you been reading, and what do you make of it? I'm very interested. You should practice sitting on the floor, because most people don't have chairs. We have 2 or 3 stowed away somewhere, but for example you couldn't eat as they're higher than the table. In Japan it's considered polite to sit up properly on the legs but it hurts most foreigners at first...

My love to you all, M.

March 18, 1981
Spring Equinox. We go to different houses to chant sutra for their dead for one week around the equinox. I try to really contact them (and Dad) so that perhaps in hearing ookyo they may be liberated. Yet often my concentration fails, and I wonder what's left to call to or to be liberated. What does happen at death? Who am I?

It's lovely going around to the houses, being welcomed in, chanting, chatting, warm and snug in kotatsus, served tea and sweet cakes. Abesan was chatting animatedly, a soft light behind her through the paper door. Perhaps it was the light, a sort of funeral parlor subtlety, but suddenly it struck me—she will be dead. So alive and vibrant now, then dead and gone. First they'll chant sutra for her and remember, and gradually not even remember as the ripple subsides into the ocean. As we went along through the traffic, all the faces seemed to me to be death masks...

I'm so impressed with these zenkai ladies. There's something in their eyes that dances. I began to wonder if all Japanese were like that (since they are mostly the company I keep), but they aren't. Galli-san noticed it at once as kensho. That was on his mind, but I'm sure he's right.

Jacuda-san was talking. I could only make out a part of what she was saying. She said something about one time in dokusan there was light coming out of Go Roshi. The fact that I couldn't fully understand her was not so important. She held me with her eyes. They didn't seem to blink or flicker but seemed to swallow me up. I felt an intense gratitude towards her. As the head of Morioka zenkai, she has taken care of so many sesshins, made it possible for Go Roshi to give dokusan. I felt not just my own thankfulness but that of every *unsui* [monk undergoing Zen training] she's nourished, every sesshin she's catered for. She mentioned Dogen, and tears began to rise to my eyes. I'm grateful to her, to Dogen, to all the Buddhas and patriarchs. But there was power in her gaze.

March 21, 1981

I've been socialized. I don't know how or who did it (I suspect Tessan-san) but now I jump up, get the tea, fetch like a servant or a dog or a Japanese wife. It is a real socialization because I wasn't even aware of it and don't really mind. But thank God I wasn't born here and will never marry a Japanese man. (What am I saying? Never marry. Period.) *Chonans* [eldest sons] are the worst.

I've been re-reading a bit of Freud through the light of Buddhism. It's interesting how his concept of the wish ties in with that of desire, instinct with craving—craving to live, craving to die—theos and eros. This craving leads to a new reincarnation (without soul), like being born with instincts but as yet no personality.

Freud thinks telepathy may be primitive pre-linguistic communication. That makes sense if the universe is really one fabric. Plants, of course, have now been shown to possess consciousness. Why do we say rocks are not alive?

March 28

Dominique came. She cycled out from Morioka through rain and then sun. Good on her. We talked and talked, 'til I was embarrassed to have talked so much. She's still not sure. One thing that really pierced me somewhere sensitive (we were drying dishes under the dim kitchen light) was when she whirled around and said, "You shouldn't be here. You should be with children, with people, where you can do some good. Look at you. You're radiant. People shouldn't have to cycle miles to see you." And of course I do love children and love people, but I'd hate it if people looked to me when I'm so immature in my practice. I'd hate to fall off. Even to her I spoke too much, saying some things I'd read rather than experienced. I felt ashamed. I told her to forget all I'd said, that I was still shallow. I could see that she took it as false modesty on my part. That night I read in Dogen that he said we shouldn't act like enlightened masters. I felt personally chastised. What can one do? In the koan "the man up the tree" I always felt he must just display his Buddha-nature. That is what Go Roshi does. But what about when it's still so dull?

Funny things have come up in my meditations—daydreams, bad concentration. One idea is to have a Zen commune attached to a monastery so that lay people could also do training, with child care facilities so that terms of 100 days at a time would be possible. Then people could also train at least three years, but if they didn't want always to be monks they could pass on into the commune.

April 1

Sesshin. I must do a good one. [Kyogen,] my koan, not good. Kyogen is all sounds. But sounds and I are not separate. I am Kyogen.

Now, after sesshin, I had an excellent session. I entered *Mumonkan*. I made new resolves. I'll try sleeping without lying down, do more soji. On the first night of no sleep, at around 11:00, I felt very tired; around 1:30, my mind became crystal clear; I could only think of my koan. Unfortunately, I guess I overanalyzed it. As I was working with it, I got so involved that it was like a dream. I even had trouble remembering it. I began imputing motives to the people in the koan; they would have been my motives. Go Roshi wasn't impressed. The second night I slept. The third night I slept about two hours sitting up and on the zendo floor. I found my knees ached, so I sat on Go Roshi's step with *Mumonkan* on my head so I wouldn't fall asleep. (The book on the head is very helpful.)

Part VII

New Resolve

Kannonji, Iwateken, April 1981

Dear Mum,

…As I was quietly sitting here minding my own business writing to you, this monk just asked me to marry him. At first I didn't understand. Anything vaguely romantic is so far from the tone of our strictly partnership relationship as to be inconceivable. The Japanese language allows sufficient ambiguity that at first I thought he was talking in the abstract, i.e., would I ever marry someone? I answered with what I thought was appropriate indifference and by thus not initially refusing outright, I got a whole plot laid before me. He says that Go Roshi had said if I wanted to marry this monk, it would be fine by him. He presented the proposal, if it could be called that, very practically. As he was sick, he needed a cook and we could continue life pretty much as before. My God, are they businesslike! I was almost too shocked to speak. He offered to support you and any of the kids here and said I could go back to Ireland every so often. I was still speechless and bumbled and stumbled and said I'd write to you. Meanwhile, Go Roshi had told me that he wanted me back in Tokyo, where I could train better with him. He had apologized profusely that I had to mind an "invalid" and promised that by July at the latest I'd be back in Tokyo. He said that if I stayed for the 3 years' course of study (I'm half-way) that then I could go back to Ireland and teach. (I know he'd help finance a dojo.)

I made a lot of progress at this last sesshin (just got back). The monk who was translating for me said that in three days I did as many koans as he in six months! Go Roshi and I work well together and it would be difficult to find someone as good. So here are my options—give me your advice. In the midst of my stumblings with Tetsugen-san and after he'd said, "Well then, it's decided. Let's marry." (At times like that my Japanese seems faulty. What had I said?) I, frantically searching for an out, said there was a boyfriend I still hadn't given up on and wanted to write to. I really hate this constant pressure to marry. Everyone worries that I'm getting old, etc.—it's only meant as kindness. But what I might do is accept this nebulous boyfriend, stay until the end of autumn (that will be two years), then go to France, find another Roshi and do post-grad work.

The other option is to calm down (I am inclined to bolt terribly when people begin talking about marriage), then go back to Tokyo, finish my term of study properly, i.e., the three years, and get the whole training solidly under my belt. I do risk messing things up by breaking too soon. What do you think? Actually, having written to you I already feel calmer. Big deal—if everybody keeps pushing me to marry I can just refuse. I just get to squirming as if there's a noose there. Tetsugen will get over it; it's not as though he's in love with me or anything. But anyway, what do you think I should do? Try to be objective—not just thinking another year and a half off in Japan but thinking also about my qualifications for the future. Tell Nana not to worry. There's absolutely no way I'll stay in Japan. Cripes, at this rate they'll drive me out!

Anyway, sorry to have gone on at such length, but he just now sprang it on me. As I said, I'm just back from sesshin in Tokyo. It was excellent; I'd say the best one yet. Toshoji has changed a bit from my days there. Someone found out about the cheap dormitory accommodation they offer to Zen students and advertised it in an English paper so now there are four foreigners, even one woman. It's much less isolating, I should think, than before. One of the foreigners, a Jewish student from Pittsburgh called Paul is over here doing research on Japanese theater. He got free tickets for a recital, so I went along. It was fantastic and the best part was having a guide who could explain the various styles, techniques, and meanings of different gestures. It was called a dance recital, but they also did many pieces from Kabuki and Noh plays. They're marathon perform-ances, starting at twelve noon and going on into the night. People drift in and out when they please. The pieces are unrelated so they don't miss any-thing. The audience chats, shouts encouragement, picnics, and generally relaxes, having a good time. Watching them all decked out in magnificent, special occasion kimonos was almost as entertaining as the performance.

The other highlight of my Tokyo sojourn was going to Tessan-san's marriage ceremony. It was my first wedding here and unusual in being Buddhist. Weddings are usually Shinto. They had only met a couple of times before the wedding yet both were cool as cucumbers about it. Her face usually looks a bit odd, like she had a mild stroke with a complex-ion the color and texture of yesterday's porridge. There's a lot to be said for Japanese beauty parlors. She looked gorgeous, serene and radiant, as she sat waiting on a throne. Her head was covered by a white hood in deference to the superstition that women have horns! Her first outfit was white silk; then she changed several times, the number of changes being an indication of the wealth of the family. Poor girl, though—she had so many layers on she could scarcely move and couldn't touch a bite of her dinner. There's another custom which says that no one may mention parting, good-bye, or separation during the day. If they do, it's meant to bring bad luck, and the couple may split up. So everyone drifts away with-out good-byes.

The actual ceremony is very simple and beautiful (no promises of love!). They used a lacquer set just like yours to serve the bride and groom during the ceremony. Then, with saké poured from exquisitely orna-mented gold vessels, we all drank to their health and prosperity. After the ceremony a lot of saké flowed with a feast that made our weddings look like Saturday night's reheated leftovers. It was sumptuous (cost about $80.00 a head), and they even weighed us each down with presents as we left. As they were getting ready to go off to Kyushu on their honeymoon they looked a funny pair. He wore Western clothes instead of his monk's outfit. Having no hair with his navy-blue suit made him look a bit like a con-man; she with her battered-looking face (had taken the make-up off) and her tight, prim little suit, could easily have been the social worker turned warden. We all went as far as Tokyo on the train together. The newlyweds sat in separate compartments without even a pretense of romance. Thank God I'm not Japanese.

So now I'm back here at Kannonji. I've just been out digging my vegetable patch, and there's great satisfaction in getting all the preparations done. I've calmed down a bit since my proposal. I'm sure Go Roshi did not suggest it, which is the impression Tetsugen-san was trying to give. Go Roshi always says he wants me back in Tokyo, where I can train more intensively…See you soon.

Much much love, M.

April 20

A bit of a gap. Let's see now. I stayed in Tokyo until the 10th. It was a wonderful time. Sesshin was excellent. There were no major kensho-type breakthroughs, but several nice little "Ah, so desu ka" [Here: "Ah, really?" Usually: "Is that so?"] jerks. Go Roshi asked me to stay in Kannonji until July at the latest, then back to Toshoji. He says if I want to marry Tetsurai-san, that's okay. I wish he'd drop the marriage thing.

Yesterday a letter from Paul and Galli-san. They said that Eshin-san has become a monk again. He may well fall in love with Sochun-san. She's marvelous, like spring sunshine after a bleak winter. She's always laughing, always bustling around working, overflowing with joy and energy. I was very touched when she wrote me a lovely letter saying how I had inspired her. If only she knew how she had inspired me. She could teach me much about true Zen practice. All during sesshin and the days that followed there was an uplifting sense of *sangha* [community; congregation; originally the order of monks and nuns]. It's something I miss here. The crazy gaijin and Yokokawa-san with her huge sensitive eyes and poetry, and Jiko-san, as daft as ever, racing down the train platform, holding the carriage. They're wonderful.

Paul-san took me to a Japanese dance performance. I saw my first bit of live traditional Japanese culture and had my first *obento* [lunch in a lacquer box with various compartments]. I've only been here one and a half years! Paul couldn't believe it. It was a marathon, beginning at noon and continuing until evening. He explained many things to me. There's Noh, Kabuki, and puppets. Noh came from the Zen mind, he said. It's very simple, with different gestures having pre-ordained meanings, like a language. Pine trees in the background of the stage mean that it used to be performed at Shinto shrines. Kabuki was a reaction to Noh. It's much more flamboyant and fast-moving, almost gaudy. It's often preceded by a striped curtain. Kabuki is a family monopoly. A few families get all the lead roles. They don't allow women, so a boy is trained from childhood to be an *onnagata* [female impersonator]. Japanese dancers usually have a repertoire of about one hundred pieces, any of which they'll do at two minutes' notice. So rehearsals are few (same pieces, over and over). If one's mother is sick, one can cancel at a moment's notice; it's not like the cut-throat competition in the American theater world.

The audience was fun to watch. In the afternoon it was mostly old ladies, elegantly clad in their silk kimonos. It was like a picnic; people ate, drank, chatted, shouted encouragement to the cast. Occasionally a pair of hands could be seen moving with it, obviously a dancer who knew that piece. By our standards, it could scarcely be called dance, just movement. The women were totally constrained in their girdle-like layers of kimonos. They kept changing costumes on stage with the help of little men dressed in black that the audience literally didn't see.

One day Jim took me to a fancy hotel. We drank endless cups of coffee, watched the bureaucrats dressed to match each other, and the decor, in tasteful, subtle, banal non-colors. Then we slowly meandered through the galleries, poking through the streets of downtown Tokyo. I really felt like a country bumpkin who'd come up to the big city. Everything was exciting, a thrill. I could scarcely contain myself.

All during that sesshin, I felt a joy bordering on ecstasy, a huge love for everyone around me. I could scarcely keep from smiling. There was an affinity with everyone, people with whom I'd never even spoken. When someone would have kensho, it was I that felt relieved. Sitting in the corridor, the young lad beside me heaved great tortured "mu's." Each one went through me, until tears dripped down my face with his anguish.

It is not that I feel a need for this sense of sangha that I said I lack in Kannonji; I can manage quite well, peacefully alone. Rather, it was that all this love welling up inside was begging for an object. I ask myself, why can't Tetsugen-san be my object? He is there. But with the language barrier and his inhibited personality, it is difficult to have a real relationship and intimacy is hard even to imagine. But he is good and kind to me, though in other moods he is bossy and demanding. Tachibana Sensei says he treats me as a thing, a temple attachment, but that is only his manner, not his heart.

When I came back from Tokyo he asked me to marry him. My stomach was turning, my mind racing. I began not to understand Japanese, and I thought I was postponing the decision, when he triumphantly exclaimed, "So then it's decided. We'll marry." I gulped, then backtracked frantically, trying not to hurt his feelings, forgetting that feelings weren't really part of the offer. Since I happened to be in the middle of writing a letter to Mum, I stalled, saying I'd ask her.

The next few days, I felt claustrophobic. He was charming to me most of the time and a cruel bastard to the cat, tormenting her, hitting her, locking her up, inventing nasty teasing games of intimidation. I'd look at him and feel blackness. When I found her locked overnight in Busshari-to I wanted to scream at him. How could I ever marry a man who'd be so cruel to a cat? The blackness was in my heart. Where was my lofty love for mankind? I felt trapped. What he did physically to the cat I felt emotionally as me (maybe I overreacted…). I resented that he could dare to think of dooming me to the banal existence I'd have with him, he who had scarcely enough life in him to look people in their eyes. But surely I should be indifferent. If I really just took a day at a time, then anyone, anywhere, any life should surely be okay. I pelted myself with recriminations. I wanted to run. Any excuse. Aagh. Then a letter came from Mum. She still hadn't received mine, but I used it as an opportunity to make my refusal plain. He took it well. After all, he had little emotion invested in the whole thing. I was amazed at how relieved I felt—amazed and vaguely shocked. Get your act together, kid!

Kannonji, Iwateken
April 28, 1981
Dear Mum,

Happy birthday to you. *Omedeto gozaimasu. Tanoshi tanjoobi da to ii desu ga.* [Congratulations. Enjoy your birthday.] A wee package is on the way but will be late. *Gomen nasai, ne?* [Sorry!] You'd better blinking well make it over to Japan. As soon as you have a definite date, please tell me. I'm still assuming that I'll be able to get free time, though if I'm in Toshoji, as is the plan, it should be easier. Go Roshi is coming here to stay for a while in May. I'm looking forward to it so I can advance with my koans. You're right that Nana seems to think I'm getting too involved. I got a come-back-home but very nice letter from her...

By now you must have gotten my last letter with my almost hysterical reaction to Tetsugen-san's proposal. Poor fellow. I did calm down, and he wasn't at all put out that I wasn't interested. I was amazed at my almost allergic reaction to the mention of marriage...

I went the other day with Mu-chan's mother to see the cherry blossoms. They're lovely. Underneath the trees sit little parties of *Ohanami no hito,* people who've gone blossom viewing. You imagine pastoral picnics, quiet family outings with Oriental tranquillity. They're mostly mobs of rowdy drunks out with any excuse to share a bottle of saké and some songs. Still, they look as if they're enjoying themselves: "Blossoms, what blossoms?" And the Japanese need these chances to let themselves go. Anyway, m'dear, the very happiest of birthdays to you...

Love to ya, M.

May 4
Tessan-san came for the night with his bride. Though there were times I thought he'd drive me batty, I really do feel a love for him. When he shows his good side, it's like a winter's hearth. The two of them seem to be doing well by each other, both a little chuffed at being married and each aware of rescuing the other from the shriveled, cobwebby shelf of spinsterhood. They seemed positively playful with one another, she

tapping his newspaper. (Why can't the Japanese touch?) They could even have married for love.

Where Christianity preaches original sin, Buddhism preaches original enlightenment.

May 13

Yesterday had dokusan. Phew. Go Roshi gave a big speech about how he'd never met a girl as diligent as me (hasn't met many girls in training). About how I was the same caliber as the old priests, the likes of Dogen. (It's more a reflection of the low quality of present-day Japanese priests.) The upshot of the thing is that he wants to make me Kannonji's *jushoku* [head priest of a temple]. I nearly died. Wants to get Tetsurai-san all trained (provided he doesn't run away) and then marry us! Leps. I glugged.

He said only my children were fit to be successors of Kannonji and though he had looked all over Japan, there wasn't a man worth me. Great, so runner-up for the stud contest is Tetsurai-san. But I finally clicked on the reason for all the marriage bit: My purpose is to make kids.

Kneeling in dokusan, the smell of incense sitting heavily in the air, made everything seem old and already cured by time, as if it all didn't matter. He was glowing, enraptured in the excitement of his plan for me and my children, he and his "baby," Kannonji. I found myself nodding— everything, anything was okay. Then I caught myself. Wait, hold it, no, that's not what I want. Stop. I thought of my ego, of discriminating consciousness, etc., but still, it's not the life for me. I told Tachibana Sensei that in Japan people don't want to do zazen; in Ireland they do. I wanted to build a dojo over there, I said. Sensei was squirming in his seat; he obviously didn't want to be the one to present Go Roshi with disappointing news and asked why I didn't call everyone over here. That's all I needed, him confounding me when I was so reluctant and so insistent. Go Roshi was laughing, said I was a plane and could fly to Ireland. Tachibana Sensei seemed to be putting things vaguely when I needed to be firm. But it'll all work out in the end, I'm sure; Go Roshi is always changing his mind.

At first I was a bit disappointed not to be going back to Tokyo, but when I came back here it was so overwhelmingly beautiful, the life so pure that I couldn't stay disappointed.

Kannonji, Iwateken
May, 1981
Dear Mum,
A very happy Mother's day…Are your Japanese plans any more definite?…More people are coming to Kannonji now that the weather's improving. Busloads of little old ladies doing the rounds of the temples. A group came yesterday and chanted ancient sutras, ringing bells. Many could no longer carry a tune, but their cracked voices wavered up and down with touching determination. Hope you get to see some of them. Do write soon, Ma, and have a good day. After six of us, you've earned it.

Love ya. M.

May 14
Lately and today specially (I was alone) I've been getting flashes of *tada* ["just," "only"]. Doing something and it's all there is in the entire universe. These arise spontaneously but are so refreshing and different that they attract attention and immediately my discriminating labeling consciousness jumps up to say, "Hey!"

May 15, 1981
Tachibana Sensei got really angry with Tetsugen-san. Says he treats me like a thing, a temple attachment, and shows no gratitude. That's an exaggeration, though he treats me often like a maid. I think it's part of the way Japanese men are raised to treat the women in their lives. Now, pretty much I just say "Hai" and do as I'm told. I reckon in the long run it's I who gains and he who loses, I who'll get my ego battered and he whose will grow more entrenched. Nevertheless, once he told me to plant *kiku* [chrysanthemums]. (I was already weeding in the rain, right after breakfast, while he sat around digesting.) I quite firmly said I'd go to

Sasaki-san's and get them, but I'm not planting them today. He looked shocked and giggled nervously, a bit embarrassed. "Why?" I said I had other work to do. I didn't feel or sound annoyed. Pushing the wheelbarrow down to Sasaki-san's for the kiku, I felt "Hee, hee, hee, I'm a bitch, I'm terrible, but chuckle, chuckle, I enjoyed that." Then I saw her—skinny, 70, down on the floor vigorously scrubbing the already gleaming wood with such earnestness she didn't even hear my call. I felt ashamed. She trundled into the garden and dug me up kiku from the ends of the rows she'd already neatly trimmed, thinned, and transplanted. She motioned me into the shed, all the time half running, her stooped back parallel to the ground like a cyclist angled for speed. The shed was dark, smelled musty. She took the lids off various barrels, pulling out all manner of salted and preserved vegetables and stuffing them into bags for me. Then "sayonara." She was off about her work. Ashamed, thoroughly ashamed, I bought an ice-cream and pushed my barrow past the rice fields with the radios, the many bent bodies at their jobs. I wondered what they thought about, if they thought at all. Were they all like so many Zen masters, living their koans—digging and digging and only digging?

May 18
Yesterday I was in a bad mood. No reason. Felt if there was anyone to interact with even a bit that it would quickly be dispersed. My bad moods usually are. Tetsugen-san came back from onsen, thrust the kettle through the window at me. "It leaks, put it in a bottle" (using the most brusque form of Japanese commands). "When you're done wipe the kettle well or it'll rust." (Again, very curt.) I bristled. Who did he think he was, telling me to fill his bottles in a manner like that? I was about to lash out, but before I could remember the word for slave or servant, he turned on his heel. "Next time, next time," I seethed. I'd had enough of him and his arrogant ways. I'm sick of silently resenting him; it's better for both of us to air it, even if he is my superior. Didn't I feel small, then, to discover later that he'd brought the kettle, filled it, and returned with it, not for himself, but for me.

Today it's pouring rain, but I'm in a great humor. Even yesterday, though, it was totally clear how all these moods just arise and fade, are empty and impotent. Yesterday I felt completely empty. Frighteningly empty. There simply was no me. Not the kind of universal me I sometimes feel—but nothing at all. Void.

Yesterday Ojii-san came on his bike, like a gentle spring breeze that you mightn't notice if you weren't paying attention. He's old and bent with a gait like a fisherman wading out from the sea. *O-mairi ni kimashita?* [Have you come to visit the shrine?] He lit incense and bowed to Kannon sama. Then walked very slowly, as if he felt the weight of the sunshine, across to Busshari-to. In his stocking feet he smiled, a golden smile of sweets and dentists and irrepressible good will. He climbed the stairs, doing one thing at a time. Every movement seemed to command his total attention. "No, no tea this time. Next time. Sayonara." Onto his bike. It was green, creaking down the tree-lined alley. The carrier sparkled in the sun. One white butterfly flickered across his path.

Am reading Simone de Beauvoir's biography. Thus far she doesn't appeal to me much as a person. Very arrogant and seems quite cut off from her feelings, or maybe they're just not the public's business, which is fair enough. De Beauvoir and Sartre had no friends and few relationships, she said. I wonder if that kind of isolation is necessary to achieve anything. (I know, I know. There's nothing really to achieve, but until I really realize that, I must go on trying to achieve, though really realizing that there is nothing to achieve.) She spoke of a woman (Camille?) who was writing from 12 P.M. to 6 P.M. every day. It prodded de Beauvoir and I think, if she's putting in that kind of energy and devotion on something like a novel, how much more I should be putting into my training?

I was thinking about Mariah [a friend in Peru] and how she sent me the cigar two years ago. Was wondering where to get one this birthday when what arrives but a big 40¢ cigar. She's great. I'm still giggling from the card. She also is trying to remember if I'm 27 or 28 (26!); it's a relief to me. Two years ago I felt very old, very afraid of growing old. Now I feel 18; I don't look it, and no one else thinks of me that way, but the world and my relationship to it feels like when I was that tender age.

I'm relishing growing old; as my body decays my spirit is only going to soar all the more.

May 19

The morning was rain. Not like yesterday's heavy, pounding rain, but a soft, grey vaporous rain. Went to Sasaki-san for daffodil bulbs. It was cold, we agreed, not like May. Ojii-chan loosened them with a big fork. I cleaned them off with a trowel. It took all his strength to lift and aim his blows but each one was perfect. He gave me purple rubber gloves for my bluish hands. He smiled and continued down the row. We filled two boxes with daffodils and narcissi. They were heavy. I washed the rubber gloves in a puddle and gave them back. He was still smiling. I picked my way back in the rain, now more like airborne dew. The mountains were scarcely visible but very present, at once rooted and wispy (like the driving instincts that show themselves as dreams...).

Today no post. Pity.

Last night I tried to stay up all night doing zazen. But I dropped off for an hour or two. I was really annoyed with myself because I missed that time of lucidity that comes after the tiredness. Felt very annoyed. However, today all day long "this mind is Buddha" which I read in the *Shobogenzo* [an important collection of writings by Dogen, the Japanese Soto Zen founder] struck reverberations in my thoughts. "This mind is Buddha, no mind, no Buddha" suddenly became very clear. They are only echoes of the one.

Strange and charming that in the technologically advanced Japan such anachronisms as the bill collectors exist. No one has a checking account, so they come around on their bikes and scooters collecting. It's much more human. Just now came the waterworks collector on her bike, her little one on her back. He bravely gave me the change. I like him better than the bank tellers.

Circumstances are forever making a fool of me. I should say "teaching me" but I'm a slow learner. Sometimes I bitch about Tetsugen-san and stupid trivial things, the way he jeers when he thinks I'm doing something wrong or silly, how he never closes the door, no longer notices what

I cook even when I make his favorite dish. I mused—he has no emotions or heart. It would never occur to him to bring me home a treat, for example; that kind of spontaneity isn't in him. Of course as I thought the thought, he closed the door behind him. Yesterday he brought me home a piece of cheesecake (Yuliko-san had said I like cheesecake), tonight raved about the curry and comfrey tempura I made. Oh, well. I've accepted that once I get to know people they're always good; I always like them (even the Shimoshinge-sans of the world). If only I could actualize Sono's "Thanks very much for everything. I have no complaints whatsoever." Truly each situation is its own perfection. I wish I could uproot the bitch in me that knows even as it bitches that it's nonsense and destructive.

I love the cat. (Actually, it just hit me that there's another example. The cat drove me crazy for ages; now she seems the best one I've ever known.)

I've been gathering wild plants and mushrooms. I love strolling with my bucket, seeking them out and bringing them back. Each one has its time of perfection, its tricks in becoming edible. Soak with the bath's ashes, boil three times, grate through the slit in a daikon...They have no fertilizers or spray; they're free and it's the same thrill as rescuing the battered chair or leaky pot off someone's rubbish pile. The scavenger, gypsy, make-do renovator in me revels. I was standing by the rice paddies with my pail. The wind was still and the waters unruffled. The sun was streaky through the clouds. Indigos, emeralds merging. Only one violent splash of yellow—huge dandelions reflecting in the water. I was dumbstruck and drawn into it. The cat ran over to me, rubbing my leg, and as I re-emerged it came as a relief to realize that I'm not separate from it. I remember the times I battered the flowers with my pleas to be let inside. Now, for moments, there is no inside and no outside.

I was tired after staying up all night. The tiredness dragged across a couple of days but seemed also to drain my usual discriminating mind. There were many moments of pure absorption. These are still rare, but it's the first indication I've had that my consciousness may actually be changing. I actually enjoy working. The first time that thought flickered across my mind, a voice, almost a reflex, quashed it—afraid someone might hear and take advantage. But Go Roshi is right. Working *isshaken mei* [with all one's heart and soul] is not work.

May 26

The other day Sasaki-san came on her bike. She looked ravishing. She sat on the step where I was scrubbing the floor. A white scarf was draped like the Virgin's veil, draped carelessly on her head. She still has all the mannerisms of a young coquette, darting her eyes playfully, laughing flirtingly into her hands. As she so often does, she brought us some of her good home-cooking. She wanted to play *goeika music* [music with hand bells and small metal gongs, accompanied by short poems of praise sung, commonly performed along with important Buddhist ceremonies] at the ceremony on the ninth. She prevailed on Tetsugen-san, employing every measure of her female charms. Her eyes were beautiful, pleading, and winning. His eyes were on the floor. He often seems to be fascinated by something inanimate when a person's eyes are too intimate, or even real. I wondered if perhaps he was listening with everything he had and if that was why he had to focus on something as undistracting as the concrete floor. She paused, straining for his reply. For a moment he was silent. Then, "Don't wash this floor like in Tokyo or the water will seep underneath and freeze in winter." A short soliloquy about cracked concrete and he lapsed again into silence. She took no heed and continued as if there had never been a gap in the conversation. I could have dumped my bucket on him. How could he be so insensitive to her?

May 28

We went to collect plants from one of Sasaki-san's relatives. It was early morning. Misty. The rice fields had not yet been planted and formed spreads of square lakes into the distance, reflecting mountains and clouds, that day a patchwork of blues and greys. We were putting the plantlings into a box. I was handling them rather roughly, thinking more that he was being rather grasping in asking her for more and more, and thinking that I'd have to plant them. My mind was far away from the plants. One tiny one went under the next sod I added. "It's alive, it's alive" she said, not in alarm, not scolding, but as if a self-evident truth were speaking itself while her lips moved. I was ashamed.

My birthday came. Tetsugen forgot. (On his birthday I'd gone to a lot of trouble to make a special cake; he only said it was better to buy one. Sometimes ya can't win.) In the morning I scrubbed windows, smiling that it was my birthday even if the world forgot. But it didn't. I was overwhelmed, tears actually brimming, with the kindness. Tachibana Sensei with four presents and a bottle of German white wine. Chiba-san made me a beautiful *samuè* [work outfit], loads of underwear, and a strawberry cheesecake. Dominique showered me with presents and good will. She seems to be getting more and more into Zen. Hope she can suspend her intellect a bit.

Life is great. Actually, my body's in bits—a cut that keeps bursting on my toe, a shin all bruised from falling through a stool while window-washing; during the cold my frostbite re-emerged. Some weird rash or biting is gradually spreading, first my arm and stomach, now legs, neck and chest. Strange. But the old *atama* [head] is ill. Am working very hard these days, about 12 hours a day without a break. Still the place seems dirty.

May 30
A quiet day. A day of wind and weeds and dirty windows.

Kannonji, Iwateken
May 1981
Dear Mum,

...I asked Go Roshi if there would be any time when it would be most convenient for your visit. He got very enthusiastic and said "anytime," even if you came in time for next month's big ceremony (when I'll be run off my feet), that would be okay. But watch out. I'm sure he hopes you'll fall in love with Japan and we'll both stay and live here happily ever after...As for my leaving here, I'm still not sure when. Your point that I should expose myself to Zen as it's adapting itself in the West is, I think, very valid. My problem is two-fold; one, how to break it to Go Roshi and second, whenever I see him actually in front of me I just can't imagine wanting to switch to another Roshi. He is so excellent and now understands me and my level in a way that would take ages to re-establish with someone else. Still, as he's not here right now, I do feel inclined to go back closer to home. Hmmm.

...You're right. Things were a bit awkward here with Tetsugen-san, but they've rebalanced. Soon at least one and maybe two from Tokyo should be staying here, which will break up the couple set-up...My plans are still so nebulous that I can't say with any certainty even what continent I'll be on next spring. Anyway, I'm busy these days. Soon Go Roshi, his wife, and two others arrive to stay. Then for the ceremony on June 7th (this temple's 10th anniversary). We're expecting over one hundred people with top Roshis, politicians, reporters, etc. from all over Japan. I always thought I kept this place clean but I see it now with new eyes and little nooks that haven't been disturbed at all during those ten years. Ah, well, I've nothing else to do but clean, so I'll have it ready in time. Am dying to see you. Do practice your Japanese. You'll be grateful for any little bit you have...

Love, etc.

June 1

Tetsugen-san made me a *zenpan* [chin rest]. The wood smells beautiful. The chin is curved; the board is carved. He inscribed my name and an old Zen exhortation that from ancient times people have done such hard training and attained *daigo* [great enlightenment]. It hangs by a royal purple string. Holding it in my hands, I feel a sort of reverence for all the hard training that has gone before. However, that didn't do me much good last night. It's hard to sleep on the bloody thing.

June 2

I wonder if the Japanese have a higher incidence of paranoia than Westerners. People are so reluctant to say something offensive that it helps me understand better why Tetsuro-san was convinced everyone was talking about him behind his back. On the other hand, it's refreshing to be allowed to be naïve, to expect the best and see good. Our culture sponsors a cynicism even in its humor.

This morning I read Dogen's commentary on Gensha's one bright pearl. During zazen, I kept repeating, "the entire universe is one bright pearl." I felt luminous. Everything really was a divine light. Couldn't help smiling. If that had been a koan, I'd have to say "There is no pearl, no universe, only BRIGHT."

Kannonji, Iwateken
June 15, 1981
Dear Mum,
…Here things have calmed down a bit after the ten-year anniversary ceremony. So, Mum, are you definitely coming to Japan? Your trip to Ireland in September is right when I was expecting you. Maybe you'd be best getting one of those "round the world with stopovers tickets" and come to Japan from Ireland. Otherwise the £99 London/Hong Kong standby deal might be your best bet. Do let me know as soon as you're definite. It's a pity you couldn't have been here for the ceremony. It was quite impressive. There was a woman priest (first other one I've seen) who told marvelous stories about when she and Go Roshi were young and training together. She set off at 20, walking around Japan, chanting "Namu myoho renge kyo" and visiting various roshis. She ended up trying to visit my Roshi's Roshi (Harada Sogaku Roshi), but was kidnapped and kept locked away by priests of her own sect. She escaped by climbing out a window and went to Harada Roshi's temple, where they all took her for a boy. She went on and on with great adventures and funny anecdotes—a podgy, little woman, full of vigor…

For the days building up to the ceremony I'd been working literally non-stop, sleeping just a few hours a night. But somehow the rhythm of everyone working together engendered new energy, and I didn't feel at all tired. So even if you decide to marry all the rest of the kids off in one huge ceremony, no problem—I'll cater! Then after the ceremony, we did the civilized Japanese thing and went to a hot springs to relax. We all spent the night. (Go Roshi paid everything for me.) Had a big feast and numerous soothing dips in the springs. But then I just went poof. Suddenly, when it was time to enjoy myself, all I wanted to do was sleep. They made all of us give a little self-introduction and sing a song. I got a mischievous pleasure from seeing all the dear little Buddhist ladies oohing and aahing and clapping when I was singing "Take her up to Monto."

Tetsugen-san must have overtired himself getting ready for the ceremony. People, like him, with kidney disorders are said to be prone to depression, and the following week or so he went into a black depression. I was ready to tell Go Roshi that it's him or me but not both of us! However, to my relief, it wasn't a permanent character change (or the real hidden self), and if anything, since then he's been brighter than ever.

Love, M.

P.S. Guess what's for dinner tonight? Whale and chrysanthemums—these were looking stale on the altar. I feel awful about the whale, but he buys it because it's cheap. Aren't you looking forward to Japanese food, Mum?

June 22

A gap. Much has happened. We prepared for the ceremony. Paul-san and Yokogawa-san came. I saved the wine from my birthday to welcome them. Paul extravagantly gave me Japanese and Zen cookbooks that cost a fortune, and he struggling to keep the shirt on his back and rice in his belly. We toasted and tasted with the wine. It sparkled, but the occasion didn't. There was a tangible stiffness between them. Paul later told me they'd had a falling out. She had been in love with him, a fact that seemed to irritate rather than please him.

The next day Go Roshi was coming. I was busy with last minute preparations. It seemed as if I had been doing nothing but cleaning for weeks and still all around me were little dirt traps, black holes. I finished Go Roshi's birthday cake in the midst of the chaos. It took ages, a challenge to my ingenuity. A cake with no cake pans and only a tiny toaster oven. Paul said it sounded like a koan—"Bake me a cake with no oven." I built

tin foil pans, held the door open with a Biro [a ballpoint pen], perform-
ing culinary gymnastics of twisting, piercing, covering, and exposing the
batter. The result looked decidedly unstable, taller than wide or long, three
uneven layers each straining to slide in a different direction. Feeling warm
towards Jacuda-san, I saved her some mediocre doughnuts from the day
before. She embarrassed me thoroughly by distributing a half each of the
by-then-hardened rings to the Morioka *zazenkai*.

Dominique came to dokusan. She seemed excited. Go Roshi gave her
muji—intriguing. Then Tachibana Sensei took us out for coffee. My own
dokusan was incredible. We only talked about the koan, nothing personal as we usually do. But Go Roshi was so beautiful, so radiantly beautiful, he really seemed to shine. Our eyes met and truly there was no
separation but it was I that was drawn into him. He told me that my
training in Kannonji was the best possible, just to throw myself minute
by minute into each job. When he said it, it seemed obvious, and I wondered how I could have contemplated training elsewhere. I think I promised to stay three years. I'm not really sure, as I was mostly trying to hold
back the tears that promptly overflowed when I left the room. I don't
know where they came from. I certainly wasn't sad but neither was I crying from joy. It just seemed to be an expression of the nameless emotion that had overwhelmed me. The following dokusans only dealt with
koans. In "Seizan, Alone and Poor" he gave me a very emphatic full
marks. In "Joshu examines the hermits," he said I couldn't even imitate
Joshu. Either way is okay.

In one of Paul's dokusans, he encouraged him to help me found a dojo
in Ireland. I was thrilled. Maybe he's accepted that alternative.

That evening Go Roshi returned to Kannonji with us. The next morning I was waiting in the dokusan line, alone, the sun soft-shining across
the tatami. After breakfast Go Roshi announced that it was his birthday
party. We got out my wobbly cake and the warm beer that Paul had given
him. He distributed both. We joked warmly about blowing out the candle, but the universe would be in darkness. "Thank you beery much" to
Paul. "Thank you cakey much" to me. We were all laughing.

The rest of the time 'til the ceremony was work without respite. But I didn't even want to rest. I had loads of energy and was riding high on the excitement of everyone being there. All had great spirit and helped tirelessly. Jacuda-san oversaw everything and yet saw to the little things, like that everyone got a cup of tea. Oku-san was there, but Jacuda-san seemed much more Go Roshi's wife and Oku-san a dear sister, whose relationship is rooted in the past.

Yoko-san, too, slaved away. Every time I saw her, she was sweeping or scrubbing a floor. When I called her Kannonji's Cinderella, she put her hands on her hips and leaned back, her teeth seeming huge as she laughed and laughed.

Paul, too, worked with every ounce he had, singing boisterously numbers from the musicals back home as he scrubbed Busshari-to's windows. His job, washing windows, had been started by a young Japanese lad the day before. He'd come asking to stay. Tetsugen was out collecting Go Roshi from the station. I said he should ask him when he got back. He volunteered to work. I gratefully accepted the offer. Things got hectic. He, Paul, various workmen all asking questions and in the midst of it all Naifari-san arrives for ookyo and tea with all the time in the world. The lad worked hard. Tetsugen returned and ordered him to clear off. He wouldn't look at him or explain but merely shouted over his shoulder as he strutted away. I insisted on feeding him lunch. He was quiet and soon went out to continue work on the windows. Tetsugen began abusing him again and ordered him off the premises. Paul and I were furious. We were all going to Morioka for dokusan. I said we should at least take him to Morioka, but Tetsugen refused to take him even as far as the bus. We pulled out. Tears of rage were in my eyes. We live by other people's kindness, and yet he couldn't even spare the kindness one gives a mangy dog in one's path. Paul was equally incensed, his eyes flashed black with what looked like hate, although I don't think him capable of that emotion. Then he cursed Tetsugen for his dictatorial ways, also for not eating the lunch I specially prepared for him. When we returned to Kannonji with Tachibana Sensei the police were moving the lad away. He had sat down in zazen, refusing to move. Wonderful. Just like the priests of old. Then Tetsugen half convinced me that he was unbalanced, but in retrospect, I don't think so. Paul reminded me about the lad that had been driven away during Takuhatsu. We both sighed and shrugged.

So we worked and then worked. Morioka zazenkai women came and took over the kitchen. They kept asking me where things were, but I didn't know.

Paul's birthday was the 6th. He had left behind invitations for friends to come to the ceremony. I wanted to do something for him but where was the chance? So at 3:30 in the morning I started baking. Only time for one layer. I went out before the dawn to gather herbs for the cake. The grass was wet with dew of last night's rain, the air misty and cool. Gion-chan followed me, jumping through the long grasses. The mountains were shrouded, revealing yet mysterious, in webs of grey sinking to black. In all the business of preparations, it was a time of stillness, of total quiet. Everyone, even Go Roshi, was asleep. It was my own little oasis in time. Then back into the fever and fun of work.

Tetsubun-san arrived from Tokyo by surprise. Before, my Japanese was never good enough to talk with him but this time we got on famously. He likes to work, to laugh, to drink beer. His heart is very young for his 50 years, younger than Tetsugen-san who prides himself on his youthfulness (prides himself with all the showiness and trappings of one desperately reassuring himself, as he fades through time).

After it was all over, Tetsubun-san and I sat drinking soda in the summer afternoon sunshine. He said he felt no difference in our ages. But when he said it, 1) it was true and 2) it wasn't to emphasize his youth but an attempt to attribute it to my "mirror Zen." Incredible man. Also the only Japanese that I'd called really sexy. When he was leaving, after a couple of beers and blushes, he asked me to say "goodbye" the European way—with a kiss. I was delighted to oblige.

That reminds me, Oku-san's face nearly burst when Paul kissed me "hello." He's still completely natural about such things, but I'm getting self-conscious with the Japanese. When he found his birthday cake and gifts, I was working in the kitchen. He came upon me from behind, whirled me by the apron strings and kissed his thanks. My first reaction was flustered. Imagine! But also I was very conscious of Yokogawa-san, who could have felt hurt.

Go Roshi was also keeping up a hectic pace. Because of my height he'd asked me to stick up various bits of paper from above. I, of course, wanted to "really do" the thing, but was so self-consciously "really doing" that the tape stuck to my fingers and things crinkled and split. Sweeping the corridor, I met him popping through the window, one leg in and one leg out, kimono hoisted rakishly. We both dissolved into transcultural giggles.

The night before the ceremony itself, we had a small party. As it was also Paul's birthday, he was heavily toasted. They asked him to sing a song. He opted for a belated "Happy Birthday" to Go Roshi. I crowed along. Go Roshi loved it and called for an encore.

That night we had *bansan* [evening sutras, chanted after evening zazen or during banka]. Go Roshi didn't come, sending instead the message that he had drunk too much *tamago saké* [saké with egg]. I loved him for that. He never gets drunk or even tipsy, so it was marvelous on the eve of this momentous occasion that he could be so unattached to his image as to send the message that he couldn't come because he was drunk! Jacuda-san was well on, waltzing around the kitchen. In fact, they all seemed to be well-oiled. I'd been doing the washing-up, but that didn't last long enough to account for the fact that I was stone cold sober and they all at least flushed.

Paul came into the kitchen. Everyone must have been pouring him birthday drinks. He looked pleased with himself, pleased with life. But then he blurted out, "They're burying you in there; they don't understand; they love you and are taking turns around the table praising you, but they'll bury you. Go Roshi's not saying a word but he must be thinking to keep you in Kannonji." He was almost moaning.

The saké must have made them sentimental. Those praises used to really upset me. They made me feel as if I was living a lie, because I certainly wasn't all the wonderful things they say. Now it just seems as if they're talking about another person, and I find it amusing. It's just the Japanese way. (One of the things they must have said is that now I look

Japanese. Two different people said so lately—it sure is as if they're talking about some other person.)

The ceremony itself went off grand. I rang the bell as they filed in. A few roshis came, but not as many as last year. There was a small, podgy woman monk. Her face when at rest looked like a surly old man nursing the ulcer he deserved from an overindulgent life. Her bald head and unfeminine features but girlish voice combined to give the impression of an aging eunuch. Then she spoke. She came alive. I couldn't understand all the words but couldn't miss her spirit. She seemed to be popping. Her sentences were punctuated by excited dashes of her fist and comic sweeps through the air. Her tiny frame seemed to balloon as she'd stretch, illustrating some yarn.

Tetsugan-san also came to the ceremony. Go Roshi thanked him for publishing his books. He was, as always, absolutely radiant. Dom saw it too, a light from him that is almost blinding.

After the ceremony we went to the onsen. Then a terrible tiredness flooded over me. I slipped into the hot mineral water with every cell in my body drooping. I was scarcely able for the party, a bit of an anti-climax.

Perhaps Tetsugen-san overstrained himself, too. He went into a black depression that seemed endless. Didn't talk to me except to ridicule me and give orders in the gruffest possible Japanese. The common greetings that mean nothing but symbolize a multitude, he dispensed with. I was biting back the resentments, chastising myself for my intransigent ego. "Good morning"—a deaf ear, still tongue, where's the difference? Tetsubun-san had stayed an extra day to help. Tetsugen-san was the soul of cheer and humor for the moment. They both exuded the fun and laughter of schoolboys on the bounce. Then suddenly into the pits of gloom. He confronted me.

What had I done? I wracked my brain. I tried to be light and normal, which he seemed to find very irritating. I almost respect him for that, for refusing to be seduced by my false entreaties. False they were, as I was choking with hurt, yes, really hurt. That "non-existent" ego was bleeding.

During that time, I spoke with no other living soul. Gion-chan tried very hard to bridge the chasm to humanity. She ran if he so much as picked his nose. Ten long days. Ten days of thinking this was his true personality; this was the future mapped out for the next year and a half. I was ready to tell Go Roshi I'd take care of Kannonji alone, that it's me or him.

Then it broke. As suddenly and completely as it came, it cleared. Last spring (about the time he proposed), he had ordered me a new set of summer robes. They arrived and with great pleasure he gave them to me. With great relief I received them. His first civil words. I thanked him profusely, but it was less for the robes (which I didn't need) and more for reprieving me.

Sasaki-san phoned. I nipped down on my bike, by the brook and across the rocky roadway. She motioned me into her dark kitchen, the bare wood beams glowing. She was rubbing salt into large *iwashi* [fresh sardines]. That room always seems timeless, as if nothing had changed since long before she was born, but she was bouncing up and down on her hunkers, flapping her hands and telling me her schedule in a hurried voice. Up at 4 o'clock, cleaning, light the rice, clean the altar, go to Kannonji, make everyone's breakfasts and lunch obentos, then o'soji. Yet she always finds time to come to ookyo and to give us her goodness. Suddenly she grew quiet and still. She was no longer speaking from agitation, looked me straight in the eye, unwavering, and says "All I ask is that when people come they say the old lady is kind." My heart wrenched. She knew all the backbiting that Morioka's zazenkai deal her even though she had donated the land and is so devoted.

I love the very same ladies that do it to her, but those pleading eyes…"That's all," she said, "and then I can be happy—now these sardines are secret; the young ones will be annoyed that I'm giving them away." She was sure I understood. I was choked and couldn't think of words. I could only bow deeply, then up and off on me bike.

Chiba-san invited me to a concert where a Japanese woman was playing the harp, Irish style. They said it would go on late. This was all a ruse so that I'd be allowed to stay the night with them. Chiba-san asked Tetsugen-san, who said they were to bring me back after breakfast, but when she asked, he said I should be back by five in the morning. Nonsense. He just didn't want to get up and do service. The concert itself was so-so, but then we went back to their house and ate dinner and drank beer. The rain was falling and the air smelled sweet. He opened a sliding door, lit an oil lamp, and in the flickering darkness we listened to the pattering of the rain. We sat drinking and chatting. It was a bit nostalgic, a thing I always love, just to natter with good friends. Don't often get the chance. The dictionary required squinting in the dark but somehow we managed, in fact 'til 3:30 in the morning. I'd been up for 24 hours by then but felt incredibly high from their warmth and the occasion. I don't really mind having to do the dishes, but not having to do them, not cooking (though I did that before I left), plus a steaming mug of percolated coffee, all thrilled me. Things I used to take so for granted. There was no way I'd be back before breakfast. Chiba-san, who makes no bones about disliking Tetsugen-san, just told me to take things easy. It was a rainy morning. Coffee and toast for breakfast and fresh tangy yogurt. We looked at pictures, smelled roses, discussed the twittering sparrows and shedding dog. I knew Tetsugen was probably getting more and more annoyed, but I didn't give a tinker's damn. Whether it was from tiredness or from joy, I don't know, but that whole morning I was in some kind of blissful samadhi. "Moment after moment." If that's what it's all about, then it's worth it. Nothing could bother. Everything, from the rain-glistening mountains to the dog's filthy pawprints on my clean kimono, was wonderful. It grew later and later. Chiba-san still didn't ring. Ah, well, might as well be hung for a sheep as a lamb, I thought, as we headed, not homewards, but to the *tamago* [egg] farm.

They had been telling me about it for a long time, but still I was unprepared for how it would take me. They had brought me to my place, to my life. It was drizzle-pouring. Black hens be-speckled the place like some insistent mildew. Everything I looked at was dotted with them and each dot would be not one but a cluster, on steps, stools, stones, an abandoned wreck, a tumbly shed, haystacks, anything stationary—strutting, calling, laying, and reminding me of my childhood. They guided me into the large dark old farmhouse.

The first room had a mostly dirt floor with one raised section of black wood beams. It smelled of the good damp earth. In the center was a huge

tree trunk turned into a table, and every surface was covered with bou-
quets of fresh or dried flowers. The man of the house spoke deep into
my insides. What was it? Maybe it was the way his eyes never wavered, so
that I was barely aware of what he said but only absorbed in the depth
of him. The sitting room was also dark, the darkness of soot and wood.
A huge square open hearth had no chimney, so the smoke curled up, up
toward the ceiling, but wearying on the journey, sifted downward. Our
eyes stung pleasantly. Then he carried in a huge pile of kindling bound
with straw and fed the fire. His smile came straight from his hara. The
woman twinkled, dimpled, wiping her hands on her apron, smoothing
it across her sparse hips. She made *matcha* [powdered green tea used in
the tea ceremony] for us, a long ritual of wiping and whirling the universe into a bowl. She knelt by the fire, dipping water from the soot-
encrusted cauldron. Slowly, almost caressing her utensils, she poured.
Her features were dim in the soft light of the room, but one side glowed
colors thrown up by the fire. I was drawn into her every movement.

I knew we should be getting back. Tetsugen would probably freak, but
truly time was hardly conceivable. Could there really be a future or a past
or anything besides this room, this woman with her frothy tea?

It was the anniversary of his mother's death. We did ookyo before a
little altar reeking of incense. Chiba-san finally decided we must leave.
Pity. The woman was busy making mochi. I wanted to stay, wanted to
work hard for them.

The scenery coming home was spectacular. It was still rainy. Tetsugen
was still in bed. He wasn't too angry. We were so very late, it was such a complete affront that he was already beaten. "*Dameda*" ["No good"], he said.

They put me on the radio. The interview was in Japanese, and I didn't
understand one of the questions. There was a very long (for radio) pause,
awkward (for the interviewer) silence. Well, that's a difficult question,
she said. I wonder what it was. I had to laugh.

Tetsugen went into another depression. First he was just nasty for a
few days. He scarcely spoke, and then it was always curt and mean. I was
getting fed-up, but was trying to tell myself that it was only my ego. Then
one time—again it was trivial and I was revolted by my pettiness—he

was snapping orders. I always obeyed, but under my breath murmuring, "I hate you; I hate you." That shocked me. Listen, Mors, you've never hated anyone in your life. You know full well he's decent. It's not him you hate but the way he treats you. Whatever it is, this isn't healthy. So I blurted it out to him, gently, apologizing, saying, "I just don't like the way you treat me. I'm human, too, not your servant or a dog." That doesn't sound gentle in retrospect, but at the time it seemed inoffensive, perhaps only compared to what I was feeling. He laughed, in embarrassment, I think. By the time I'd finished banka, he'd gone to bed.

For three days he stayed locked in his room. At first I thought maybe he was dead. I felt shockingly unperturbed. Several times I called to him. He answered that he was okay, but he didn't come out. Was he trying to punish me in some way or just so sick of everything that he wouldn't come out? It was peaceful. When he finally appeared he was surly, his skin a sickly grey, stubbled. For the next 48 hours, he only snarled at me to wash my filthy feet and get him the sensei's money. But something had snapped in me. I didn't care about him anymore, so I was free of him. He could say what he liked to me, hate me if he liked. It didn't matter so the whole thing became rather amusing. I felt a bit of a cruel bitch to be laughing at his misery, but it was a lot better than going under with him.

Then he came up from it.

Go Roshi came for zenkai. Dom came to consult with Go Roshi and asked a million questions, wanting everything to be rationally amenable. It wasn't.

After zenkai, coming home, the light was on in the kitchen. Strange. A bald head. It was Shimo-san. I couldn't believe it. It was late and I was tired, but I managed to throw something together for him to eat. The next day, early, Tetsugen phoned Go Roshi, who said to throw him out. Easier said than done. He had no money, he said. Tetsugen brought him to the station but Shimo was back at Kannonji before him. There's something in him I admire. He's a very free man. Doesn't give a damn about much of anyone or anything. But his being there made allies of Tetsugen and me, us against him as it were. We sat on the roof chopping stray branches and laughed about mad Shimo-san. They say it's Zen sickness, that he used to be normal but overdid his Zen training and went a bit bonky. He was marvelous, though. Here we were busily throwing him out, and he had guts enough to do banka. I do enjoy that kind of guts. I stopped feeding him, and he left peacefully enough, first ascertaining exactly when sesshin would be.

It struck me that cats can do no right or wrong. Is that because they have no ego, or because right and wrong are our mental constructions? Even when Gion kills, it is not wrong.

July 11

Several mornings of samadhi. For the first time I woke up, still actually sitting. Got the news that Galli-san was coming early to prepare for sesshin. He came and we had fun. Tetsugen went to hospital and left Galli a pile of wood and an electric saw. We climbed a tree, listened to the wind blow and the rice grow. For lunch I made an improvised spaghetti with *soba* [buckwheat noodles]. We sat on the veranda of the head of the Soto sect's room, looked across the rice paddy and toasted each other with lunchtime saké and ice cream. Then he went back to work and I pulled weeds. I heard him shrieking, "Maura-san! Maura-san, my finger!" At first I thought he was joking, but the saw was still running and his voice sounded hysterical. His hand was gushing blood. I put on a makeshift bandage and we ran to the road, his hand up in the air. I stopped a car and got him into the hospital. Everyone was staring. We must have looked a sight, both filthy and ragged, his T-shirt spattered with blood and me in my wellies. It was a very nasty cut, right through the bone. They patched him up. He still worked hard, helping me prepare for sesshin.

Yokogawa-san came. She was preoccupied, worried about how her dog would settle in. She slept in the shed with the dog so he wouldn't be upset. I had promised to help Mia-chan, a semi-paralyzed girl; the kitchen was understaffed; I had the official priestly serving duties, and I badly wanted to do dokusan. But so often I'd be nearly at the head of the line when I'd have a job to do. I got in about three times in all. At night I stayed up doing zazen, scarcely sleeping, and any free time seemed to be absorbed.

Tessai-san wanted his clothes mended. Dom or Mia-chan needed a shoulder to cry on.

Dom fizzled out. She had some incredibly strong resistance in her. She had to phone her mother in London and talk for 45 minutes. Several times she ran away, became very vehement. Mia-chan, on the other hand, at first didn't seem to be putting herself into it, but by the end had gotten a lot out of it.

I was tired and still pushing myself. It was great having Galli-san as an ally. In the zendo he'd be doing *jonin* [meal-server for meals eaten formally in the meditation hall], walking slowly with dignity (and a plastered fist) round the hall, holding the *kyosoku* [keisaku-stick used to compassionately strike sitters who might be sleeping or losing concentration], me carrying the buppan. We'd catch one another's eyes and suppress smiles. At those times it felt as if we were everyone's parents, taking care of them, helping them on this great thing. He said, "I can't be serious with you around." It was mutual. He went to dokusan, and Go Roshi said he should marry someone doing training, like Yokogawa-san. Galli-san said no, that he wanted to marry me. He told me, warning me that Go Roshi might mention it.

I was waiting in the dokusan line, frustrated because Tekkan-san wouldn't let Mia-chan cut in and she could never make it to dokusan. Galli-san was at the front of the line. Tetsugen-san wasn't there, so Galli told me to take his own place. I asked him to give it to Mia-chan. Chiba-san struggled up the stair slowly, like some dogged animal, with her on his back. Galli-san was helping. They bowed. That bow was so beautiful that tears involuntarily streamed down my face for 10 minutes. I listened to the mu's, felt their pain and their hope, a pain and hope of my own, a nostalgia and joy. Again I wept.

In this overly sensitized state, I went to dokusan. Go Roshi told me I was to marry Tetsugen-san on September 18th and stay in this temple. I said I didn't want to. He was pushing me, pushing hard. It was killing me to refuse him. I loved him so very, very much, and he was being so insistent, thinking of everything to induce me. I begged him not to ask, no, not that. Finally I broke down and told him something of Tetsugen's two characters and of my dreams for Ireland. He said he'd think it over. I went out in tears, became quite hysterical. Tachibana Sensei was upset and so was Galli-san. They took me outside. I knew I was being ridiculous.

All along I realized my reaction was all out of proportion to the situation. We were walking back towards the zendo when my legs gave way. I fainted. Galli-san laid me down in the entrance to Busshari-to and shouted to Takuda-san. I only wanted a cup of tea. They brought me inside. Everyone was fussing. I couldn't understand—just a cup of tea. I tried to calm them, tried to stand up, but collapsed twice. They were worried, massaging my feet, applying carbon and discussing cures.

Something left me, some huge oppressive weight that I'd never even known was there and only recognized in its lifting. I felt so light. I was laughing and crying. Euphoria. They were alarmed. I assured them I'd never felt so wonderful in all my life. (Tetsugen-san had nothing to do with it any more; he was merely the trigger.) My breathing was a kind of panting as if mounting to some emotional climax. Galli told me to breathe deeply, to do zazen. I tried. My breathing stopped. My mind never felt so clear or lucid. The voices were very far away. I was in a crystal paradise. Galli was screaming at me to breathe. From somewhere I heard my voice softly answering, "Hai." In the distance Tetsugen was calling the hospital. What an effort. But I'd have to show them I was okay. I snapped out of it, sat up, normal as hell. "You see, I kept telling you I was okay." They were relieved, but I only wanted to do zazen. I stayed up doing zazen, but I was too tired for it to be much good.

Next day, Go Roshi said, "Until last night you were human trying to become God; now you're God. I'm Buddha." He shook my hand. "We must help the others."

He said it would be all right for me to go back to Ireland after three years.

I was looking forward to living with Yokogawa-san. She has a very quiet, strong, and beautiful nature. When she smiles, it's like the August sun in February, and even my toes have to smile back. At the end of sesshin, during the big party, I was pouring her some beer. She began to cry, threw her arms around me and said she was crying from happiness. I was confused. She didn't seem happy—maybe it was all the build-up and not getting kensho. I was very moved, though, to see her, a Japanese woman, openly displaying such a depth of emotion (though everyone else seemed to find it ridiculous). The next day she left to bring her dog home and never came back. Tetsurin-san (with whom she was apparently having an affair) phoned several times and said it was decided at shosan that I'd return to Tokyo and she'd stay at Kannonji.

For the first time, I really believed I'd return there, and I put my luggage in order, started to bid my good-byes. Tetsugen was freaking, asked me to refuse. I said that if Go Roshi told me to go to Toshoji, I'd go there; if he said Kannonji I'd stay there. He said he needed me. I was his Kannonsama. He mourned the garden that would fall into ruin, his health that would collapse. I was aloof to his protest and felt that life with just the two of us there was sucking at me like the whirling vortex of a drain dragging me down, to swallow and drown me. To have had three of us there, almost any three, to break the couple structure, would have been a relief.

But of course all this was only imaginings of my own construction. Yokogawa-san didn't come back and Tetsurin-san ran away from Toshoji, so I mentally sketch in a romantic elopement and feel happy for them—but stranded myself with a rising tide.

Sasaki-san was also very put out when we thought I might be transferred. It was understandable, what with all the bitching and back-biting that goes on, that it would be natural for her to want an ally here. As a result, when the politicking for a successor at Kannonji arose, Sasaki-san agreed to accept Tetsugen under the condition that for as long as I remain in Japan I'd be kept at Kannonji! And Go Roshi gave his consent.

Strange...Yokogawa-san didn't even stay one day beyond sesshin yet her presence brought me closer to leaving Kannonji and left me further from leaving than ever before. I had a sinking feeling, a trapped feeling. Tetsugen couldn't suppress a slightly smug smile. I refused to admit I was a bit disappointed, to acknowledge that in his pathetic way he'd won. But then, the stirring thing—whether the thought of losing me, the security of being given Kannonji, or whether something happened in sesshin, I have no idea, but he was a changed man. Still occasionally bossing me, but also actually treating me with respect. We became two equals cooperating in a partnership. His whole disposition is sunnier. I keep waiting for it to pass, for the depression to set in, but it doesn't seem imminent.

After sesshin came the massive job of cleaning up, of hauling out all the futons and covers, pillows to be aired (twice), washing all the sheets, *oryoki* wrappers [eating bowl wrapping cloths], futon covers in the tiny, not-automatic washing machine. It took days and before it was really finished I had to start cleaning in preparation for Go Roshi's return and *obon* [Summer Buddhist festival for summoning forth restless spirits, and also the remembrance of deceased ancestors or loved ones, in order to nourish and appease them].

Shimo-san arrived again. I have to laugh and admire his bull-dog tenacity and thick skin. Roshi permitted him to stay for obon and help us as *rusuban* [caretaker] with Abe-san. In Toyko everything had gone mad with everyone either being asked to leave or running away. No more priests.

I was busy. Some mornings we left as early as 5 or 6. I'd have to get up the buppan, fix the day's food for Abe-san and Shimo-san, offer ookyo, come back, start cooking, light the bath fire, do washing and mending, soji, etc., etc. I did the soji in Go Roshi's room as I waited in dokusan line. It was hectic but okay.

Roshi asked me how many hours I slept. He said that since the war there was no one my equal. I was Irish, he Japanese, but since the war I'm the only one who is his equal. Of course, I'm not. Not at all. But in a sense it gave me something to live up to. Since obon, my practice has improved. We eat earlier, so I have more time for zazen, each day 4 to 5 hours, once a week all night. (Well, last night I did doze a couple of hours.) I ram a desk up in front of me so I really do sleep sitting up and have stopped eating in the afternoon. I'm sleeping about 5 to 5 ½ hours a night. Some days I feel as if I'm near some kind of awakening, because my consciousness is different, spontaneously, truly losing itself in menial tasks. Other days, more cynical days, like today, I think I'm closer to a "sleepening." That's only because I'm tired and too half awake for my mind to make the effort to run around; it's all I can do to guide my hand peeling the potatoes.

Of late I feel ridiculously happy. No reason. Just bursting with joy. I remember when I was young, deciding to commit suicide at 26. Once one hit 30 one was over the hill, so 26 was far enough to live. I reckoned that if I hadn't got done by then whatever there was to be done, I never would, so I might as well end it. Now I'm 26, and I feel as if I've lived my life. Strange sensation. Almost as if I'm close to death. Any desires, ambitions, hopes I may have had have either been fulfilled or spontaneously dissipated. I'm totally content. Of course I want to get deeper, see clearer, but even if I could only have this paltry, shallow awakening, I'd be quite satisfied. Facing into a long, cold winter is not only fine, but I know I'll enjoy it. Everything seems wonderful. Even undesirable, painful conditions have a poignant beauty and exaltation. So in a sense I feel I have died; for myself there is nothing else to strive after, nothing more to make my life worthwhile or to justify it. At 26, a living corpse and such a life!

I'd be embarrassed to tell anyone, it sounds so wishy-washy, but now I have maybe 50 or 60 years (who knows?) of time, of a life, open, blank, ready to offer. I want to live it for other people. What else is there to do with it? Not that I expect to change the world or even a blade of grass, but it's as if to give myself is all I can do, as the flowers have no choice but to blossom. At the moment the best I can see to do is to give to people this freedom, this bliss, and how better than through zazen? So I must go deeper and deeper and work hard, no longer for me but for everyone I can help. And still I can't save anyone. They must work themselves, and not every one will. Thus I should also work politically, work to make people's surroundings that much more tolerable, work for a society that fosters more spiritual, more human, values. A society for people, not profits. What better way to instill the Bodhisattvic spirit in people? But they should work for each other, not for personal gain, and they shouldn't have to worry about economic muck.

Who knows but God-as-a-person may be tentative. We as people don't exist, nothing exists, yet for ease in conversation and life in general we use names and ascribe a tentative existence to ourselves and things around us. In such a way, perhaps, a personal God could be said to exist, but only in this labeling, not fundamental, degree, but existentially.

In a sense, though not his sense, Descartes was right—I think, therefore I am. It is the reflexive thinking that creates the isolated subject.

Part VIII

Mum's Visit

Kannonji, Iwateken, July 25, 1981
Dear Mum,
Great to hear from you and to know that you are still coming. Things
have become a little complicated at this end, but being adaptable as you
are, things should work themselves out…

Poor Go Roshi is really near the brink of death. He has lost a tremen-
dous amount of weight from stomach cancer. His doctor says he's already
a unique case in the medical history of Japan, to have lived this long. It's
pure will power, but at the last sesshin he collapsed and said it might well
be the last one he could give. But he doesn't stop pushing himself, keeping up a teaching and ceremonial schedule that would defy two young,
healthy men to keep up between them. He told me that he's only extend-
ing his life to wrap up unfinished business. That's why I feel really infu-
riated at the ingratitude of the Toshoji priests who ran away. However,
sorry, I got into a diversion. What I meant to explain is that there's no
one to send up here. (He may get new monks but they would be very raw
recruits.) So I won't be very free for touring. However, suppose I came
down to Tokyo to meet you and we spend a couple of days doing Tokyo?
(We could stay in Toshoji if you can stand the schedule.) Then we could
come to Iwate. There are many day trips and local excursions we could
make from here…I'm wondering if you'll still be here October 1st to 5th.

MAURA AND MUM
ON THE TEMPLE PORCH.

I had signed up for sesshin then (thinking your visit would be in September). Aside from the fact that with no priests I'll be needed, I also really want to do this one. I was so busy in the kitchen at the last one that I scarcely got to dokusan and, as I said, this may well be the last one. If you were still here at that time you could do it, too. It would be a unique "inside glimpse" for you. About a third to a half are first-timers and it would also probably be very good for you…I won't be coming back with you. I'd like to do one more *takuhatsu* (begging) before I go back, though if Go Roshi doesn't last that long, I might just return before then. At the moment we're right at the edge of a typhoon. [Here Maura made suggestions for gifts to bring each person she's mentioned]…Also, it would be a good idea to have a small stash of gifts for the people who will inevitably overwhelm you with kindness. How's your Japanese? During sesshin the TV people came out and did a stint, including me doing dokusan and a small interview. Not only did I have to make a fool of myself with my wretched Japanese, but they also had me translating for Galli-san. Wisely they added sub-titles for his bit.

See you soon…M.

Kannonji, Iwateken
September 10, 1981
Dear Mum,

...Remember my casually mentioning that we were at the edge of a typhoon? Well, it hit. The worst one in 33 years (they seldom come this far north). I was enjoying the warm winds and feeling of excitement. We had to do a special sutra-chanting for about 60 people in Morioka, so we went into town (I did *Ino* [Sometimes the priest in charge of the monks, and of all ceremonies. Also used for the leader of service, who calls out the names of chants.] for the first time before such numbers.) On the way back, we were quite amused by the flying chimneys, downed sign-posts, and overturned bus shelters. It wasn't quite so amusing when we got back to Kannonji and in the pouring rain with pathetic hand saws had to saw our path in. Loads and loads of trees are down, my poor lit-tle garden quite leveled, branches and dirt everywhere and all inside the building, too. What a sight! Me, enjoying the winds so much, had left my window wide open. It was so full of tree bits and leaves that you'd have trouble recognizing it as a room at all except for the soggy remnants of human habitation. We'll be ages cleaning up after it. Anyway, it's over and it was exciting...

Hurry over, etc, M.

Kannonji, Iwateken
October 14, 1981
Dear Nana,

...Mum left the day before yesterday and now I'm back in Kannonji...She will fill you in on all the details of what we did. I freeloaded on all her entertainment and did more feasting and sightseeing in that time than I've probably done all told. Poor Mum started with a dose of culture shock but bounded back admirably so that even the Japanese were com-menting on her adaptability...Mum's last week was a wild whirl as we had a retreat in Tokyo. The kitchen was understaffed, but Mum jumped right in. She was a born turnip beveller, mushroom fanner, and even with-out a knowledge of Japanese she would nip off on the bike (terrorizing the neighborhood) and pick me up the last minute bits as the meal approached count-down. I'm sure she'll have plenty of tales with which to regale you.

Love, Maura

Kannonji, Iwateken
October 1981
Dear Mama-san Rootu,
When I got back the place was in a right mess. The "gnome" [Tetsugen] hadn't done any housework and had left up the same offerings, so even the tea was turning moldy. A lot of the leaves are turning and they're taking in the rice. Wish you could see it. The mornings, however, have been dipping down below freezing. I got my salvia and a few other things up and drying, the begonias inside, widened all the flower beds at the front of the house, put down a ton of bulbs, and now I'm trying to clean up the typhoon damage, so I'm out chopping wood every day. I got the log border made at the back. (Me and the wheelbarrow—very long logs. It was hilarious.) But it looks great, as if it always belonged there. We're going to try a sand garden in the square between zendo and hondo. So I'll make my mistakes here and do a perfect job at home. Tachibana Sensei (who sends his best) and I have started translating Go Roshi's book, so I seldom get to bed before 10:30 and he, poor man, a good 45 minutes later. It's very slow going but my Japanese and his English are improving. I've started teaching English at the Yoshida's (remember the concert people?). It's great getting out once a week and she's been teaching me a lot about traditional temple cookery. I never knew her that well before but I find stimulating, in fact, inspiring, company—extremely enjoyable and civilized evenings…

Yomiuri Shinbun, one of the three major national newspapers, did a half page special interview with me. Actually I said almost nothing. The gnome prattled away, full of exaggerated praise. Now the TV people are pushing me to do an interview on a morning talk show, but I really don't want to. I'm sick of all this publicity nonsense—though there are some advantages. When I came back from Tokyo, I got a terrible craving for *ramen* [Chinese noodles] and searched all over the station for a ramen shop. Anyway, on the bus home, a neighborhood fellow who'd read about me in the local magazine came over to me. He owned a ramen shop and insisted on bringing me for a meal and then driving me home. It really quite took me aback.

I've started my novel, though I really don't know if I should. Remember at first I was stuck for themes? Now I find there are loads of things I really want to say and the characters are taking on a life of their own. It's really strange. One feels almost like a medium as some of them, based originally on people I know, are just spontaneously insisting on their own personalities. Even the heroine, who was originally based on me, now, although she has many of my experiences, has quite different reactions to them. It astounds me for I wonder where they are coming from. Funny feeling. So all around the temple I have odd pages where I jot down notes as they occur to me. I've also started to write the thing itself, and this is why I say I don't know if I should. But that there are things that I care about saying, and communicating properly, I find it disturbing that my English has turned so strange. As I read what I write, it has an awkwardness that is coming from having Japanese sentence patterns foremost in my mind. This seems inevitable as long as I'm here.

...As for the poor old suitor [a priest owning a temple in Sendai], when I came back here from sesshin, I decided I'd had quite enough of this mooning business. So I wrote him an express letter making it quite clear that I wouldn't marry him. I didn't go so far as to point out the irreconcilable differences—like that I could never keep up with his laundry. But I was to-the-point, and the poor thing got such a shock that mysteriously the muscles of his Achilles tendon or something seized up, and he's been hospitalized for a month. He blames it entirely on his "great disappointment," but I'm relieved that he'll have a month to get over his "great disappointment" before I have to face him again. Anyway, m'dear, I've prattled on long enough, and I want to clean the hen house before the rain that's gathering...P.S. It seems you, too, may be in Go Roshi's next book. In one of his lectures he was criticizing

the Japanese for only being religious for ceremonies and at their con-
venience, and he praised you for being determined to go to mass even
when away from home, without the language, and at the risk of getting lost...

Love, M.

(undated, late autumn 1981)
Dear Sean,
...I'm delighted that you're staying back in Ireland for a while because
that's where I feel drawn myself at the moment.

...How's Ireland treating you? I really enjoyed it last year. Of course a
lot was revolving around Kate's wedding but it made me feel I could really
go back to something of which I was not at all sure before. It was strange
that everyone had grown up. Do you know what I mean? People were
doing adult things like having families and working in straight jobs that
they hated but...If anything, instead of my future narrowing into a set
path, Sean, I've now regressed to the stage of not having a clue what I'll
do. There seem to be so many exciting possibilities. Everything seems
open, almost dazzling.

Speaking of new things, Sean, don't tell anyone—I've only told the Ma
and now you, and I might never actually get it together but I've started
writing a novel. I realize just what a rotten writer I am but I'm enjoying
it. (Am still only on the first chapter—life's been busy.)

Mum has gone back recently. She was here for a month—happy, hectic, and heavy. We had a lot of craic [fun] together, but the whole religion
thing came up very forcibly and painfully...I felt bad that through no conscious intention of my own I was causing her all this suffering. The other
side of the coin was that we did enjoy the mutual company more than we
had in years. The timing was unfortunate in that for her last week we had
a retreat on in the Tokyo dojo. I was doing all the cooking (my first time)
and she jumped right in beside me in the mornings and trotted herself
around Tokyo in the afternoons. But it was one of those 20 hours a day
without a break routines at a time when she was feeling very out of things.

She was horrified to see instead of her daughter, someone in black robes bowing to idols and shouting mumbo-jumbo to the beating of drums…It was very hard for her…

…The summer too was busy. The various factions here consulted and decided I was best suited to become successor to this temple. They put on a lot of pressure for me to marry this kidney-machine monk and live here and start a dynasty. Was I not into that! In fact I fainted, blanked out three times at the very prospect. All of this triggered some psychological mechanisms of which I have neither understanding nor control, but there seemed to be an actually physical weight lifted off me, followed by an ecstatic euphoria that I wouldn't mind repeating— but without the threat of marrying Tetsugen-san. Anyway, that resolved itself.

It's getting colder every day, though you can still put your feet on the ground without them hurting and the fingers don't freeze on to the doorknobs yet. (Oh, the little blessings to be grateful for!) In all the politicking during the summer, trying to tie me eternally to this temple, I felt a bit of a rotter. Every week someone else was running away 'til of all the trainees I was the longest trained there. Roshi is meant to be at death's door, though he neither looks nor acts it, so I felt bad letting him down and refusing the temple. I finished by compromising and agreeing to stay until my three years are up—that's December of next year.

So unless he lies down and doesn't get up (which is highly likely), I'll be here another bit yet. Sure & I know it's good for me and I really do love it here, but I wouldn't mind a good dose of the real world myself…

Kannonji, Iwateken
November 1981
Dear Mum,
Things certainly sound hectic at your end and I imagine will stay busy right through Christmas. My book is slow, only about 4,000 words to date, but really the hardest part is beginning. I still can't decide on whether to use the first or third person. I feel whichever one I choose will

make it a different book. So far, I keep switching—1st person seems more vivid, but I actually enjoy writing more in the 3rd person. Strange…I feel the lack of literature in my own background. While I always read, I preferred non-fiction as being somehow closer to "truth," "reality," etc. Of late I feel tremendously excited. I always thought that writing analytical books about Zen seemed so un-Zen. It set up structures, distinctions, and invited argument and speculation. The novel, on the other hand, requires the sympathetic understanding of the reader. If it's successful, he'll leave his own ego and "become" the character suggested, at least for the length of reading. This is much closer to a Zen understanding (intuition, even?). Really, Mum, I've seriously been considering studying English. That must seem funny to you.

T.C.D. [Trinity College, Dublin] sent me the standard boring forms about post-grad. At least in Sociology and Oriental Religions there's a deadline for applications. These are also formal courses, a fact which has its advantages and disadvantages. I really can't decide anything without talking to the professors involved and being clearer myself about which is the discipline through which I can best express my nondisciplinary ideas…We got a nasty cold snap, snow and the lot. Even the old-timers were surprised, and some of them were caught without the rice in. I'm frantically chopping wood. Tetsugen-san is very thoughtful about standing looking over my shoulder and pointing out what I'm doing wrong. Still, his heart's in the right place, and he shocked the life out of me yesterday by helping me sweep…

Love, M.

Kannonji, Iwateken
Dec. 5, 1981
Dear Mum,
…Try to do a bit of zazen every day, even if its just ten minutes. You really sound great. When I first came to Toshoji and the researchers tested me (remember?) they were surprised I'd only been at it for three months and thought I had surely meant to say three years. They concluded that I had a "natural" talent for it. I'd say you do, too…You asked about Go Roshi's

health. Not good. At the end of October they found 5 new lumps. They don't know whether they're benign or malignant but want to open him up immediately. He says he's too busy. (He just had a sesshin in Kyushu; now it's one in Toshoji and New Year's is the busiest time for a temple.) So he won't go in until January…This translation stuff is very slow. My own book is also slow, but I have an appointed time each day and whether the muse flows or not, I write…I've found a classical station on Okusan's radio. This morning I was making pickles, watching the snow fall and listening to (believe it or not) the Boston Pops—heaven in my own dingy kitchen…

Love, M.

Kannonji, Iwateken
Dec. 1981
Dear Mum,

…Thanks for the books. I'm half-way through *Zen and the Art of Motorcycle Maintenance*. Rather than making me all Zen-ized, I'd love to get a motorcycle—or at least have access to one to repair it. The other books look as if they'll tide me across many a pub-less evening.

I really missed you and Paul during sesshin. Even that strange old lady last October was another pair of hands. This time it was just me and Kondo-san, with larger numbers. Still it went off okay. One or two fiascos, like when I was using the carbon lamp to treat Go Roshi before dinner, but I didn't have the time to stay there, so he asked me to arrange newspapers to avoid a draught. Since it was chilly, I put on loads of them. Then the whole load went up in flames. Got the fire out, cleaned up the mess, but with only 5 minutes 'til dinner, I still had no soup made or meals on plates. What an exercise in concentration in the midst of chaos! But we made it in time. Afterwards I just lay down on the floor with a sack of rice as a pillow and fell asleep. Kondo-san (remember? always fixing you sandwiches) was marvelous, like an extension of my own arm, often anticipating what I needed done and totally responsible. A blessing.

The Deguchis came up from Nara for the occasion and send their best. Tetsumon-san and the little lady who gave you the fan send greetings, too.

Thanks to Tetsumon-san, who always sent me up to the top of the dokusan line, I got my share. Dokusan was also very stimulating, perhaps the best yet. I've gone on to a more difficult book of koans (and skipped one). Go Roshi is being quite severe about the koans but explains "A Roshi is like your mother, who comes half way round the world to make sure her grown-up daughter is all right; so no matter how good a student is, a Roshi will worry and push and push." (Although he always tells me in dokusan that I'm useless, apparently in one of his lectures he said that I'm the only successor to the Zen heart in Japan today!) He exaggerates, but it's nice…

A little old lady just came for a ceremony. Then another one came bringing me pickles. She's been out of sorts lately, and the bicycle trip with the pickles seems to have been too much for her. I told her to lie down for a while, and she's gone sound asleep.

When changing for the ceremony just now, I put on the leg warmers you sent. They're brilliant, make a world of difference. (My pickles lady just popped her head up and down. Life in Kannonji is as thrilling as ever.)

The greatest blessing you sent will be that can opener. During the sesshin I cursed a string of curses such as would put all Japanese tin openers out of action eternally. Right at a very busy time I had eventually to bash my tin open…

I'd love to be with you at Christmas. In the supermarket in Tokyo they were playing "Jingle Bells," but there was no holly or tinsel or turkey or Christmas spirit. I know that dear Tachibana Sensei will play Santa Claus, but it's not the same. I suppose it won't do any good my brooding over it; still, I love Christmas. New Year will never take its place. Have fun and a good big feast and a peaceful family Christmas.

Love, M.

Kannonji, Iwateken
December 30, 1981

…We're in the middle of a funeral. The procedures last for days. All morning yesterday was bedside sutras, then at night 'til very late the mourners gathered in his home and more sutra. Today is the cremation—more sutra and tomorrow the funeral proper. The funeral and a big meal (I only found out last night!) are to be held here, so I'm up to my eyes in cleaning, sutras, New Year preparations, a mountain (no exaggeration) of beans that must be shelled, and I have to teach tonight. Never a dull moment…Hope you all had a brilliant Christmas.

Love, M.

(undated; Dec. 1981/Jan. 1982)
Dear Sean,
Happy Christmas, New Year's, and all the rest…You really sound in great form…As for my own bit of writing, it's slow. The last 10 days I've hardly had a chance to touch it (some days working from 4 in the morning until 12 at night—so much for the peaceful monastery myth; have nearly forgotten what it is to have time to myself). But it's craic. I've written about 30 pages and about as many pages (not quite) of notes. It's all formed, in a general way, in my head, so it's just a question, either here or later, of getting a chance to get it down…It's such a psychological effort to get over the idea that to write one must be a "writer," so I'm not insisting on great literature or the final statement on anything. I'm thinking of it as my first book and not requiring a whole lot more of myself. Still it'll need a lot of re-writing (says she, before even writing it—).

Right now I'm suffering from a smoky fire and am freezing but not much else to complain about. Tomorrow we start begging. *A bit later:* Been washing leaves for salt pickles. The log's burnt down on the fire, so it's not smoking and I'm perfectly happy…I was amazed, even not being with anyone at all, I didn't feel at all lonely or spooked as I had last year. So I just glided around at my own pace and my own time, getting things done, but when I felt like it. Not having to cook for him [Tetsugen-san], serve him, make his bath for him, or clean after him—it's certainly a new me, being a man's servant, but that's what I am, Sean. I'm beginning to realize how the majority of women in the world really live. Liberty, equality—I never knew just how much of a middle-class Western luxury it was. Here men actually order their (possessive case) women (including me)—get that, do that, carry that, "baggage, baggage" (and I quote). The irony is that even the men will admit they're weaklings compared to the women. Yet this too had seemed strangely liberating. (At the moment it's something of the abstract freedom of Hegel's slave.)

Really, Sean, the thing is, I can do it now...I'd never choose to bind myself into such a relationship, but I feel free in that I can actually do it. (Are you following me?) It's crap; it's unjust, but I'm living it and totally happy. Don't get me wrong—it's no perverse, masochistic, always-secretly-desired-the-whip joy—but in spite of that I'm quite aware that the universal implications of such a view would be reactionary and I would hesitate to recommend it, but it sure makes life easier...

While he was out of hospital I went down to Tokyo to cook for sesshin...Had some excellent sessions with the master. It's funny, Sean, I'll work on a koan, be sure I've wrung out every last drop of meaning, then present it to him and be stunned at just how low and shallow my understanding is. He really is an inspiration. Anyway, I dashed back on the night train. ("Move over, dearie, and let the little nun sit down.") Klunk. I slept 8 hours until my station. Came back; the monk went into hospital again, mostly for rest. I got a bit of writing done and studying Japanese.

Practically as soon as he came out we had "the funeral," our first one here. It was fascinating. Funerals involve loads of sutra. We chanted from the stage where he was still in his bed with a hanky on his face and the body warm, through a late-night service, a cremation preparation service, then the cremation and post-cremation service, then a funeral service, the next day a pre-burial service, and finally a burial service. The idea is not to get divine intercession but rather to try to stimulate whatever consciousness (not soul) that lingers, into enlightenment.

Then we belt back here to get ready for New Year celebrations. Decorate the place with tangerines, pine branches, and lumps of glutinous rice. All the neighboring people pour in for a bit of a chat, light a stick of incense, and enjoy a cup of saké. At midnight we bang the bell 108 times (to try to bring all drunken Irishmen to enlightenment) and more sutra. I'm losing my voice. (I'm also losing my paper. The cat keeps shifting to where I'm trying to write.) Anyway, Sean, before tomorrow I have to get ready a load of things—the begging gear and get these pickles finished…

Take care, Love, M.

Kannonji, Iwateken
December 1981
Dear Nana,

…Mum may have told you that I'm teaching English to a temple family that she met. While, to be honest, I wasn't crazy about the idea at first, it has worked out wonderfully. The girls, three of them, are extremely intelligent and cooperative, a pleasure to teach (though the differences in levels is a challenge). It's not only an enjoyable evening with an exquisite dinner and a taxi home, but they have adopted us. They have an extremely wealthy temple and enjoy being bountiful; we're by far the poorest in the area. Since I started teaching, though, we haven't had to buy food. She loads me down with goodies that she searches out as not being sprayed, shot, or artificially anythinged (rare in Japan). She's really almost embarrassing. She heard I had a cold so came all the way out on a snowy day, laden with presents, and she gave up her afternoon to wrap me in steaming ginger plasters. She knows all about old oriental medicine and has been teaching me that, along with cooking. (The ginger plasters really did seem to help.) Now she's trying to arrange that I study flower arranging with her teacher. He's an elderly master trained in Kyoto. She speaks very highly of him, and if her own arrangements are anything to go by, he really is a good teacher. It would be fun to learn…I think of you often with very much love.

M.

Part IX

Completion

Takuhatsu, February 1982

Rescued this notebook from a fire. Tessai-san said I should keep a diary. I felt there wasn't time to write feelings and analyze reactions. He said feelings were *moso* [something that can distract]. I said they were not and he agreed, but said a busy person should just write events. Events will recall feelings. This seemed a fitting notebook to use.

The day I found it was in January. I got up at 3:00, shoveled snow, did zazen, woke the others, made breakfast, cleaned up, went out to beg. We had lunch at Okawa-san's (tempura...she is kind, remembered that I love it). I came home, gave Ojichan ["uncle"] lunch, cleaned temple, lit fire for bath, made dinner, cleaned up, sorted *momi* [chaff] from rice, talked with Tessai-san (admire him profoundly), did zazen and went to bed. Takuhatsu was a busy time.

Kannonji, Iwateken
February 1982
Dear Mum, Scott, and Beth,
Phew! Finally I have a moment to slow down, catch my breath, and write home. I'd been going at the same pace as sesshin for a whole month. Tessai-san came up from Nagano to beg and then stayed 'til the 31st. We walked [begged] every day, and then I finished it after he left. Tetsugen-san

walked on the days he wasn't being drained [dialysis], and I hustled people who helped when they could. Two gaijin came from Toshoji and walked four days. Tachibana Sensei, after much initial reluctance ("but Maura-san, I'm over 50"), led us during the winter school vacation and every day he was free from school. He looked so comical squeezed into my robes, his spectacles and grin under the huge straw hat and a polo neck sticking out from under the layers of kimonos. Whenever we needed a smile we'd only have to shout "Sensei! Student, student," and he'd duck, squirming, pulling the hat down over his face. "No, no, where?"

Mum, you remember Megumi-san, my temple English student? After we'd been walking a few days, I was bemoaning our lack of numbers. She looked up instantly and said, "Well, maybe I'll help." She's a marvel. The next day she was out on the streets looking more of a veteran than any of us, never seemed affected by the cold or the wind, just smiling and chanting. At the end I asked her if she'd do it again next year. This time there was no hesitation. She positively roared "of course." We're the only women who have ever walked in this area, and I suspect she's the youngest to have walked.

Tetsugen's case was close to miraculous. The first couple of days he was wrecked, but after that the walking did him good. Tessai-san also had a positive influence on him. He was shocked that I was literally doing everything while Tetsugen hovered over a stove crying "invalid." Tessai-san wouldn't put up with any self-coddling, and night after night he lectured him. Tetsugen was inspired on the days he was due for dialysis. He'd walk an hour to the hospital, even in storms before paths had been beaten in the snow. I was dumbfounded.

Last year the challenge had gone out of takuhatsu for me, so this year I decided to push myself further. We're allowed to wear socks with the straw sandals so we usually wear several pairs plus plastic bags to keep out the wet. In the old days, though, the monks used just to go barefoot with the sandals through the snow. I wasn't sure if I could. When the snow melts and refreezes it's just like walking barefoot on crushed ice, but, as Go Roshi says, if you just take one step at a time you can do anything. And it's true. It was fine. The others, except Tessai-san, tried to

discourage me; they said it would be too much. He only said if he wasn't
so old he'd like to try it too. Then one night we were sitting up late by
the woodstove, drinking tea, with him telling me stories about Go Roshi
when he was young. It was then a week before the end of takuhatsu and
Tessai-san said, "You see, your limits are mostly in your mind." Then he
gulped, as if only realizing for the first time what his words really meant.
Then he said, "I've only a week to go, but I'll do it barefoot," and he did.

So we all learned something and maybe got a little stronger. It was also
a lot of fun, maybe the most enjoyable takuhatsu yet; all the walkers got
on very well, and it was just plain good fun. Many people gave us meals;
Megumi-san's parents did so four times. It was a help, especially for me.
I'd be up most days at 3. Then if there was snow-shoveling to do, I'd get
it done before zazen time, then sit at zazen, make breakfast, put the offerings in front of the statues, go out and walk, start lunch as soon as I'd
walk in the door, get it all cleaned up and start cleaning the temple, bring
in the wood (give the chickens their hot water bottle), light the fire for
the bath, take down the offerings, make dinner, clean up, wash the rice,
prepare the next day's vegetables, do laundry, shell beans, take a luke-
warm bath, and conk out for a few hours.

The climax was yesterday when all the temple supporters and Go Roshi
came for a ceremony and dinner, but the day before was zenkai, so trying to keep the whole place in order and the new snow all shoveled out
was near miraculous. But it's over, and today I'm just taking it easy. A
Swiss friend is going back soon and is having a big "do" at the Grand
Hotel—an 8000-yen-a-head affair. It seemed a bit extravagant to me, but
Jim insisted on paying for me, so I'll go mad tonight.

Scott, it's a pity you couldn't have been here to walk too. As it was, this
year I got even more publicity than before (the radio once, papers twice,
and local and national TV four times) but they would have loved Scott.
The bit I enjoyed the most but hadn't looked forward to at all was a TV
current-affairs interview spot. It was in the studio and a bit awesome
with all the cameras and mikes and things, but we really had a great
laugh—even in Japanese. Everywhere I go now, strangers point at me and
run out to shake hands. It's weird.

One of the gaijin who came up for takuhatsu, a Scotswoman, Allison, had reached one of those "life turning points," tried everything but was not satisfied, etc., etc. After a couple of late-night heart-to-hearters, she decided she wanted to try being a monk, at least for a couple of years. When she went back to Toshoji, she had her initial ceremony. She's supposed to come up and help me here next summer. I presumed I'd just continue here "as is," but I'll probably go back to Tokyo after Tetsugen-san's ceremony proclaiming him the head of Kannonji temple, probably in September. Allison phoned from Tokyo frantic that Go Roshi wanted her to come up immediately, and she wasn't sure if she wanted to be in such an isolated position. I still don't know her decision. However, apparently the monk who was translating for her didn't want to disappoint Go Roshi so he made it sound as if she was more willing to come than she is. Anyway, Go Roshi came up here, full of plans for my remaining time. He wants me to do my remaining two ceremonies. (To do this I'd have to spend a period of time in Toshoji, so Allison's coming here would free me.) Then I'd be all official, registered at the head temple and qualified to head a temple or dojo, though not yet to teach.

Up to now we have our busy times here, then the calms while I recuperate. But Go Roshi wants me to help cover both temples and go back and forth between Toshoji and here as well as doing various ceremonies with him around the country. At the moment the schedule is March and early April in Toshoji, then back up to Kannonji, down to Kyushu in May, then maybe Nagano. Back to Tokyo for my ceremony in June, in July sesshin at Kannonji, then July obon [Buddhist All Saints Day Festival] in Toshoji, August obon at Kannonji, etc. He says he wants to bring me around Japan as an example to others, but I'm seriously wondering if I can keep up the pace of this 72-year-old cancer patient. Anyway, I'm game to try.

Up 'til now the only thing I've regretted about Kannonji was only being able to do dokusan once a month, but Go Roshi says that while we're together he'll do extra ones at noon and in the evening. It's very kind of him; it would be as often as sesshin. I'd certainly finish Hegikan Roku [book of koans called The Blue Cliff Record] and maybe the next book.

He says when I leave he wants it to be with a certificate to teach, but that usually takes 10 years. It's unprecedented to be given one after 3 years (as it is for him to do all those private dokusans). I feel very touched but very unworthy. He only sees me at my busy times, when I've no choice but to do my best. Anyway, it's very exciting but completely depends on Allison.

Mum, he seems to be taking his discussion with you seriously. He hasn't even jokingly suggested my staying on next year (even when one of the papers mistakenly printed that I'd stay 2 more years). I was wondering with all that activity how I'd work on my books. My novel is okay, as I've pretty much figured it out and it's just a matter of getting it down, which I could do when I get back, but the translation needs to be done here. We hadn't mentioned it to Go Roshi yet, so he stunned me when yesterday he announced to the supporters that all the contributions they'd made were going into an account he'll open in order to publish his books in English if I'd be good enough to translate them. So I've a busy few months ahead. Scott, I hope you won't be bored if you come over, because I won't be able to devote myself to you as totally as I'd like. Anyway, all of you take good care.

Very very much love, M.

Wednesday, February 24
Overslept. Meditations not very good lately, but feel incredibly indefatigably happy. Still, should try to get more proficient in samadhi. Miko-san came and taught me about seika flower arranging. As always many presents. Dominique phoned; I will meet her tomorrow.

February 25
Morning meditation was good at the beginning and end. Even when not concentrating, I felt suffused by an incredible joy. It amazes me that such a physical thing—no supernatural gods interfering—as just sitting, maybe breathing a bit differently, can fill one with such elation. Did a

million things at once and left early to meet Dominique. Talked in tiny, cozy, intimate cake shop. She worries so about nothing but has fantastic heart. Got her to agree to try zazen daily for 6 months. She always asks a million questions and explanations are useless. I spent a long time with Umezawa Sensei. He's deeply enlightened, sees everything as flowers. All existence in threes: *shin, jin, tome* / past, present, future. He had that one koan but came to understand everything.

Friday, February 26
Tessai-san at hospital. No one came; didn't get a ton done. Tessai has really changed, become much nicer. Yesterday he actually did some cleaning. Today he brought me home a slice of cheesecake. Evening meditation drowsy.

Saturday, February 27
Morning meditation awful, three quarters asleep. Must improve. How? Went to *Fukudoji* [Happiness Hall Temple] where Go Roshi was raised. His elder-brother-*deshi* [disciple] and family were there. The scenery was exquisite. Very cold. The stories of Go Roshi as a child clipclopping down the road in thin geta (no socks) through the wind and snow, crying from the pain, came alive. Of being awakened and beaten at 3 in the morning with snow on his futon. We also went to nearby Tendaiji, high on the mountain. Very remote and peaceful. Heavenly for training. Nice day. Night meditation good. Lately I always get sleepy about halfway through, so I took a break, had a cuppa and a bit of a read, then was able to continue well. I haven't solved the koan but had some samadhi. Around 11 o'clock, I heard strange laughing—howling like a woman's voice. Very eerie but I presume it was owls or something.

February 28
Phew, time is flying. Morning meditation bad. Gion-chan was sleeping with me. In my semi-slumber I was loath to move her and got up late myself, 4:40. Got loads of work done. Fell asleep at 9.

March 2
Morning meditation only okay. Allison came, it was nice to see her. We had a little celebration. Bad meditation.

March 3
Go to dokusan but miss the bus, so we walked. It was a nice day; we did it in 80 minutes. Roshi says that in thirty years of training I'm the only one of his students who trains as if *inochi o steru* [to abandon my very life]. I messed up the koan a bit, but it was generally okay. Home very late.

March 4
Gidaji [name of a temple], flower-arranging. Home late.

March 5
I'm a bit tired but have to do ookyo at home of dead neighbor. The woman, still in *nemaki* [nightgown], could have been asleep except for purple ears and hanky on her face. Disconcerting. Her child lay on his stomach in kotatsu and stared at the corpse on its futon. Relatives kept wiping her lips with water; it shone on her dead mouth. A single tulip, a candle in line so the stem and the stalk coincided, the flame rising from the base of the tulip. She had a cold that didn't get better, so they operated on her throat in the hospital and killed her. 43 years old.

March 6
Met Reiko-san and had sumptuous lunch, then went to a magnificent flower-arranging exhibition.

It seems to me the difference between life and death is consciousness (even plants are conscious), and the difference between human and other life is self-consciousness. In Zen the narrow subjectivity of consciousness is transcended, becomes pure subjectivity rather than relative subjectivity.

Allison is sick.

Sunday, March 7
Morning meditation mostly drowsing, but I solved the koan that had
been annoying me. Go Roshi pulled a great one. When Kondo-san's people came looking for him, Go Roshi first tried to persuade them not to
pursue him, then he pretended to give up, hid Kondo-san in the pre-fab
and had one of the monks pretend he'd run away from Toshoji. They
then gave up but threatened that they'd be back in touch. Then someone
stole Jean's money, and Go Roshi, suspecting At-chan, went prowling
around in the dark to check on him. He fell and hurt his leg. He's sleep-
less with concern over the theft.

Monday, March 8
Allison is still quite sick. She went into hospital. They say it's enteritis and
give her pills that only make it worse. She's brave.

Toshoji, Tokyo
March 18, 1982
Dear Mum,
A huge package of books arrived from you the other day. This is the first
moment I've had to write and thank you. I'm dying to launch into them.
The Kadowaki one, *Zen and the Bible*, looks particularly fascinating. Just
leafing through it, the man seems very illumined and obviously has
grasped and lived both worlds. I was extremely impressed with just the
little I've read.

It seems to me that every day something happens and I say "Oh, I must
tell Mum that," but now I don't know where to start.

My ceremony has been moved from June to April 25th. Go Roshi says
he's not sure if he'll be alive in June, so he wants to do the ceremony as
soon as possible. I'm going bats trying to learn all the stuff. It's old Japanese and has completely different tonality and pronunciation from regu-
lar conversational Japanese.

For a week I was doing ookyo at the different people's houses…(just by
myself I did about 70 houses). It was fascinating. The people around
Morioka are really pretty much all of one type, but here [in the Shinagawa

section of Tokyo] I got much more of a cross-section, from modern, luxurious, Western-style concrete, with plate glass and a dining-room table, to tiny, dark, second floor hovels. Some were weensy little garrets where, after stepping over boxes and up a two-foot-wide staircase, there would be a single room where a whole family lives in oriental harmony. The people were very good to me, and I was amazed at how broadminded they were. (How would you react if a young girl from Bombay dressed as a priest walked into St. Joseph's Church to offer Mass?) Quite apart from my being gaijin, most had never even seen a woman read ookyo before. It was, however, exhausting. I did a house an hour.

I got around by bicycle and have become adept at misreading Japanese maps. No one can come up with more original ways to get lost. Meanwhile Go Roshi was bombing around on his bike—you know, like the big, black, 2-wheeled armored tanks that the Irish police, down the bogs, use. Other mornings he'd be out at 5 o'clock when he had to catch the subway to a distant house. That part wouldn't be so bad except that he's doing it on a sprained ankle which has now become extremely painful and swollen.

He got the sprained ankle while checking up on a young "delinquent" we had here who used to borrow money and get jarred over in the prefab every night (the little house where we stayed when you were here). But it is because of another fellow that we are in bad odor with the police here. The guy was from Morioka and had committed offenses that I'm sure any American policeman would smile at, but they were real shockers in Morioka. His mother was a wreck (her only beautiful boy—and he is gorgeous), so she begged Go Roshi to take him. She didn't mention that he was on parole and not allowed out of Morioka. The police caught up with him just after they found out about Kondo-san. (Remember the sweetheart of a monk who was always fixing you sandwiches?)

Anyway, the young man was a friend of Reiko-san (the temple mum where I teach English), and his father was a monk who re-married after Kondo-san's mother died. It was a classic Cinderella tale. The stepmother hated him, favored her own son whom she wanted to inherit the temple, rather than Kondo-san who, as eldest son, was in line for it.

So she succeeded in making life miserable for him and in promoting her own son in the father's favor. Kondo-san, from young childhood, had to do most of the cooking and cleaning in the temple and sell newspapers after school. On the one afternoon a week he had free he worked with hand-icapped kids. Well, after 20 years and no sign that things would improve, even Kondo-san was starting to get discouraged. Reiko-san stepped in and helped him to run away. (Imagine, 28 years old and having to run away from home, but such is temple life in Japan.) It was summer. Bit by bit he smuggled out boxes of clothes, mostly winter ones so that it would look as if he was going to Hokkaido. Reiko-san, as wife in a very prominent tem-ple, was putting her neck on the block. They got him to Toshoji.

For a month the police didn't get wind of him. Then one of the dor-mitory students got stopped for drunken bicycling and Kondo-san went to bail him out. They asked his name and birthplace. Not having a sly bone in his body, he 'fessed up. Explosion! His people came down for him (after many intense phone calls). Finally Go Roshi hid him in a cup-board and had another monk let on that he had run away from here too. I don't know what will happen next, but the police have black-listed Toshoji. There's certainly never a dull minute here.

I've kind of adopted that poor mutt Guru. (Remember the one with the unearthly howls?) I never thought of myself as a dog person but dogs are really great. They give you so much more of a reaction than cats.

I'm blasting through koans these days. I can scarcely keep up and sel-dom have time to prepare them properly but Go Roshi figures that if he at least gives me the key to them, then I can digest them later. Phew! My head is spinning a bit.

A couple of days later…I'm very excited about the news that Scott is coming. I only wish he could have been here in time for my ceremony. We're busy preparing for sesshin. Right now I'm up on the roof mend-ing futons. It's a beautiful sunny day, a change from the weather of late. It's so very pleasant sitting up here in the sun and wind, sewing, listen-ing to the children playing in the streets below.

Today a woman from some Tokyo magazine came for an interview, and before I left Morioka, I did a long radio thing that was to be played in installments for a week. I wouldn't be surprised if Scott ends up on radio or TV or in some magazine. I haven't worked on my novel for weeks, but it's in the works. How's about Christmas in dear old dirty Dublin?

Much love, M.

Toshoji, Tokyo
April 1982
Dear Mum,
Happy Easter! It's a glorious Easter Sunday here but without a bonnet in sight (in fact, only conspicuously bald heads). They'd give anything for Easter weather like this in Ireland—seems a shame to waste it on infidels.

Sesshin is over, and practice for my ceremony is in full swing. I'm going over, and over again, the same meaningless syllables (ancient Japanese that even the Japanese don't understand). I have to do all the tonality and pronunciation in a peculiar oratorical style resembling the Kabuki narrators. It's going to be unusual anyway…

Scott, I'm as excited as can be that you're coming. For clothes, the young Japanese casual uniform is a track suit, though that may be hot in a Tokyo summer. You may want to ship back most of your baggage ahead, as we'll travel light in Thailand and India. My ideal is one of those weekender packs, a sleeping bag and rain poncho that can open into a ground sheet, a set of clothes on one's back, a set in the pack, and a light jumper or cardigan. (Maybe not necessary, I must check the likely weather.) I don't believe in money belts. Everyone knows about them, and the pros all know how to relieve you of them. Get both large ($50.00) and small travelers' checks so you don't need to carry too many. Bring a nailbrush. Where do you want to go? Flights within southeast Asia are cheapest from Hong Kong, so we should start there, and flights back are cheapest from Thailand. Also bring Lomotil in case of tummy problems. So start researching and dreaming, and let's have some fun.

Love, M.

March 30

Put out futons to air. Dug garden. Made oryoki. Six hours zazen. Naka-mura read me koans on the floor by flashlight. First hint of any interest in me.

March 31

Changed address at *yakuba* [ward office]. Preparing for sesshin. I feel an incredible joy, incredible energy. The koans are still hopeless.

> Somewhere a door creaks
> I crane for a
> certain footstep.

April 1–5

Sesshin. Kitchen great, I wasn't tired, it became the heart of the temple. Everyone streeled [sauntered] in in dribs and drabs if they needed a chat or a cry, an ookyo book, rice balls, a cup of tea, if their legs hurt or they had a headache or cold, if their kimono needed sewing or their rakusu, if their dokusan needed translation or if their address book had to be fished out of the toilet; they all came to the kitchen. Me and Kondo-san were the mother, Go Roshi the stern but beloved father. During their meals I'd lie down on the kitchen floor with my head on a rice sack and a smile would creep across my face. We were very happy, worked very hard, and laughed very hard. My koans weren't great, I had scarcely time to prepare them. Still, Go Roshi says that of all his disciples I stand alone. Politically, we could never agree. I appreciate his points, and if everyone felt like him, as apparently they used to, it would be great. I doubt he'd ever appreciate my point.

April 1

Allison and Mike got kensho. It was very beautiful to be with her then but later she was disillusioned and depressed. She still doesn't really know she's Buddha. Mike had no expectations or disappointments.

April 2
Kiguchi-obasan from Morioka had kensho. In zendo she could hear my voice doing ookyo (but I wasn't); then she was crying and got into the dokusan line. I was watching Namura suffering and failing dokusan, and Kiguchi was crying beside me. It became too much. I began to cry, too. She was deeply moved and had kensho. I ran downstairs, collapsed in a heap in the corner by my rice bag, sobbing uncontrollably. They were all suffering so. Stuart came in, was shocked and comforting. I left meals outside Namura-san's door. He wasn't getting kensho, and I was afraid it might bother him to think I was watching. He tried with his heart and soul, and mine, but he didn't get kensho. Even in the kitchen I'd call "Mu, mu," to him, but my concentration was bad. He seems sad these days, hasn't been doing zazen. I'd like to reach out to him but he often seems strained in my presence.

Go Roshi was an inspiration. His leg is still dreadful but he struggled to sit on it. I begged him to use a chair but he refused. The leg has swollen to twice its size. In dokusan he was continually shifting because of the pain of sitting long hours on it. This sesshin I was right weepy. Tears just streamed down my face, touched that he'd do this for us, pained to see him. He says I'm not to go back to Kannonji.

April 7
Roshi went to Morioka, Yamaguchi goes home for a couple of days. Drizzle day, mostly sewing.

April 8
Count Basie concert with Yuriko and Hiroshi. Roshi still in Morioka. I knocked down an old shed. Went for a drive with Izaki-san. It was pathetic. Surrounded by concrete warehouses, a towering official with a walkie-talkie, Izaki-san looked up at him and said, "We just want to see the sea." A gull circled overhead. "Impossible." We drove for ages and finally saw a bit of the sea by the airport. I talked to Namura a bit, but he seems very cold. He hasn't seemed well since sesshin. In torrential rains

in the afternoon, met Roshi at the station. Yen phoned, Allison frantic that I won't be returning to Kannonji.

April 10

I chopped up the shed and put the wood away. Put ashes on the garden. My practice for *Hossenshiki* [koan graduation ceremony] not very good. I'm sleeping four and a half hours with no problems. Feel good.

April 13

I decided to approach Namura. He looked so mopish and depressed. He hadn't been doing zazen in zendo. But I came on like a bulldozer. He didn't know how to react. I asked if he was okay and he said he didn't seem right. Then, Japanese style, he started apologizing. I ranted and raved about the Japanese repressing their feelings, etc.

A new American woman, Jocelyn Ford, entered. Seems she may be serious.

Izaki brings me cheesecake.

April 15

I put mondo to Go Roshi.

"The stone that is now preaching the Dharma, is it living or dead?"

He said, *"Ishi, konna ishi?"* [*"Stone, this stone?"*], indicating.

I said "Hai."

He said "I don't know," then laughing, "ask the stone."

I said, "I am asking the stone." We were both laughing.

He said, "I'm not a stone. I'm Ban Tetsugyu" and we both dissolved into laughter.

Jiko-san came, back from India.

Bad zazen, very sleepy, disorganized. Couldn't do dokusan in the morning. Pouring rain.

April 17

Abe says he'll help, and I have written to various people asking them to visit Allison.

Actually had a five-minute conversation with Namura. Since my outburst, he seems in much better humor. I don't know if there's a connection.

In the evening went to zenkai with Go Roshi. Maezumi Roshi was there. Seems good. The whole thing was great fun. Roshi was in a very good humor. We went by subway with Maezumi Roshi asking Go Roshi, "Where's your car?" Go Roshi wouldn't let either of us carry his bag, so Maezumi shared it with him. They fought like little boys going down the street in the dark, and finally both carried the minuscule briefcase. I walked behind in undignified convulsions of laughter. Roshis!

April 18
It was Go Roshi's grandchild's birthday. They invited me over. I was very touched.

Allison phoned, she's not getting on with Tetsugen.

I went to see Kiguchi-san. His mother was returning in the morning, and I wanted to stay and give her an obento. Turned out it was Kiguchi's birthday, too, and Namura was there. I left to phone Allison, planning to come right back. He left.

Allison was asleep, but I asked Tetsugen to give her free time each week. He didn't seem to mind. Sounded good.

I felt disappointed that Namura was gone and annoyed with myself for being disappointed. Zazen was bad, so I went up on the roof. It was getting late, and Namura's laundry was out, so I was putting it away just as he came for it. We talked for a long while. It was nice, but when Izaki and Kiguchi appeared, Namura scarpered.

Kondo is a sweetheart, brought me an eclair.

April 19
I decided to try three hours sleep. I was exhausted. I tried reading the paper, next thing I remember it was 4:00 and Go Roshi was knocking on the door, calling me to dokusan. Things went wrong all day. Really seemed jinxed. I suggested to Roshi that Gen go to Nagano, Mio to Toshoji, and Allison to Kannonji. He said he wanted me to marry a

Japanese man and run one of the temples. He's given that a rest for a while. Another goof: I tried to give Kiguchi a late birthday present, poised it atop his window ledge and it fell. Highly breakable. It was Roshi's 33rd wedding anniversary.

April 20
Go Roshi stunned me in dokusan. I'd been thinking about Namura being seven years younger than me, and that really this attraction is absurd, when Go Roshi told me the story of the woman who jumped into the toilet to save the cat. From all the priests she had picked out the best one, the one most serious about training, as she herself had been. The one she chose was seven years younger than herself. Roshi looked at me meaningfully. "I want you to follow her, that is, choose for yourself."

My hossenshiki *renshu* [practice] is 120 percent thanks to Abe-san, who drills me very kindly.

The funny, drunken former tenzo came back again. He sat with his sandals outside the gate, heaving big sighs. He became a bit violent.

April 21
Go Roshi is pushing me hard to stay in Japan and become his successor. I feel disoriented. All my previous principles, goals, opinions seem totally changed. Whether I'm here or in Ireland, married or not, none of it seems a big deal. It seems I should assent and truly throw my life away for training. Mum would be upset. In the real world, Roshi's and my ideas are so different. But it seems I have no criteria left by which to make a decision. Anything is okay. It's a strange feeling, not a problem, but definitely disorienting.

I did *insatsu* [printing] in the evening, with the rain falling.

Roshi said my interpretation of the koan was deeper than the koan. Then he thanked me. I was touched.

Allison phoned again; it's hard for her.

April 22

I planted flowers, weeded, did insatsu, sewed. I love all the people in Toshoji, each and every one of them. They're all excellent, not a bad apple in the bunch.

April 25

My ceremony.

I practiced too hard the day before so my voice was not at its best but was okay. Wonderful day. I had prepared a good speech, but when asked to speak, could only burst out crying. I got very emotional and kept bowing and thanking people. (I spent all my money in a frenzy of gratitude, buying things for everyone.) Many beautiful gifts to me; I was extremely moved.

In the evening we had my party. Kondo-san hurt his back, so I had to do all the cooking. Tired. Up at 2:30, great energy in hossenshiki, then no break. Cook and clean.

They all dedicated songs to me. Yamaguchi was roaring, looked as if his blood vessels would pop, thumping his leg. Izaki, swaying, romantic, asked Namura for a song, but Namura said he couldn't sing. Later he stood up shouting, "Everyone's done a song for Mora; only I haven't because can't sing." So he did a wild, impassioned, cheer-leading type of thing, punching the air, creating dazzlers, screaming my name. I wanted to run to him.

Later I couldn't meditate for thinking of him, so I went to the roof. Kondo-san was lying on his back, drunk, singing powerfully to the stars. He then calls into the night: "Mora-san, I made a mistake (in the ceremony). Sorry." He's so pure, beautiful. I sat on the steps. I was a bit worried about Kiguchi, so I headed that way with the dog, met Izaki, Namura, and friends going to the baths. I asked directions to the park; Namura didn't show me the way.

(undated; probably spring 1982)

Dear Sean,

Finally a spare moment in the merry-go-round of events and happenings in Toshoji Towers. I'm in a train station, waiting to go to the head temple. In Toshoji, even with only 2–4 hours sleep a night, I never seem to have a spare moment...They told me yesterday morning that I'm to have my final ceremonies and pay respects at the head temples. Frantic washing and ironing of kimonos, shave me head and borrow the accessories I don't own, and onto the night train. The seats were at 90 degree angles so I fell asleep on a drunk next to me, who didn't seem to mind.

Now it's eleven in the morning with the sun nearly overhead. The feeling here is very different from what I've experienced anywhere else in Japan. It's Southern and feels Mediterranean or Latin American. It's a pleasing combination, Japanese and Latin. A tiny country train station, pink flowers between the tracks, sun beating on scalloped clay roofs. Outside the little waiting room I can see into a house—an old man's sitting on the floor, bamboo screen moving slightly; he's very slowly peeling what looks like a summer pear. Beside me a kid is playing with a musical calculator. None of the hurry of Tokyo. The air smells like mountains, and though it's hot, it's not muggy. I'm beginning to get excited at the thought of visiting the head temple. Part of the ceremony involves my becoming master for a day. It's the follow-up to a *gyo* [a particular practice, short for "shugyo"] I was doing when I got your letter, so you were in my mind although I had to do 3,000 prostrations while chanting.

...Later, slightly overwhelmed, but into it. This is a very old temple up in the mountains, about 200 monks scarpering around. Feels strange. I wear red slippers, sleep in a gold room, and all the monks have to come to a full stop and bow so their face isn't seen when I walk by. Splendid (vegetarian) feasts. In the dark last night a monk led me around the stone passages by a candle lamp. He showed me what to do for all the ceremonies. It was eerie—pitch black, stone slabs and tatami, smelled of incense. At first I thought he was blind—he just gazed into space, not focusing on anything in particular. Then I wondered if he was retarded— he spoke so slowly and deliberately. (But I then surmised he probably thought I was retarded—a foreigner and all that. Speaking of which, that and my sex took them very much by surprise.)

The ceremonies are nearly over. Have just had a nice cup of tea, brewed on a hibachi with spring water. Beats Tokyo any day. Don't know if I made many mistakes or not. I felt so sleepy that the whole thing happened as if in a dream. The day after tomorrow I go to the other head temple; then Cinderella is no longer a red-slipper person and I'm back to the old grindstone. Leaving probably Oct. 7th, planning to be back in the Western world around Christmas.

...Later again. First temple's over. On my way back to the big city. Da da de dum. Train stations and a packed lunch with salt pickled plum. Back in Toshoji and nothing much has changed. No one fed the dog and Roshi got a rip in his bedclothes. I'll be back in my never-a-moment-to-write schedule soon enough...

Love, M.

April 26
Poor Kondo-san, still maimed. Abe-san is doing massages and needles. I am doing the kitchen.

April 27
Namura is definitely not interested, so to hell with it. I'll just forget about him.

I spent hours getting Roshi's *tabi* [white socks with a split between the big toe and the others] dry by the morning, then he didn't wear them.

There is nothing dead. Everything alive is in movement, if only in time.

May 15
Did sesshin in traditional temple in Kyushu. Allison shaved her head. Go Roshi was happy. Her poor legs gave her agony. We ate and slept in zendo. I made many mistakes in protocol, but Tetsumon-san helped me.

It was the best sesshin I'd ever experienced. I had two minor awakenings. On the second day, in dokusan line, I realized—really experienced—*Ten ni mo chi ni mo tada ware hitori* ["In heaven and earth, there is but I, myself," a statement attributed in legend to the baby Buddha Shakyamuni]. That "ware hitori" includes everything.

Later, during teisho, I felt such intense gratitude toward Go Roshi, I could only cry. I cried for about an hour and a half.

On the fourth day, my awakening began in the corridor and became intense while I was eating. Everything is perfect. Everything is enlightening, just as it is by virtue of being. As it is, it is *narikiteru* [totally being], even *bonpu* [the mundane unenlightened state of delusion] is narikiteru bonpu. It was revelation, the perfection within the imperfection. Many times Go Roshi's words of remonstrance penetrated to my very core. "Is there even one of you truly narikiteru?" I'm not.

At the end, Hukokuji's Roshi made a speech and referred to the fact that, like Dogen Zenji, I hadn't slept lying down for a thousand days. I was so ashamed and also inspired to do better during the final *Shiku Seigan Mon* [Four Bodhisattva Vows: to awaken all beings, to end all delusions, to master all teachings, and to accomplish the Buddha Way]. I was weeping again, intensely grateful to have the opportunity to experience this sesshin.

I forgot about Namura. I must just do good training, no distractions.

Tetsumon-san made a weird speech. He likes me (loves me, he says) but is justifiably put out by Roshi's exaggerations of my worth and his condemnation of the Japanese. I wish Roshi wouldn't do it.

Allison is to come to Toshoji in July; I wonder how Namura will feel. People have started doing zazen. At first it was only me, now there are five of us in the evenings.

I feel ecstatically happy. It's a gorgeous May, warm and breezy. I love the world.

May 14

Last night I stayed up late talking with Namura—very good, very open, spontaneous, and relaxed. I realized many things. I grew to like him more, and I feel closer to him, but am put off him as a man. He's still too young. I'd hate to either dominate or mother him, as would be inevitable. That leaves me freer to concentrate on training. But he's a wonderful person.

Go Roshi returned. He seemed tired but strong.

May 15

Reiko-san and Megumi came to visit. I was very happy. Megumi is unsure about her future. (A Morioka woman who was apparently moved to tears to see me in takuhatsu, wants me to help her son tread the right road, return to school, etc. These are strange cases. I feel wilder than the kids.)

I have started cleaning the toilets again at 3 o'clock in the morning. Three hours' sleep. I am pretty much asleep sitting up, but still bad.

The weather threatens rain, but it is beautiful.

Toshoji, Tokyo
May 17, 1982
Dear Kate,

…Just had a phone call from Jane. Nearly dropped. It's May 17, I wished her happy birthday, she said it wasn't her birthday. Beginning to wonder if I had 2 sister Janes or was going soft in the head. It's still yesterday there (and Go Roshi always says the past doesn't exist).

It's sunny. I'm watching the beans grow. It's a happy, peaceful day, neighborhood. People all doing Oriental neighborhoodsy things, and the kids are feeding shoes to our dog, who is called Guru, and kept on a chain. This morning we did a funeral for a cat. (I became an official priestess on Ruth's birthday. I'm Soshin osho, or omasan, depending on your inclination.)

The funeral people brought us a big feed of sashimi in thanks. Seems appropriate to get raw fish for burying a cat.

I'm sitting in May sunshine and winds overlooking Tokyo. If it was a clear day, I could see Mt. Fuji but it's not, so I can't. I've been sitting up here mending Go Roshi's patches. He's been wearing this robe for 50 years, so I'm putting patches on the patches, and it's all fraying in my hands and these heavenly May winds. So I'm taking a break and writing to you, without much to say.

Days fly past, cleaning and sitting and having a laugh. It's nice living with people again. All good people, but like any bunch living in a small space, many undercurrents. The Japanese aren't big on face-to-face encounters, etc., yet everyone just seems to know what's afoot. I've shocked more than one by saying the unsaid, out.

Go Roshi is good. Had planned to die this year. It's the year of the dog; he was born in the year of the dog, so he wanted to have a big bash and pass on. But his book's been delayed, and half the text has gone amissing, so he's putting off his retirement.

* * * *

Another day. It's three in the morning. I've just finished washing all the toilets, pulled up the poles, and opened the gates, put out the offertory box and the outside offerings. Some drunks are staggering home, and I still don't feel quite coherent but reckon you've been waiting quite a while for an answer.

I guess the most exciting thing that's happened to me lately is the sesshin in Kyushu. Kate, it was great. I got to just be a participant. No cooking, serving, or patrolling, but loads of zazen. Anyway had a couple of real breakthroughs. Very overwhelming, tears and laughter and a long sit in a pebble garden. Now they seem tenuous. Old habits die hard but the experiences are there, I now really know what I had theretofore assented to as being true. Anyway excellent, though as excitement it probably seems boring in the context of what you're doing. (Well, to hell with contexts.)…Kate, I have to go. Write again.

Take care, M.

May 18
The clock stopped, and the dog broke a bag of garbage. I saw both and took care of neither. *Funbetsu* [This is a reference to a Zen story which emphasizes importance of detachment.]—I'll do it later. I haven't the responsibility here.

May 19
I'm making myself do jobs when I'm willing to turn a blind eye. Made juice, sewed clothes on the roof. I began work on the *Mumonkan* translation again.

May 21

I had an incredibly wonderful walk with the dog through the streets. They were playing music; I wanted to dance. A mother watched her child eat pink ice cream. The summer plastic festoons have gone up, silver and blue. The streets seemed to be in festival. Smells of soba. Vegetable stalls. Old man on a bicycle. Young lovers not holding hands.

Ichigawa-san was afraid to sleep in her room, so we traded. Had a laugh. I heard funny noises and thought Namura was playing tricks on me. He'll be a fine man, but not right for me. Nice to really know it and nice that he's relaxed with me. The dormitory students have been coming down with things. I like mothering them. Everyone takes care of me in so many ways—fixing me treats, giving me papers, helping me with my koans, shaving my head. They're all patient, kind. We love one another beyond nationality or sex.

I have been tired for the last couple of days, almost no sleep. I am ashamed though of my shoddy efforts. I read about the old masters, bow to the living Buddha before me in dokusan, and try, but I am still very far from *risshin* [success], from narikiteru.

It was a rainy day, very nice. Greens intense, pink roses.

May 23

Jim and Dominique are in town. I stood bald under the *Star Wars* sign in Ueno Park. Many stares in the razzle-dazzle of the night. I met Jim's mum, her birthday is the same as mine.

May 24

My birthday. Paul sends instant birthday kit from Dublin: Guinness, cake, and tapes. We have a hell of a party, dancing on the roof. Lovely gifts. Crazy night. Tired next day.

May 26

In the morning I felt exhausted to my bones. I feel I will surely collapse, I have reached some kind of limit, breaking point. I wanted to sleep 24 hours. I will surely collapse in sesshin. The tiredness has accumulated.

Sleep after breakfast for an hour. During the morning the tiredness falls away. I can scarcely believe it. At lunch I feel alert enough to write letters. Really strange. My shoulders feel tight, but my body no longer seems tired either. (Izaki-san, so funny, doing zazen he feels strength he says came from me, sitting opposite.)

June 6

We had sesshin from June 1–5. Time flew. Allison and I in the kitchen. She's moody but a very big help. Kondo-san has kensho. I'm delighted. Also Ichigawa-san and a German, Helmut. I was translating for four people. Very busy, often began at 3:00–3:30, clean toilets, work all day.

June 8

We went to the park, danced barefoot. Kikuchi and Izaki-san played the guitar and sang. In the distance we could hear a baritone and flute player. We raced bikes home. I fell asleep in zendo.

June 10

Namura's folks came, worried about him. Made us promise not to tell.

June 12

Galli-san phones, trying to come to sesshin. No expectations or anxiety. I can't imagine. His voice was good. I am working on *Tetsugyushi* [Go Roshi's book] and *Mumonkan*. In the evening I met Namura on the roof. The air was heavenly. We had a good chat, open. I told him some of the problems I had at the age of 20; he seemed eased.

June 13

Izaki-san came back, did some *Mumonkon*. I was starving. Kondo-san is doing the wedding arrangements. I cook for two ceremonies. Did a fantastic zazen on the rooftop.

June 14
For the first time since he was sick, Namura did ookyo the energetic way he used to. I'm delighted.

June 18
I begin *Denpo-shiki* [Dharma transmission ceremony]. Three thousand full bows. Have one week to do it in. For the first ten minutes or so it felt good. Breathing deep from the hara, *"Namu san ze sho bu(tsu)"* ["Homage to all the buddhas of the Three Worlds"], again and again. Up and down, head bowing, blood rushing to the head, hyperventilating. Then I began to feel dreadful. Everything hurt, breathing, legs, stomach, dizzy. Kondo and Izaki gave me treats. I continued, barely took breaks. Was drenched in sweat. I began to lose awareness, felt there was a noise, a movement, vague sustained awareness of heat, but no "I." If I stopped, the pain in my legs was excruciating, but doing it again, I became unaware of them. Fifty wooden chopsticks from side to side. I finished 3,036 the second day. Everyone was incredulous. Do banka, then straight out to zenkai. I was falling asleep there. The stairs were hell.

June 20, 1982
Fathers' Day.
Up early. Legs dreadful.
   I have my Denpo-shiki. Very moving. Early in the morning, 50 bows. I do *doshi* [priest officiating at services]. Hardly notice my legs. I have to concentrate. I can scarcely do all the bows. We bow together. Abe-san attends. Go Roshi removes my *okesa* [outermost patched robe of the fully ordained priest] and gives me a gorgeous one. When it finishes, I cry more.
   I sneak into his room and leave pens, goodies, a card, and roses.

June 22
Usha, an Indian Hindu, comes for the night. She's a very wonderful, intelligent, unusual woman. I'll visit her again.

(undated; Kannonji 1982)
Dear Maureen,

...there's little as satisfying as a big dinner after a good day's digging. It's great; there's loads of wild things to eat these days. A couple of old ladies and a monk from the mountains have been teaching me where to find and how to cook various weeds and mushrooms. All kinds of funny preparations—like soaking them with rusty nails or ashes from the bath's fireplace. Then there's herbs for the bath itself.

Go Roshi decided not to transfer me back to Tokyo after all, at least not for the moment. Last time I saw him he was pushing the idea of giving me this temple and a husband he had in mind. Eek. I said "Thanks, but no thanks, I'd like to go back to Ireland." He just laughs, "You're an airplane" he says "you can fly back and forth when you like." Him and his bloody Zen logic. He thinks me and this monk of his would be a good match because—get this, Maureen—we're both tall!...

Well, Maureen, I'm trying to think of what there is in the way of news around here. Today a little old farmer's wife with a bent back and a green bike came by with a scarf-ful of sweet rice bean cakes. Two days ago a housewife wanted her epileptic child blessed. The fourth floor has wasps and the back corridor leaks. The postman came; the milkman didn't. Not much happens. It's peaceful. No complaints...

Have a great birthday...Write sometime, Maureen, even if you only sign your name 17 times down the page—at least I'll know you weren't hit by a bus...

Take care and I love ya,
Maire

(undated, probably summer 1982)
Dear Maureen...

Delighted to hear from you and to hear that you're so happy. Regret that, tho' I really want to be at your wedding, you won't be in Dublin when I get back. Have made travel promises so the earliest I could be in Dublin is Nov. If your dates are postponed, TELL ME. Am very happy for you. Have had to re-think many of my ideas on marriage and realize I never really believed in love...I wish you the very best and hope that by some miracle things get delayed and I can be there. Do you want a Buddhist blessing?

Love, M.

June 24
I spent the day getting photocopies. I lost and found my dokusan notebook. Izaki was incredibly kind to me.

June 25
I returned a book to the Zenkai temple. There was a letter from home. I phoned Scott's host family to let them know when he would arrive.

Toshoji, Tokyo
June 1982
Dear Mum,
...Hope Scott comes soon, as from the 10th of July until the 6th of August will be hectic for me with the summer equinox sutras. I have to do 80 houses in 5 days, then race up to Kannonji and get the place ready for sesshin, then do sesshin, rush back here to prepare for the August sesshin, cater that (sweltering Tokyo in August). So anyway, I hope he comes soon. Did you get my letter telling you how Paul, from Ireland, managed to give me a brilliant birthday party? On Go Roshi's birthday he phoned from London. He said he had a great time in Dublin...I've been working every day on translating Go Roshi's book. It's very hard. When I go back to Ireland, I want to study Japanese seriously. In order for proper Zen (not "pop Zen") to take root in the West, there are a lot of vital texts that simply must be translated. All present translations are really inadequate. I'll explain another time. I'm not crazy about translation work but it has to be done, so...

Koan study is proceeding at a dizzying pace. Quite a few foreigners are coming these days, so I translate all their dokusans. This is a great opportunity for me because I see again and again how to deal with beginners and to adapt one's approach and one's answer to the needs of the person. So I'm thriving, but by October will be ready for a break...

Love, M.

Toshoji, Tokyo
July 4, 1982
Dear Okōchan [Mum],
Well, your son has safely arrived and quickly acclimatized. There was an accident on the runway, so his plane had to circle overhead for ages. I was there at 3:30. He finally arrived at 8:10. It gave me plenty of time to talk with his host family. When he arrived they recognized him; I didn't. I insisted that that grown-up young man wasn't Scott. Like Peter, I denied him three times before it finally hit me that it might indeed be my brother. He's much changed, very likeable. The poor kid had been awake for 28 hours but managed in a foreign culture to be very gracious, helpful, attentive, and extremely positive. Really he was delighted by everything. He tucked right into the raw fish with relish, likes his family very much, and when he finally got to go to bed, he wanted to unpack and put away everything from his suitcase first, so as not to be messy! Really, I was very impressed with the way he only saw the good side of everything and made a real effort (though it seemed effortless). But I can't get over how very American he seems.

His family let me spend the night there. They are lovely. The father is gentle, with smiling eyes, very intrigued by Scott. He only knows how to say "thank you" in English.

Scott took to the whole thing like a fish to water. No awkwardness, as if he'd been in Japan for years. He seemed to know all the right things to do, how to hold his glass, to pour for others, how to sit politely, etc.

The mother is delightful—one of those super duper Japanese housewife types. She had worried awfully about Scott coming, afraid he'd be too tall for the futons, etc. She actually lost weight worrying. The older son is 24, has spent over a year in the States, so speaks fluent English and understands how it is to be away from home and in a strange culture. The girl's English is good, though slow. She's outgoing and fun. They've arranged for Scott to attend her school. All the girls there are dying to meet him. In short, things got off to a very nice start.

Scott wants to give sesshin a try though he'll miss the Kannonji one on account of school. It's a pity. I wanted him to meet all the folks up there. We were both dismayed by our mutual dates. The very earliest I can leave (doing all my packing, buying, goodbyes before sesshin) would be October 7th. Scott feels he must be back at school by mid-October.

A wonderful Indian woman came to stay here recently. She's 50, single, a lecturer in psychology, and the student of an Indian guru. She has a house and servants on the Ganges. We got on extraordinarily well, and she invited me to come and stay as long as I wanted. In October there's a festival of lights and one of good and evil that she wants to show me. She says that October is most pleasant and she'll take me to various places of Buddhist interest as well as a visit to her ashram in the mountains. I wish there were some way that Scott could work things to come with me. I think I'd really enjoy his company.

Love, M.

Toshoji, Tokyo
July 16, 1982
Dear Mum,
…We are into obon now and suddenly two 69-year-old parishioners passed away. Remember, that involves wake, service at home, one at temple, one at crematorium, and one at the grave. We're going bonky. One of the dormitory students who has been growing out his hair came home last night after a few drinks, merry, singing, and rubbing his new hair, only to be told that we're desperately short of priests. Would he mind shaving? God love him. Not a grumble, just where are the clippers? Today I do ookyo from 8 in the morning 'til 7 at night, then out to the wake. I hope someone feeds me. Will write when there's more time…

Love, M.

September 1982

Dear Mum,

…We can't get info here in Tokyo on flights back to the States from Thailand (the bargain ones) for Scott, so we'll wait till we get to Thailand and then see what the story is there.

[Later] I've been having terrible trouble cashing our dollar checks. Don't know how the Japanese handle international banking at all. It's unfortunate that all this coincides with *ohigan* [the spring equinox]. I'm unbelievably busy. (It's now 3:37 in the morning, and I'm stealing time between jobs to write this.) It looks, however, as if the checks will pass through by Monday.

I tried to contact Sr. Ruth Sheils, but our schedules didn't fit well enough so we could meet, but we had a very nice long phone chat. She's a very interesting and intelligent woman and will look me up in Ireland next summer. She told me a lot about Sacred Heart, Tokyo, and it sounds excellent.

Days and days later: We've had ohigan, then a sesshin, in between my trying to organize packing, posting, visas, shopping, money, goodbyes— am totally exhausted, but it's almost over. The reason this took so infernally long was that I was waiting for definite news on our travel funds. It was hell. Anyway, I must post this NOW or not at all.

Sorry! You can't imagine how busy things are. Will write.

Love, M.

Appendix

In answer to the requests I have received from readers seeking more information about Maura's earlier life, I have attempted to transcribe and put into chronological order the remaining papers that she sent home or left with me before embarking on her last adventure.

Almost all of these pieces were written before Maura left for Japan, with the exception of Part X of the appendix—the first portion of Maura's never-finished novel. This single chapter is both an entertaining and harrowing account, obviously only slightly fictional, of her own life as she plunged as a newcomer into the customs and routines of Zen monastic life.

Another addition to this collection is a transcription of the notes she kept during a year-long trip alone through Latin America, including several months in Peru. These notes reveal a fearless, unconventional traveler, deeply attuned to the people and physical environment of South America.

The remaining contents of this volume consist of a journal she kept of travels, job, and romances in Canada, California, Boston, and Dublin in the '70s, all of which I have attempted to link together by excerpts from letters and explanatory comments.

Many years ago, when Maura was in her late teens, an acquaintance commented to me on what an extraordinary girl she was. Although I don't often remember my own casual remarks, for some reason I recall my reply: "Yes," I said, "if I ever achieve recognition in this life it will be as Maura's mother." Now, as her literary executor, I find myself in the unenviable position of fulfilling my own prophecy.

—Ruth O'Halloran

I. Poetry

3/8/79 Boston

How dare you place my life beneath the microscope of yours?
Demand to know my plans, contemptuous of my dreams?
My diffuse career, my wasted talents
are my business and pleasure.
Insensitive to uncertainty's charms, you
Insist on an edifice of definitions and destinations
And time gnaws at all edifices.
They tumble
And only the bramble blowing tossed
    free in the wind remains intact.
I do not lead my life, but gently,
By the hand, whispering sweet tales
It leads me.

3/11/79 Boston

They're soon to be married
It's a meaningful relationship
It seems like the thing to do
It's for the folks
We have so much to give each other
We'll both keep growing
Saprophytes, constrained to a life-sucking life,
By mutual consent
Should I say congratulations?

Two wanderers

Pursuing places
Faced back to back
Explored each other's roots
Missing each other.

He, with his pressing

past and future.
She, left holding
Only her
present
was somehow poorer for his gift.

Now returned to her world

Of insurmountable separations
Weaving once again
Through minds and bodies,
Weary of every meeting's
Inherent gap
Resentful of this parting's
Imposed gulf
sighed through all of her places
that he had no time to touch
but deeply moved, *(unfinished)*

3/23/79 Boston

Pushing prams in the park's sunshine
Round and round in monotonous meanderings,
Slowly past perfumed daffodils,
Faster past wino dreaming,
Dwelling idly on the price of milk
Cooing at each other's goslings
The women grow older.
Proudly rocking her son and heir
She winces for the somewhere mother
Of that world-weary frame.
He cradles the bottle in blissful oblivion.
"Such a waste"
They cluck.
"A life of emptiness"
He lived a life of abandon
Knew the joy of surrender to a
Something greater than himself.
Was strong enough to release
Dared to relinquish self
To drain, yes empty, into
Wastedness.
The matrons circled once again
Paused from pity
The brakes of pity that filled their vacuums of passion
Never having been an experience
Never having known what it is not to know
But to feel, and be
Without subject or object,
Feeler feeling felt
Without feelings
How could they but pity.
Blessed are the pitied.

"His life had lost all meaning"
They affirm
"He's killing himself"
In their meaningful words
They cannot even kill
But slowly
Merely
Passively
Are dying.

3/28/79 Boston

Awareness awoke
arose rosy
circled the world and set
knowledge knew
it slept
while the world circled
it,
til it set.

Wisdom was
motionless
in the stationary
understanding
it saw neither
rising nor setting
but the
movements of a
mirage.

1980 Tokyo

Mu
My skin is raw from the biting cold
My skin burns from my tears' salt
It drops onto my chest
Runs wet down my breast
I think
Nothingness

1980 Tokyo

My blood drips icicles
I stand in early morning's winter sun
it kisses tenderly
my naked
feet.

Untitled

'Cigarillos, cigarillos.'
Little boy his jumper torn, shoulders hunched against the cold calls in
the darkness.
Unfeeling streetlight reflects on the drips of his nose
Cigarillos in a dirty battered box clenched
In wind-stiffened dirty battered hands
Little bent shape pleads at café doors
'Cigarillos, por favor.'
Grey jacket stretched across bulging belly
puckers around the straining button
Silver siding on black briefcase glistens.
With customary tightness his elbow clenches
the evening news.
'Cigarillos, señor?' The ripples of fat
momentarily tense as newspaper, like flyswatter
strikes the ever bending head.

Untitled

I sat alone with the dawn
Preparing the tea
On a kerosene stove
I sat in the shelter
Inside the alcove
Black arc through the raw grey

I awaited my spirits.

She came from the right.
I knew her
It was Cathleen
Black shawl hooded fair face
Stony feet felt no cold
A stride of graced determination
She sat beside me
A smile's ghost acknowledged me.
She accepted tea

I basked in the warming glow of her strength
Watched her firm grip position the mug at stove's edge
Every movement consciously concluded.
She stared, piningly, peacefully, to sea.

1980 Tokyo

In the bamboo grove
Sun and sounds filter in lacy patterns
   Crow cries, brook burblings
   and in the distance the low sweet rumble
   of the
   trucks.

   Was the world always this
   Perfect
   Or did I just never notice
   Before?

   I feel a love
   pulsating
   in the air.
   Why so blind?

   He said
   "I have no time."
   She whisper-smiled
   "But my dear we're
   waltzing through the corridors of
   eternity."

   Gentle breeze
   changes
   to blustering wind
   while I search for
   the Divine Mover.

   Line for dok'san
   Acid stench of stale piss

wafting on a wind
Merciless floorboards gnawing into my bones
    I only shuddering
    shuddering
    shuddering.

Mind, as full as the sky is empty.
Show me the evil man and
I'll show you a mirror.

At last I found
My teacher.

        It was myself
Understood the doctrine
there is
noself.

Your love has petrified
And melted.
I'm sorry
The sun still makes its
Morning climb
coaxed by the callous calling
of dawn's creatures
unheeding of my desolation
the broom and heather still
smell sweetly of
sticky childhood summer
afternoons, licking
toffee

MAURA IN HER FIRST COMMUNION DRESS,
MAY 13, 1962.

II. Her mother's recollection of Maura's childhood and youth

I am sometimes asked whether I recall anything in my daughter Maura's childhood that would give any hint she might one day be regarded as a bodhisattva in Japan. This is an extraordinary question, because in our Catholic Irish-American household I don't ever recall having heard the word "bodhisattva," let along foreseeing such an unlikely and premature form of immortality for our eldest child.

"Bodhisattva" is an ancient Indian word meaning "enlightened" (bodhi) "being" (sattva), so in theory there are as many bodhisattvas as there are enlightened beings. After this life, according to Buddhist belief, the bodhisattva chooses to defer from *nirvana* [liberation from all suffering] in order to help all sentient beings achieve enlightenment. Thus the distinguishing characteristic of the bodhisattva is compassion, a quality that the Buddha instructed all his followers to cultivate.

In the Buddhist tradition, compassion is often portrayed by a Kannon bodhisattva statue, a female figure wearing a long kimono-like garment that extends down to the large lotus blossom on which she stands. This representation of compassion is as familiar a feature of Buddhist homes and shrines as a statue of Mary would be among Catholics, and is regarded with similar reverence.

In April 1983, with my son Scott, I was invited to attended the unveiling of a Kannon bodhisattva statue dedicated to the memory of my daughter. With Roshi Tetsugyu Ban and his wife as our hosts, we attended the unveiling ceremony and the reception that followed. Here many of Maura's old acquaintances had gathered to meet us and talk about her, a profoundly moving experience for me. All the guests spoke of her industriousness and intelligence, but in particular of her compassion. I believe it is for this quality that she is remembered and for this reason that pilgrims still visit her shrine.

Did I see this special quality in the young Maura? A home movie taken the day we brought baby Kate to our Wellesley house shows two-year-old Maura rushing to shower the newcomer with all her favorite toys. Though in every way a normal child, her concern for her parents and younger siblings seems to me to have been unusual in someone so young. She had just turned fourteen when she came wholeheartedly to my support in the early days of my widowhood. I would say that generosity and a loving disposition were her outstanding characteristics as a child, characteristics that grew more pronounced as she practiced meditation in Japan.

Recalling her childhood in the Boston area, I see her assuming a motherly role, running errands or keeping an eye on the newest baby.

When she was 14, she was flung into the grownup world for good when I woke her up on a July morning in 1969 to tell her that her father had been killed in an accident the previous night. Her first reaction was to look at me in horror, saying, "Mom, that means you're a widow!" Her sympathetic reaction did not even consider the likelihood of a much reduced lifestyle.

Indeed, a reduced income was one of several reasons for our decision to return the following year to Ireland, a project which I could not have undertaken without Maura's energetic help.

In the summer of 1971, aged 16, Maura worked as an au pair in France.

After Maura's return to Ireland in September, Madame wrote to me to say she was *"tres heureuse"* ["very happy"] with Maura and hoped she would return next summer. However, seeking a change the following summer, Maura took a similar job in Belgium, coming home genuinely fluent in French.

Soon after school began again, Maura (now aged 17) with her sister Kate (aged 15) took the bus in town to attend a performance of "The Playboy of the Western World" at the Abbey Theater. The so-called "Troubles" in Northern Ireland had not yet reached Dublin at this time so we

MAURA IN HER EARLY TEENS.

were stunned to hear in our suburban home the sound of explosions as three terrorist bombs went off in the center of Dublin beside the Abbey Theater. The entire theater shook and the frightened audience, including the two girls, hurried out into the street. There they found all phones disabled and transportation suspended. Seeing no alternative, they proceeded to pick their way over fire hoses and through debris for the long walk home. Meanwhile, we waited helplessly, unable to approach the scene and not knowing where the girls could be. I needn't have worried. About an hour later the two bedraggled youngsters came trudging up the street, apparently no worse for their experience. Looking back, I regard this incident as an indication of Maura's early ability to face a crisis calmly and to take prompt and appropriate action.

Her own account of her youth lists her school interests and accomplishments, including early acceptance at Trinity College. Given her facility at mathematics it is perhaps not suprising that she thought of becoming an actuary, a career so unusual in pre-feminist Ireland that the local newspaper sent a reporter to interview her. However, the leftist leanings bred by her college studies in mathematical statistics and economics soon effaced any such potentially profitable ambition.

A last gesture of conformity to the social customs of middle-class Ireland was her debut with her Mt. Anville classmates at Dublin's Shelbourne Hotel. This elegant event—the girls all wearing long white dresses—now seems almost unreal to me in the light of her later rejection of so many conventions she had once accepted. The next four years, 1973 to 1977, which she spent at the University of Dublin, Trinity College, molded the liberated young woman that her later journals and letters reveal.

College Years

She smiled at the jagged circle. She was 18, sitting in Mulligan's with Paul Mulligan and Tony. Mulligan's had the best pint in Dublin. They sat around a great wooden table, savoring the great black stuff. The yellowing walls seemed to breathe the smoke. The pub was full of old men with drawn-down caps, buying rounds, casually leaning on one another's shoulders, punctuating arguments by the slight spilling of the pint—a lance of foaming liquid curling across the wrinkled boot, its only polishing. Students of pseudo-proletarian leanings huddled in their groups, philosophizing or trying to escape it.

They formed one such group. Paul considered himself socialist. He has since tried to establish his own little enterprise. To her socialism was only corporate capitalism. She wanted no part of it. She was much more concerned with her own development. Liberation cannot be imposed; there can only be personal liberation. She was caught in the debate of whether a school was necessary or not—and did nothing. It is easy to do nothing but she knew she must do something. "We can 'do' nothing; we are only capable of reacting. I am reacting to my recent reading. Read again tomorrow and you will react yet again." Three years of traveling outside to arrive at the same place inside.

The few sentences above appear to be the only surviving sentences that

Maura wrote about her college days. Her remaining college papers, entrusted to a friend for safekeeping, have disappeared.

Even while attending college from home, she became involved in student and extracurricular activities. During her first weeks at Trinity College, Dublin (TCD) she joined a student protest against higher tuition fees. I remember gazing in horror at the front page of the *Irish Times,* where she could be easily recognized charging up the steps of the administration building, intent on achieving justice for her fellow students—but risking her future status with the powers that be.

In 1974, still living with us but hoping to spare me further tuition expenses, Maura set her sights on earning a scholarship. A very comprehensive "Foundation" scholarship is granted by Trinity College to its most gifted students. To qualify for this she formed the habit of retiring for the night after our evening meal, then rising at 3 A.M. to study intensively when our busy household with all its noisy children, guests, pets, and repair projects was finally quiet. I find it significant that her habit of going off by herself to meditate began at this stressful time.

When her success in the exam was announced in May 1975, we were all ecstatic. I considered it the proudest day of my life—though I half-feared she would disgrace us all by wearing her usual tattered garments to the formal presentation. In fact she looked quite presentable in a long white dress seated beside Provost F. S. L. Lyons in the group photo taken at the "Scholars of the Decade" dinner.

Despite the exception she made for this one occasion, her generally disdainful attitude toward fashionable clothes and possessions may be seen in the following incident. Soon after being awarded her prestigious scholarship, Maura, who nearly always wore skirts in preference to pants, was waiting at a bus stop when an unknown student approached her.

"Aren't you Maura O'Halloran, the scholar?" he asked.

Flattered to have her celebrity status recognized, Maura replied, "I am, but how did you know me?"

"By your unmatched socks," he said. "Everyone on campus knows that."

She, thoroughly chuffed, rushed home to announce to us her real claim to fame.

However one incident should have given me a hint of the direction in which her thinking was taking her at this time. To celebrate her getting the "Scol," Maura and I took a bus tour through Italy in September 1975. Stopping in Assissi, we had just come out of St. Francis' Basilica when she announced, "I'd like to stay right here and meditate."

T.C.D. SCHOLARS OF THE DECADE
TRINITY MONDAY, 19TH MAY, 1975

MAURA APPEARS IN A WHITE DRESS,
CENTER-LEFT OF FRONT ROW. MAY 19, 1975.

In fact, the Franciscan attitude toward material possessions seemed close to her own voluntary poverty. So reluctant was she to become the owner of any real property that she immediately gave a legacy she received at this time to her younger siblings to help pay for their education. I have often conjectured over the intervening years that if I had encouraged her to follow this impulse and stay in Assissi, her meditation would have remained within the Catholic tradition and she might not have taken her fatal trip to the Orient.

After touring Italy, a country she came to love, we returned to Dublin, where she moved into the sunny suite of rooms overlooking the college quadrangle, which were provided by her scholarship. Here she entertained her many friends for vegetarian meals—though fasting herself every Tuesday—and exasperated the college groundskeepers with her habit of putting food on her windowsill for any passing bird. Even those messy pariahs of the feathered world, seagulls and pigeons, were welcomed.

During her college vacations Maura either took a job, as she did the summer of 1973 for her uncle in Maine, or she traveled. In 1976 she came back freckled and broke after a month in Greece, Yugoslavia, Austria, Switzerland, and Eastern Germany.

She spent the summer of 1975 caring for troubled children at the Rudolf Steiner School at Glencraig in Northern Ireland. Aware that her grandmother in Maine might be concerned about her safety, Maura sent her the following soothing letter in an effort to paint as calm and normal a picture of her life in Northern Ireland as possible.

Dear Nana,

…I get up at 6:15 in the morning and then don't stop until around a quarter to nine at night, and from then to bedtime one is still on duty. I became a "dormitory mother" last week, which means that in addition to cooking, cleaning, and helping in class, I'm responsible for the dormitory.

The thing I really like about this place is that they become "my boys" in the sense that they and everyone else considers me to be the next best thing to the boys' real mother. Many of the children, though very young, might only see their parents a couple of times a year, so this kind of setup suits them.

It's really an ideal place—peaceful and quiet, overlooking the loch and surrounded by our own fields. We grow much of our own food here biodynamically and the handicapped adults work on the farm. It's wonderful for the children to be near the horses and cows and to take part in the other workshops. For example, in the class where I was helping this morning they are all making clay mugs, which will be fired and glazed in the pottery here. Other children help in the fields or have a lesson about chickens right down at the chicken coop. It's nice to have our own fresh eggs and milk, fruit, vegetables, etc. Then we make our own jams, juices, cream cheese, bread, and such things.

Mum is coming up to visit me on Thursday and it will be good to get news from home. One is so busy here one becomes immersed and everything else seems really remote...Keep well (and give Toby a pat for me).

Much love,

Maire

This visit presented me with two contrasting views of Northern Ireland: idyllic Glencraig but a much-changed Belfast. The peaceful city where I used to shop had become a tense scene with gun-wielding soldiers, barbed wire, and armored cars everywhere.

During her college years, Maura's various jobs and travels had increased her maturity and compassion, especially her concern for children. She had already demonstrated this at home with her younger siblings, by volunteer work at the local orphanage, and by doing *au pair* jobs in France and Belgium. The journals of her Latin American travels reveal this concern even more vividly as she became the honorary mother of street boys in Cuzco. Whatever type of social reform she might have chosen to undertake if she had returned to Ireland, I feel confident that it would have involved children—maybe her own, but certainly others.

In the early '70s, the "Troubles" in Northern Ireland burst over the borders into the Irish Republic. Car bombs exploded in Dublin's shopping streets. The British embassy, close to Trinity College, was burned down by furious mobs reacting to attacks on unarmed civil rights marches in Derry on "Bloody Sunday" in 1972. Trinity students had never remained aloof from local or national turmoil. In their pubs and lodgings the political and social problems of the time were hotly debated by Maura and her friends, often coming to the conclusion that only a social revolution could ever solve Ireland's problems.

It is not surprising that Maura became thoroughly politicized while studying in the TCD Department of Economics. Among her senior texts are listed such titles as *What Is Orthodox Marxism?*, *Political Power and Social Classes, The State in Capitalist Society, The Nature of Fascism, The Age of Imperialism, The State and Revolution* by Lenin, and many more in a similar vein. In spite of her statement above that "socialism was only corporate capitalism," she later calls herself a socialist. And given the depressed economy in Ireland in the '70s, this potential solution to the injustices of Irish society must have appealed to her at this period of her life.

The important point to keep in mind is that whatever Maura decided to do when she returned to Ireland from Japan, she was convinced that nothing could be accomplished until she first changed herself. After that she could see about changing the world. Her training in Zen meditation and her intention of teaching it in Dublin would, I believe, have been one of her contributions to a better society back home.

Her college classmate, Sean O'Suichru, agreed. Speaking of Maura on a radio broadcast for the fifteenth anniversary of her death, he said, "She had got to a major milestone in a massive learning process. I can't think of anybody that I know of or have read of who has done that amount of learning at her age and has done it so well…She was really going to do something and I'm really sorry she's not around to be here with us so we could see what she might have done."

The four years between 1973 when she matriculated at Trinity College and 1977 when she completed requirements for her honors degree were some of the most exciting and productive in her life. Without waiting for the November TCD conferral, Maura left Ireland in June of 1977 shortly after her outstanding results were announced. With several of her college friends she set off for the U.S. and Canada to try her hand at working in the "real world." The following letters and journals from Canada and California provide a lively guide to her development during her first year of independence.

III. Canada

Letters from Toronto

June 1977

Dear Mum,

So much has happened in such a short space of time that I can't believe it was only a week since I saw you. Let me try to describe all my adventures (nothing exciting) since first we arrived in New York. As I told you already, we stayed with Sean's friends' family. The mother was Irish, from Kells, and was going on Wednesday back to Ireland for the first time in 25 years, so she loved just sitting and talking about Ireland while drinking millions of cups of tea. She was the kind of woman with whom you just had to nod your head once in a while and she was content to chatter on.

Anyway, we decided to go to Philadelphia to buy the car as a guy from our class lives there and his uncle is a mechanic. We stayed there for a couple of nights. Hank's mother, called Max, is one of those New York Jewish mother types. She decided I was hiding my beauty under a bushel so to speak, and insisted on giving me an entire new wardrobe of clothes—about 4 or 5 times what I had already brought over. Well, needless to say, I couldn't use so many clothes so I gave most of them to Goodwill and kept a few. We had a very enjoyable few days there, as we really got on extremely well with Hank's folks. Anyhow, his uncle bought the car for us—a beautiful blue Belair Chevrolet. It turned out insurance-wise [Maura was the only one in the group who was an American citizen] to be cheaper to have the whole thing in my name. I had to laugh to think that I'm the legal owner of two cars and yet I'm scared to drive two blocks. (That's a nice bit of Americanese, isn't it?)

We got our blue beauty out on the highway and within an hour it had a nervous breakdown. First one of the tires blew out and then, when we fixed that and tried to start the car, the battery was dead. The turnpike people gave us a new battery and from then on it went like a bomb, although for an awful hour or so I was afraid we had a dud. We drove up to Niagara Falls and, my God, was that an experience! First we went to what they call the American Falls and they had the best viewing spot all fenced off. We jumped over the fence and hid behind some bushes. Then we went over to the other Falls and went right down to underneath them. It was absolutely fantastic; I just couldn't tear myself away. I stood there for well over an hour, absolutely hypnotized.

As you probably know by now (I presume Nina's parents will have rung you) I'm safe and sound in Toronto. Sean and Phelim have gone looking for tobacco jobs but I think I'll try around here first. Nina's living in what's called a co-op, i.e., several young people rent a house, each having their own room, but share living room and kitchen. There is a room coming vacant here and I think I may be allowed to move in. Unfortunately, this is the long weekend and I haven't been able to go job-hunting but I'll start as soon as the weekend's over. I'm afraid you won't get this letter for ages. Nina says it takes about ten days.

She has been really good to me since I've come. We went all over the markets nearby. I really enjoyed the markets—you'd never think you were in North America. This city is a real melting pot, loads of Caucasians, Caribbeans, Jamaicans, etc. You know how such mixtures can often be a bit sinister—not so here. The people are really integrated. The market was all full of different fruits and vegetables, thousands of grains, beans, dried fruits and nuts, many that I'd never seen before. Eggs were sold from the chickens that laid them before your very eyes. Nina and I went in to buy two lemons in one shop and they insisted on giving us two crabs for free as well.

The little shops were full of tanned, smiling foreign faces and reminded me more of Corfu than North America. They even had cheese shops that sold nothing but cheese, which they let you sample ad infinitum, until you were satisfied. It was a great way to shop—joking with the merchants and faced with loads of selection. There's quite a cosmopolitan flavor to this part of the city. I know some people who live out in the suburbs, however, and I visited them and didn't care much for the area.

Yesterday we decided to go to the country—imagine, you have to drive nearly fifty miles to get to the country. We got nearly drowned in a thunderstorm, but once wet, actually enjoyed the rain and excitement.

Today is Tuesday. I decided to wait until after the long weekend to let you know how things went. It's only one o'clock and I've been offered the spare room in Nina's house, opened a bank account, and landed three jobs (in the space of an hour!), with the option of a fourth job starting tonight that involves selling paintings door to door. How's that for organization? The room in Nina's place is a real bargain, though by Irish standards $82 per month is a lot. It does, however, include all utilities and phone. My address is 277 Richmond St., West, Toronto. The only trouble with the jobs is sooner or later they'll want a social security number. Eoin told me before that I could use his, so I think I'll write and see if he meant it.

The people around here are very friendly. One of the people next door offered me a load of his plants if I stay in Richmond Street, and would you believe, I've already been asked out to dinner. We went to a lovely Israeli restaurant where I tried out falafels. This town is an eating-out paradise. There's every kind of restaurant imaginable and a lot of them are extremely reasonable. I'm sitting in a park now relaxing after my job hunt. I hope everything's going well for you and for heaven's sake, don't worry about me. Besides having tons of common sense, I'm also very lucky. I hope you're not frantic by the time you get this. Nina says the post from Ireland to here is much quicker than vice-versa. She says the Canadian postal system is in a mess as they are going computerized. Take care and give me all the news of yourself, the kids, and my plants.

Tons of love and kisses to everybody,

Maire

Dear Everyone,

A week has gone by since last I wrote to yis and I wonder if you've even gotten that letter by now. As you can see, I'm now living next door to Nina until about the 24th of August, when I'll move back in there. It was a really nice stroke of luck for me—there was this Greek bloke living here at 275 and he had two of the best rooms in the house (he's an artist);

anyway, he was going on his holidays so he's letting me sublet his rooms for only $10 a week. They're beautiful rooms and full of nice art.

Nina got a job working at the same place as me. It's a jazz restaurant and also has a sidewalk café section. It's lovely on warm summer evenings and that way the boss isn't looking over one's shoulder either. The tips are good; we earn as much in tips as in wages.

I'm meeting a lot of interesting people—artists, dancers, actresses, sculptors, a costume designer, and various "thinkers." It's quite stimulating. Of course I don't get much time off. Last night I went to a dance demonstration at one of the universities. There were some absolutely excellent pieces. It varied from modern jazz to classical ballet. Then there was a party afterward for the cast and audience. Lucky that last night happened to have been my night off. I enjoy living next door to Nina and working with her. She's a great laugh and we've really been having fun. She's also been very useful for telling me which shops to get various things in. We get our main meal at work, so that cuts down on expenses a bit.

The day before yesterday, Nina and I went out to an island in Ontario Lake. It was a lovely sunny day and great to be able to walk to a ferry and go out on a beach. The water was not the healthiest looking. Pollution spreads over from Detroit. I'm enjoying myself here quite a lot. Things have worked out very well as regards job, place to live, nice people, and lots of laughs. I'm also managing to save a bit of money.

Needless to say, I miss you guys. Everyone over here has heard all about yis. Could you send me Jane's address? I seem to have lost it and also, if you got copies of those recent photos, I'd love to see them. Take care and do write. All I've had for news since I left was that much appreciated letter you wrote just after I parted. I'm sure there's been loads happening since then, so write.

Much hugs and kisses,
Maire

Dear Mum, Margy, Scott, and Wiggins [Beth],
Well, I'm sitting here indulging in sentimentality looking at my photo of you guys and wondering what you're up to. Did Margy get nursing? Jane,

how did you enjoy Belgium? I hope things are going well for you. I have a curious kitten on my lap who keeps attacking the pen (in case you are wondering about the writing). I'm very happy here. Things are going well...Did I tell you I'm working in a jazz club doing the outdoor patio section? I'm thinking of getting another part-time job as well, though I'm managing to while away any extra hours very pleasantly. Yesterday a few of us went to "the beaches" on Lake Ontario. It was a beautiful sunny day with a warm breeze. The water was a bit polluted but still looked lovely. It was great fun rolling down hills, paddling, and eating ice cream. (Mmm, lovely gunk!)

I've met loads of people over here. In fact my next night off is so booked out—a dancer I met has invited me to her house for dinner and two fellows I've gone out with have asked me out! One is an architect and sculptor. He made me a beautiful dinner today—chicken done up with loads of spices and vegetables, another mixture of onions, peppers, mushrooms, tomatoes, and—believe it or not—cooked cucumber, all in sauce, plus rice and beans and homemade corn bread, all washed down with lovely wine. And then I'm supposed to go to work! (In fact I got off work tonight. The boss rang up to say it was so quiet I needn't come in.) The other fellow I'm going out with is a physiologist, presently studying chiropractice. (Is that a word? It has something to do with the back.)

Nina and I are leading a very healthy life. We've been getting a swim in before breakfast (not every day) and unless we're late we walk nearly two miles to work. I love the job. The management are very nice. They can be a bit stingy but have decided that the Irish are great. I enjoy the customers, too. They're much better tippers over here. I can earn nearly as much as my wages on tips. We're never too busy so we get a chance to stop and chat and have a laugh with the customers.

I haven't a lot of news as things seem to have settled down for me, which is nice as it makes things seem homey—not that they could ever be as nice as home! I feel as if I should make up some bad news or you'll think I'm only writing the good bits, but quite honestly nothing has gone wrong. I'd love some nice pictures of you lot and also, if there's a copy of that gorgeous one of Dad, the one where he was working on the roads in America.

Did you know that Toronto has the highest structure in the world and the longest street in the world? They also must have the worst newspapers in the world. I'm getting no news. Is it possible to get a subscription of *Hibernia* when one is abroad? Anyway, take care of yourselves and scribble a line when you can.

Much love and kisses,

Maire

Dear Mum and all,

…Things continue to go well here. Last week was cool and rainy sometimes so business wasn't all that good at work. So I've gotten another job starting next Tuesday that's indoors and not dependent on the weather. I might keep up the old job part-time. I don't know yet. I like the old job. The management are from Gyana (how do you spell it?). They're stingy as hell but we still get on extremely well. They want me to work there all winter and do the inside. The new job is in a sort of Captain America's place. There's loads of young people as customers and college students working there. It's in a big emporium that sells loads of wicker work and plants. It makes me positively ogle. Anyhow, I'm really lucky to get the job as it's famous for being one of the best places in town for tips.

I'm sitting in the back yard now beside a huge pear tree. The sun is pouring down and I'm being piggy on halva. Did you have any in Greece? It's a candy of sesame and honey that we get in the market. You can get so many delicious and exotic things here—I love it. I'm having a lot of fun these days, going out a fair bit. There's lots of exotic restaurants and pubs with music, etc. I was lucky to move into a house like this for I've met lots of Canadians, though I've also made friends through work. Nina's and my exercise plan of swimming every day went a bit by the board (no pun intended) during the bad weather. We're still walking a lot…[more about meals, family, savings, etc.].

Hugs, etc.

M.

...I'm sitting at the moment in front of city hall on a bench by a fountain and pool, bathed in glorious Indian summer sunshine with music floating in the air. It's absolutely heavenly.

Things are still going well here, and while I won't be a millionaire I'm still saving...I left out a page of my last letter. In it I explained I was going to California with Nina's boyfriend (very trusting, isn't she? Hee, hee) around the 7th of Oct. We are probably going to spend a week or ten days going across Canada and down the West Coast. I'm dying to see the plains and the Rockies. That way I could also stop in Vancouver and see Cathy Cawley, Jim and Catherine, Barry Saunders, etc. Deirdre Casey, who was out there with Cathy, has been staying with me for the last three weeks. She came to Toronto for 2 days and loved it so she stayed. There's a friend of mine here trying to get me a job with CBC as a researcher on a documentary about the leftist movement in Europe. He reckons with my French, my sociology, and European background that I could be some help. That would be May or so. (There's a creep trying to chat me up, so I'm ignoring him and writing merrily away.)

I should tell you about some of the things I've been doing. I went to the Canadian National Exhibition here in Toronto. It was great fun. [sections of this letter are missing]

...We found a fountain where someone had put bubbles into the water, so we had great fun having a bubble fight and wading in the fountain. Anyway, a guy from the paper ended up coming and taking a load of photos of us. I also went up to the CN tower, the tallest observation deck in the world. It was a great thrill to look down and see everything so small. In fact we could even pick out my house and window. I've also been to a few good parties and lots of bands and things. One of the best parties was one we gave ourselves. We have a backyard with Nina's house, so the two houses gave a joint party. We put a tarpaulin up over a table that served as a bar. Then we put speakers out the windows. We built a bonfire out the back and had roasted corn and homemade pizza. It was really great fun. We also got out all the instruments in the two houses—guitars, a saxophone, a flute, etc.—and people just jammed a bit.

...What of Kate? Is she doing art at night? How does Miggins like the nursing? How did Jane find sixth year? And what of Scott and Ring?... Thanks for the photos and the *Irish Times*. It's great to see some real news. Everyone here was impressed by the standard of the newspaper. They also marveled at the beauty and handsomeness of the family (but then that was to be expected). Take good care of yourselves.

Much love,

M.

Journals of Toronto and Her Travels to California

Oct. 1977

So my stay in this city draws to a close. I sit in the house of C. I'm listening to the not-quite radio, drinking the too-tannin tea with goat's milk, from half the cups, from the tea caddy. It's a lovely, cozy, shabby house. A yellow bucket beneath the cold tap, blue beneath the hot, and everything in the sitting-room post-bath. It means a quarter hour for a cup of tea, a tin foil toaster, a brick iron, a mattress bouncing on our heads on Queen street, fruit boxes on the tram, and an eternity of laughing memories. (Posters and burlap, garbage and hydro men, wild dogs and wandering winos—I love it.)

It's been a materially beneficial time. I've never had so much money. A man is as rich as the paucity of his needs. Denying myself nothing, money just accumulates. Wealth has a very emotional import for me. It revolts and repulses me. I derive great pleasure as I sit here on a milk crate cuddling cheap tea in a plastic cup, but I can luxuriate in a velvet chair cradling cognac in a crystal snifter. Decadence delights me. I love the extremes. Middlingly comfortable elicits little in me. But intellectually I could not rationalize leading the life of the rich. Ha! Fat chance I'll have the option.

So materially I profited. I think I'm also gaining inner glimmers. I'm thought of as a nice girl. What a totally despicable creature is the nice girl. I'm glad I'm leaving all this messing behind. It dawned on me—I was running away from these situations. Why? At first I thought of my ego and vanity—that perhaps I wanted all the admiration and hence didn't discourage it. But I think I find it hard really to hurt someone.

Taking myself in hand I steeled. I phone S. and told him I didn't want to go out with him. I felt terrible—it was so difficult, his disappointment, not to hurt him would have been easier all around. Had I the right to do that? Yet I lied. I didn't, couldn't tell him that he didn't interest me or attract me. Then the H. fiasco. I would go out with him and explain where I stood. I couldn't get a word in. That night I could have explained but not now—I couldn't do it to him as I see the infatuated trust in his eyes. So I have seen the liar that lurks in my soul. But the lie is created for me. There is the assumption in the man-woman relationship of feelings that enter me rarely. I must respect a man—his spirit and his mind—but I must also enjoy his company. Otherwise my flirtation involves little emotional commitment. So the lie is always already ever present. I must in the future make myself clear. Though I tried with T., he couldn't have listened.

Oh, such seriousness. I feel like just going my way, following my intuitions. Why must they always involve a web of complications and emotions?

Chuckle, chuckle—the hydro man just called. Horror registered as he realized we had no heat, followed by veiled hints about the department of health. Oh, how soft these Canadians are!

I have learned a lot from the women I have met in Toronto. E. taught me about getting up and doing what you believe in. I must be more active in my life. I believe so firmly in my good fortune that I'm inclined to leave things to fate. N. and D. both taught me to be more assertive. Normally I say what I mean, but often I don't know what I mean. I can be too accommodating. Perhaps after meeting T., I may get involved in some kind of psychotherapy group. She certainly opened my mind much more to it.

Toronto was quite a sensual time. Many of my pleasantest memories were purely sensory—like being at the ex, wet, laughing, throwing bubbles into the air and colored lights, or walking along in the old Jewish part feeling the crisp and crunchiness of bright autumn, or the Kensington market, its smells and sounds, or the back steps bathed in the sun, and so on.

I met G. two days before I left. T. felt we should meet. He asked me not to put a hex on anyone as once I had been a witch. He played endlessly boring tapes of a man in a trance as we sipped herbal tea. He drew a very flattering picture of me and asked would I return the next day as he really wished to sketch my hair. I spent the next day with him. He was a psychic and could see my aura—red and orange on top surrounded by blue, going down to green. He said I wasn't just lucky but blessed and had a white spirit with me. He gave me a jacket from a lama in Tibet under the condition that I'd never give it away. As promised it was deceptively warm. At first he attracted me, but then he became too much, overwhelming me with compliments I couldn't believe about my spiritual and physical beauty. This is beginning to sound like an ego trip—I don't feel like writing about it.

My journey across Canada entailed the most beautiful sunset and the best egg salad sandwich of my life. P. gave us a lift to the highway and we got out of the car at around 10:30. The air was bright but chilly. We both felt tremendously excited and very free. We were ready for adventure, having been warned of the possibility of dying of exposure on the plains. The second car gave us a lift and we were off. We had excellent luck, never waiting, bringing us to Elloit Lake by teatime. It was beautiful there, all the tall orange trees. B. collected us and we returned to drink wine and eat spaghetti 'til all hours. Our last lift had said that if we were at the corner where he left us at 7:30 he'd give us a lift to Blind River. We arose early but were still hurrying. I asked some people going to work for a lift to the corner. They obliged and we waited quite a while for the other fellow. Then we decided to hitch. An old guy in a battered lorry picked us up. He was interesting, talking about democracy and ideology and how he's been brainwashed by the Nazis, the Eastern German communists, and the U.S. We got to the highway and he asked did we want breakfast. We weren't into speedy get-as-far-as-you-can hitching, so we accepted.

His house was simple. It smelt like country houses at home. He woke his wife and she gave us coffee and sat down to wake up with a cigarette. Then she produced a filling breakfast and we embarked on one of the most interesting discussions of my life. While they were still very anti-semitic, they were also extremely intelligent. Hence they didn't merely hate Jews but also sought theoretical backing. Interestingly, as sympathizers with a fascist regime, they had come to reject much of capitalism and its attendant state. He theorized that Newton's second law and the law of conservation of energy were in contradiction, something to do with equal action and reaction, force and resistance such that x=2x. Also he invented a frictionless wheel. Water being heavier than air it has down force on right and air upward on left. They were middle-aged but into self-sufficiency, she knitting and tending goats, he building. They were very fine and interesting people.

Back on the highway the sun was actually shining and both our heads were buzzing from their stimulation. We figure there's no way we'll get to Thunderbay but we're not stopping between Soo and Thunderbay for there lurk the infamous Wawa and Nipigon. A fat lusty American type brought us to the Soo. He told us a story, oft to be repeated when we were desperate for conversation, about field mice nesting on his carburetor. There we ate at McDonald's. It, the people, the food were totally synthetic and unsatisfying. Mr. McDonald's himself was there and our next lift was from Mr. Submarine, and can you believe it, he was going all the way to Thunderbay in a big, black VW van. He was a gentle bloke who obviously found conversation (and keeping wives) difficult. We wound our way up around Lake Superior, watched a beautiful sunset. The maples and silver birch gave way to fire. We had a snow flurry and in the dark the pines were laced with snowdust. It was as if the fairies had sprinkled it. One imagined the seasons to be competing, each showing its more alluring features—the incredible exploding fires of autumn, the delicate snows of winter, the warming sunshine of summer. We arrived in Thunderbay and stayed with slightly neurotic, very warm D. Next day, typically, we didn't get out on the road until afternoon. It was clear and crisp and too warm for jackets. Everyone had said we'd freeze but even the weather was with us.

The big lift of the day was our mad Arab. He spent the first five minutes explaining why he never picked up hitchhikers; then he said I could talk to him for five minutes; then he was playing some Eastern music. He proceeded to tell us about his thirteen-year-old daughter who had to be in bed by 7:00…He was old, would never say his name. We came to a beautiful village with boats in the harbor and the sun went down a violent sanguine color. The Arab said it showed the rage of the Indian for what the white man had done. He made it seem slightly sinister and very powerful. He took us through Winnipeg (where the wind in winter can kill) and on past Brandon…Out on the road again we found ourselves in the prairies, surrounded by flat dry silent infinity. We stumbled up to the nearest café for coffee and chattered for ages.

When we finally got around to hitching around one, there was hardly a car on the road, just wide empty highway. Our first lift was to our destination, Calgary. He wasn't a particularly interesting person, which was only appropriate to a journey across the prairies. It really was cowboy country. We stayed in Calgary with friends of S. and I met a friend from Dublin. They were very good to us. They lived a funny life of lots of money, more than they could spend, yet boyish wildness. They worked in the system, profited by it, yet had to live the contradiction of rejecting it. I had a beautiful day there. It was late afternoon and we were in an old-fashioned western-style town. No one else was there so our footsteps on the wooded paths rang out like a ghost town. I sat on a rock and looked over the lake at the Rockies, as the sun began its descent and I thought, Maire, what are you at? What was I doing when all that was perfect to do was sit on that rock? I stood at a corral with my hands on a fence. It was wrought wood and my hands felt tingly. I could feel every rise and fall of the grain. I could smell the horses, see the view, hear silence. I felt surrounded and engulfed. After a while I followed the others. I certainly didn't want to listen to P.'s silly chattering.

We left in the afternoon for Vancouver. They slagged us, "We'll see you back again tonight," for it was a fourteen-hour drive. Our first lift wound us into the Rockies. It was a young couple in a van. They were extremely interesting. The girl and I were just getting into a great rap about Findhorn when we had to leave. There we were in the quiet of the Rockies on a gloriously sunny day where they rose in white magnificence into a clear-blue sky. S. smoked a cigarette and I lay on the ground by the highway just looking up and breathing the freshness. We recommenced the impossible hitch and in no time got a lift straight into Vancouver. Our driver was an earthy, lively warm man. We had some good laughs though he was a bit put out when I began to nod off. We wound our way through the Rockies with me sometimes unable to speak for the beauty around me. We arrived too late to phone C. so we crashed in Queen Elizabeth Park, under a red maple. Next day the sun was warm and bright and played dancing games with the dew filagreed on the grass. C. had gone to school, so we spent the day in a Chineser and swinging in the park. C. gave us a sincerely warm welcome. She bought wine for the occasion and enjoined us to stay for a week. We relaxed, washed, and had food fun.

IV. Latin America

Maura had begun the study of Spanish while working in San Francisco and planned to travel through Latin America with friends she made there. When they dropped out at the last minute, Maura took off alone, making acquaintances as she went along.

The first item is an unpublished article she wrote soon after returning from her travels. This article is followed by transcripts of several letters and journals.

Appropriately, it was April Fools' Day [1978]. I was sitting in the [Boston] station, scared. In half an hour I was to start my five-day bus journey to Mexico City, very alone…Possibly nothing would happen. Then I reminded myself that if "the worst" happens but is not fatal then at least I'll live. If it is fatal then I would be beyond caring and I will have enjoyed myself going. I won't be eighty, rocking my chair to the rhythm of "if only."

So off I set. As I sat in the bus station I felt butterflies in my stomach. If Marie was there and we were going off together we'd be excited, laughing and delighted. So I realized that the butterflies were from my head. I pretended there was someone with me and I felt better. Then I went, bought my ticket, had a beer and felt like myself again. I caught the bus on a Wednesday and rode night and day 'til the following Sunday. The bus went through some lovely countryside. I especially loved Virginia around the Appalachians. All the dogwood was in blossom. In Tennessee we ran into a so-called Dogwood Festival. The town was covered in dogwood but it was all cardboard and plastic reproductions of the plant. There was one lovely dogwood surrounded by a tarmacadam parking lot. I went on to Dallas, then Alice, then Laredo.

The ticket-seller in Boston was Irish. He went to infinite trouble to arrange my connections so I wouldn't be hanging around bus stations at

248 ～ PURE HEART, ENLIGHTENED MIND

awkward hours. In the hospital they liked my accent and had given me
free shots and prescriptions. In NY, too, the station attendant was Irish
and took great care of me. I enjoyed the NY bus station; it was full of
characters and of paranoias. In the ladies room was a black woman with
the most hideous, tatty, reddish wig I'd ever seen. It looked as if she'd
scrubbed the floor with it before putting it on. With her was an old-
before-her-time woman sincerely admiring it. I had to refrain from
laughing as the former woman went on at some length about the process
and fittings involved in getting it.

As I traveled through southern Texas I kept thinking, "This must be
what Mexico is like, arid and run-down, full of lean-to shacks." I was soon
to realize fully the difference was one of culture rather than geographi-
cal setting. The Trailways bus was an anemic journey, an almost stereo-
typical American alienation; strangers rarely talked. The woman in front
of me consistently nagged her child, filling his head with morbid possibilities. "The bus might crash and you'd go through the window; don't
do that, you'll fall; sit down and keep quiet; don't wriggle so much."

Arriving in the Laredo terminal, I had ten minutes before departure
time. There was a little old lady scurrying back and forth with parcels
and suddenly I found myself with my rucksack, bag of books and food,
a huge sack of assorted rubbish and a trolley, tripping over another bag
of hers. Women were pushing and shoving parcels everywhere. I was
struggling to get my rucker up on the rack. Lupa, who would become
my neighbor, threw it up like a load of feathers. *Bueno, vamanos.* I had
to fill out papers at the border. When I came back I tried to figure out
which bus was which. Lupa hung out from the window, signaled me,
then came to fetch me. Customs men came on and ignored some of the
obvious merchandise. I can only imagine it was to elicit bribes later.
Lupa had been reading comics, but when the customs came on she
switched to a book about saints. She was caught. Immediately the bribe
appeared. She abandoned the holy book in disgust. They didn't find her
cigarettes behind my mochilla; I sat on her radio. After the inspection,
the money-exchangers and the girl with smuggled whiskey did their business. The driver stood outside the bus, looked at his watch, raised his eyes

to heaven and made the sign of the cross over the bus. I was all the time trying to resist the urge to laugh right out loud.

We were off. I entered another world. Everyone stood around on the bus chatting, the radio whined Latin lovesongs, children ran around the bus and I played hide and seek behind the curtains with Juan. How different from antiseptic Trailways! Lupa and the other ladies showed me dirty magazines they'd smuggled (deftly hidden from the men in the bus). They giggled with an honest sense of fun. We wound our way through the mountains which made striking silhouettes against a fiery sun. As we turned we were able to watch it set again and again. I felt very high.

I found a little hotel, then walked for a long time out to Chapultepec Park. Saw the anthropological museum. On the tube on the way back it was extremely crowded and several men tried to push up against me—these men seemed to be stuck in a really childish, kind of Peeping-Tom mentality. Mexico City itself would have been attractive were it not so overcrowded. I went out to Teotihuacan and climbed the Pyramid of the Sun. Their pyramids weren't hollow but extremely dense and were used only to hold up a tiny temple. They were built without the wheel or beast of burden. I could only wonder why and feel they must have had some knowledge, perhaps about energy polarization, that we didn't have.

When I finally had a shower it felt so good after five days that I was laughing with delight. But that made me realize how normally I must not be present when I shower. I bought a beer with lime and climbed into bed.

My Spanish was atrocious and I had a mild dose of culture shock. I decided to study Spanish for a week or two and get some kind of basis. So I arrived in charming Cuernavaca, full of flowers. They were very decent at the school, let me start immediately and waived the $50 registration fee. It was a pleasure to sit on a balcony in the warm, quiet air under a huge rubber tree for classes. The whole place, however, felt very much as if constructed for rich American kids. We went to Taxco and I had decided to go down to Oaxaca. Paco was giving a lecture on the subject. He was an anthropologist who had lived with the tribe for many years. His lecture was fascinating. Members of the tribe are the Sons of the Clouds and live high up in the mountains. They weave intricate red dresses, each one distinguishing a certain group. Property is held in common. Paco explained all about the religion, about how early children grow up. The Tribe are the only group actually diminishing in stature— malnutrition. I thought my questions must have interested him because he invited me to join him the next day for a chat. We met in a little open-air café by the plaza. He showed me all around the town and invited me out again. He insisted I should accompany the group free of the $60 charge. I was thrilled at the idea of going up among the Tribe. I felt glad to be traveling alone.

Most of Maura's letters and records of her experiences in Central America have been lost. In several Central American countries she got involved with local police or military in possibly misguided attempts to help the people she met there. In at least two cases a revolution erupted just as she was leaving the country!

...I made my way through Central America, picking up fragments of Spanish. In Colombia I met a plucky, penniless woman. We decided to hitchhike to Bogota together. Our first ride was with Umberto and Carlos. They were driving a scrap metal truck. It took four days to make the ten-hour journey to Barranquilla, four blissful days winding high among the wonders of the misty Colombian mountains. We'd sit atop the broken fenders and rusting bedheads, the wind in our hair, the sun in our faces. When it rained, all four of us sat in the cab of the truck. After hours of sitting with one hip precariously balanced on the gear stick, I soon knew every shudder of its shifting. Three times tires blew out. Umberto would sigh, sweat flowing across the arc of his swollen gut. Carlos' huge, brown eyes registered resignation, "Tranquilla, tranquilla," he cooed. He slung a hammock under the truck so we could rest in shade, then spoiled us with sweet, sticky mangoes.

In South America, a woman is whore or sister. They accepted us as sisters (with a little persuasion). We weren't allowed to pay for a meal or a hotel room. Even when we would try surreptitiously to pay, people refused our money. It was for gentlemen to pay!

We parted sadly. They were worried about our hitchhiking. They needn't have. Colombians continued to overextend themselves with generosity. They seemed almost to be trying consciously to disprove Colombia's reputation for thievery and assault. After misunderstanding directions, we elected—on the flip of a coin—to hike to our destination. We trekked for five days.

All along the way the mountain people welcomed us into their homes, fed us what little they had. We met a woman on the path with a basket of green baby parrots, kittens on each shoulder, and a puppy struggling to keep up with her stride. She and her husband lived in a windowless shack of mud and sticks perched tentatively on the side of a cliff overhanging a roaring river. They took us in. Their furniture consisted of one child-sized stool and a makeshift bed. They insisted that we use both in turn. They slept on an arrangement of planks so that we, the guests of honor, could rest in a bed.

Little wizened mountain men, who had seldom seen an unfamiliar face, fed us, extended welcome, proposed marriage, and guided us, leaping across stones, down the river bed. Families let us sleep with their children. They sent their children or menfolk to guide us where necessary. In places this involved hacking paths through the vegetation. Word spread ahead of us. "We expected you yesterday," said a stranger riding by. We were the first gringos to have passed that way. So strange did we seem that a little girl was brought just to see my exotic blue eyes. "Alone, how brave," they'd say. "Not alone," we'd say, "there's two of us." But there, to be without a man is always alone. They admired that.

My friend and I separated. Gradually, over the months of gaining confidence and understanding the culture, I found I could hitchhike alone. Nothing bad ever happened to me. A couple of times I was asked to leave a lift when I made it clear that I was not a prostitute. No one ever tried to force the issue. This is not to say that nasty incidents could not occur, only that they did not.

I felt a great freedom, the freedom of the road, of doing what I want, when I want, without being afraid. There was a surge of pleasure that comes from unconsciously putting your hands to your face and realizing that you are smiling and that a smile is now your natural expression.

People picked me up and brought me home or from concern or curiosity stopped to converse. Hospitality came from all quarters, from campesinos and truck drivers to hacienda owners. Each day was different—sleeping in a thorn bush, a cave, a park, a bus station, a marsh, an adobe hut, or tucked into linen sheets by one of the maids. I was wined and dined on course after course or ate a banquet on the back of a truck or made do with a bit of stale bread.

As a woman traveling alone, with few funds, one is invariably cast into a role. In Latin America people feel either the urge to protect you or to degrade you, depending on their conception of you. Occasionally you are treated with respectful awe either as a witch or a gypsy. There is little choice regarding the culture's definition of the unaccompanied woman. Nonetheless, it does give one access to a world that is never so available to other travelers. Once accepted, you will be invited to meet children, grandmothers, and the village. Doors are constantly opened to you that are less often open to the seemingly self-sufficient couple or potentially threatening single male.

People, in introducing me, often said, "She looked so alone that we had to bring her home." What had seemed to be a disadvantage, to be a lone woman, was in fact a decided advantage. No one is afraid of you. Now, to be accompanied by a man no longer seems such an unmixed blessing; he may be an actual drawback. My fears were my real enemy. The imagination is much richer and crueler than reality. To travel alone in South America is not difficult. To sit in the States and seriously contemplate traveling alone is the first and greatest difficulty.

Mexico
May 1979
Dear Mum and Jane,
Felicidades [birthday greetings], I bought hideous cards for you but I

can't find them at present so this is all you get. We're in Oaxaca at the moment, soon leaving for Guatemala. I've picked up survival Spanish and am managing okay. This visit to Oaxaca has been incredible. As I told you, we went with the anthropologist and some of the students at the school. We saw things we could never possibly have seen otherwise. We visited the Trike Indians who live high up in the mountains where it's very green and misty. It was market day in the village we visited. Trikes had gathered from all the neighboring villages. They were all dressed in magnificent woven red wraps. They were very gentle and quiet. There were over three thousand of them there, but if you closed your eyes it seemed like maybe half a dozen. They're a very small people (declining in stature due to malnutrition), but I don't know when I've seen so many beautiful faces all together. We went to the school in the village. Their teacher is really gifted—you should have seen all the children standing at their seats trying to learn Spanish when they still can't even read.

Paco (the anthropologist) took us around to all sorts of markets and craft centers and to visit friends of his in the countryside. We saw an old woman of ninety years, Dona Rosa, demonstrate for us how to make the black pottery of this area. She's quite famous and has won awards, including free air travel anywhere! She didn't even use a pottery wheel but two curved plates, back to back. I found it really touching to see her skinny frail arms working the clay so expertly. She knelt on a little woven mat, held her hair back with a twist of her shawl and worked away in total silence, scarcely even needing to look at her pot. She's been doing it since the age of ten.

We went to see the ruins and pyramids of the Zapotec and Mixtec Indians and to lots of museums. In fact I even saw the widest tree in the world—over 2,000 years old.

Well, I'm sitting right now in a little restaurant eating delicious guacamole and still-warm tortillas. From the corner of the door I can see the market where the women are seated doing their backstrap weaving. Everything is bathed in sunshine.

Paco has been really helpful. He has given us addresses for along our route and insists that we call him collect if we have any problems along the way. Can you imagine my embarrassment when, saying "goodbye," I called him Pablo instead of Paco. Oh, well, even in Spanish (should I say especially in Spanish?) I can put my foot in it.

The students in our group were great fun. We made some life-long friends and if half the people who promised to come and visit me in Ireland do so, we'll have to hang out a bed and breakfast sign. We're going to Guatemala via San Cristobal. It's one of those situations where we all know it's famous for something, but we can't remember what. I hope there's a letter in Guatemala from you lot—I'm dying for some news. It's going to be strange having my birthday so far away from home. I'll never forget last year when you all came trooping into the Buttery [at Trinity College, Dublin] armed with Chinese food. I suppose it won't do me any good to go around getting all nostalgic…

I must tell you how amazing one of the ruins was. Using only instruments of stone and wood, these Indians could tell not just the seasons, solstices, and equinoxes, but could predict eclipses and constellations. I crawled through a dark, three-foot-high tunnel between the ruins. Pretty creepy. I didn't intend to go through but just kept wanting to peek around the next corner.

Once again, happy, happy birthdays,

Much love,
Maire

V. Maura's Boston Year [Most of 1979]

Maura was prolific as a letter-writer during this very fleeting chapter of her life. The bulk of her Boston-era communications are highly personal, and are largely infused with references to friends, places, and events for which we have no context. Instead, we present here a summary of the period, which was of just under a year.

It was for Maura an interim period, between travels in South America and her move to Japan. She was saving money for her trip and enjoying a bohemian lifestyle. Her sister Beth remembers visiting her in her one-room apartment in downtown Boston, which was over an antique jewelry store. The building had one of those ancient elevators with a metal sliding grate as a door. Her room was furnished with only a mattress, which she had rescued from a Dumpster. Beth remembers restless nights, as the place was home to an ant colony. But the building was full of artists, dancers, and writers, and Maura thrived on the stimulating company and rooftop parties.

There are many references in her letters to difficulties with the management of the restaurant where she worked, and a disappointment at the lack of result at an attempt to start a union to protect the staff. It was at this time that Maura started to mention her interest in a "personal revolution" as a method of bringing about change rather than solely through group socialist action.

She followed her time in Boston with a solitary and meditative stay in rural Wayne, Maine.

VI. Maine

The following notes were written by Maura at age 24 during the last four weeks before her departure for her new life in Japan. The three years she spent in Japan introduced a greater element of introspection and discipline into her life. This led to a maturity at 27 that is not yet evident in the following self-portrait at 24.

In the last year of her life, her beliefs, especially with regard to politics, mellowed considerably. In fact, there is almost no reference to politics in her Japanese journals, let alone to revolution. Her religious view underwent a similar mellowing. Although she became deeply immersed in the Zen tradition of Buddhism, she clearly came to regard it not as a religion, but as a highly effective way to achieve enlightenment.

Maura O'Halloran was undoubtedly a profoundly changed person by 1982, but this glimpse of her in 1979 gives some hint of what she was to become.

Wayne, Maine
September 1979
I sit down on the banks of Pocassett Lake to ask myself all the questions I find so objectionable when asked by someone else—the future-past-meaning-direction questions. And they seem so irrelevant. The water is making its eternal lick, lick, the sun turning soft on the breeze, stroking the end of yet another day. This year's sweet-smelling pine needles drift down to join last year's. I return to the woods of my childhood where my mother wandered enrapt—a side of her I always loved though she scarcely shows it now…

Yesterday everything was clear. The future stretched with tangible clarity, incorporating pleasures and passions. She glanced benevolently across her shoulder at her past, smiled benignly on the course of her present grapplings and allowed this to be planned. She passed a euphoric day, a day sweet in satisfaction. She would go to the Orient, work (humbly, of course) in a monastery, learning a way with which she could return, armed, to the world. Then she would go to Paris, write her brilliant and monumental thesis. Already her mind was excited, churning the variables to be explored (as the front of this notebook attests). So stimulated was she that the next year before her research could begin seemed almost a pointless delay. Then from Paris, where of course she diligently continued meditating, she would finally return to her homeland.

Back in Ireland she would build herself a small cottage in the country, but near enough to Dublin to go there each weekend for political and social activities. She would dedicate herself to the social revolution, while keeping time for her reading, writing, meditation, and photography. (So talented she could have been a "photographer" but so committed to higher ideals that she didn't.) Last night, falling asleep, she planned her home—where she'd put a desk, what flowers to plant, where to hang window-boxes, position windows, wiring, even what pattern she'd like the cups to be. The future was comfortingly, promisingly, clear and satisfying.

This morning she arose early, conscientiously. She phoned her mother, arranged flowers, tidied the house as she would her own little nest, then smugly strolled down to the lake. The sun had the come-home warmth of fresh baked bread. The breeze was strong and playful, boisterously trying to steer the boat.

She stared at the mental screen she had so finely tuned, the vivid, pleasing picture of her future. "What do you want?" the technician on the screen asked. Do you want that jumble of voices? There always was some interference on the set, an annoying jangle, a fading in and out of pictures. But a moment ago it had been so clear, no interference, no background humming and so much more attractive than the gloomy squiggles now before her. You can suffer, the figure said, work with me, work hard and we can change the tuning of your machine. You can control it. You can make your peace permanent or you can continue as before, confused by the voices, distracted by the commercials, the fuzziness and jumping of the screen (your moods), but you cannot do it alone. You will grow frustrated, settle for the rattling. There are other technicians—some are good, some are ignorant, some are deceitful. What do you wish to do? Your vision has already been disturbed. You know there are other possibilities. Can you ever be content again?

One small voice within her assented. Another joined and yet another. Soon there was a cacophony of voices, some agreeing, others loudly dissenting. Some wanted their peace; things were adequate, even pleasant before; some doubted her ability to work, one questioned him. She clapped her hands to her ears. She was drowning in voices. It proved his point. She could not stand it. About to commit herself, the program changed. It was only a commercial. Should she dismiss the whole notion, change the channel and try in her own bumbling way to get a good picture? Watch another show, read another book, be consumed once again, fixated by yet another picture?

Her peace could always be merely tenuous. What to do? The voices rose again—some selfish, some calling her to work for others: "You cannot mend another's machine until you control your own. You should struggle, not with individual machines, but in the factory where defective ones are produced. If you can improve even one small mechanism, you have helped." She tried to mollify the voices. I will look for a technician tomorrow. Sleep a while yet.

In her heart she knew this was not satisfactory. She would go to Paris in a year to pursue her studies. It was still a postponement but gave her time to accustom herself to the thought of spending some time in uncomfortable squinting and trying to concentrate through all the contradictory chattering and clamoring of the voices.

It would doubtless call for a reassessment of her work. Some of the more esoteric lines of research would probably be more compatible— the concept of time in language and how it relates to religion, a dialectic reconceived on the notion of three forces. She wanted to write and research on the notion of revolution in the 20th century with a view to pursuing such a course. This they would say was a part of her personality, assumed, taken from others. That was true. But one must fight against a system structured on and perpetuating injustice. She could already hear their laughter, already felt indignant, already felt a real problem of her involvement. In Paris I can study and draw my own conclusions. My future can't be on the screen but in the outcome. I will be produced.

VII. Maura's unfinished novel, 1982

It was dusk when she first arrived. She walked from the station through the village to the outskirts where the temple lay. With each step closer, the urge to turn and run became greater. Alone. She knew not a living soul in this land of inscrutable Orientals, not a word of the language that could somehow breach the barrier and establish humanity as a bond.

The stone steps were steep. She had to stoop her gaijin head to pass through the entrance. This humbling posture robbed her of her little remaining confidence. The temple was perfectly silent, self-contained, awesome. She stood still just inside the gate, too still even to tremble. She clutched her small bundle of possessions closer, staring, locking her arms around this one token of familiarity in an unknown world. A dim light flickered on. She supposed she should head for it since the other buildings were in darkness. Yet her feet did not move. She began to shiver in the evening chill, gulped and marched quickly forwards. She stumbled and her bundle rolled from her arms. She gasped a muffled scream and tried not to cry.

Eventually she reached the light and entered a dim room. "I'm Annie Shaw, Annie Shaw," she pronounced it clearly, as if it would somehow add information that her freckled Scottish face withheld. "I'm expected." The little monk didn't wait for that. He was already flinging papers about, shuffling and muttering in excited Japanese. His black pajama-like robes flapped around him as he searched under the desk and on top of shelves. He looked comical. "Penguin on a hot tin roof," she thought and, repressing a giggle, felt much relieved. "Ah, atta, atta, atta!" he shouted triumphantly and banged a paper on the desk before her. There, penned in a childish scrawl, was "Please come this way." He peered at it, strained to pronounce it. "Pleezu kumu deesu waiyu." He was off, waving the paper before her nose like a carrot before a donkey, and making gestures that to a Westerner looked like "go away" but obviously meant "follow me."

Stumbling down the narrow dark maze, she felt like Alice chasing the Mad Hatter, he still shuffling and mumbling, "pleezu kumu deesu waiyu." Ducking around yet another invisible corner, he braked. After pulling and straining at a door swollen in its tracks, he slid it open to reveal her room.

This little monk, Hogen, was proud. He had cleaned the room himself in anticipation of the lady gaijin. He had scoured the temple to find a spare desk with legs aligned and had chosen the prettiest cushion cover he could find. It was floral, huge magenta roses. He was delighted to discover it. Everyone knows Europeans love roses. He found the light. With a majestic sweep of his arm as if displaying the palace to the queen, he ushered her into her new abode.

"Oh my God." The bundle nearly tumbled from her arms. The single dingy bulb cast sinister shadows. "It hasn't even a window and it's only four mats wide. I can't stretch my legs out across it." She wanted to collapse into an armchair, or onto a bed, but there was only a hideous magenta cushion and a Spartan plywood desk. She thanked him.

He watched her reactions, her pause as her eyes dwelt on the gaudy cushion. Oh, she likes it! How wonderful! A European lady right here, here in Shodoji—incredible. The dinner bell sounded, and before the full horror of it engulfed her, Hogen was whisking her back into the black of the temple labyrinth.

He was running, scurrying, oblivious to the gloom. "How can he possibly see," she wondered, bumping the wall yet again. "He's just like a bat—yes, quite batty," and she smiled at her bravely pathetic attempt at humor.

Hogen led her to a large bare room. At one end, as if huddling from the cold, stood four wooden benches. Against the wall were piled four more identical benches, no other furniture. Two monks were watching her shyly. "How are yoo?" "You berry welcome," they tittered. The sound of clappers. Their faces were transformed as they grabbed their oryoki. Hogen gave her a similar parcel. He was distressed that he hadn't time to show her the procedure before the meal, but indicated that she must imitate him. They stood to attention, lined up around the benches, the oryoki balanced at eye level on the thumb and first three fingers of both hands. A bell. The master entered. He bowed. They bowed. More ringing and clapping of sticks. They sat and unwrapped their parcels in inhuman quiet. Two bowls, a tiny side plate, a pair of chopsticks, and a cloth square were all wrapped in another square like an Oriental version of the mess kit she used to use in Girl Guides. She unstacked the bowls. The words "Oto sasanaide" ["Don't make noise."] were roared into the quiet. With a blush of confusion Annie realized they were directed at her but had no idea of what they meant.

Hogen demonstrated how to place the bowls so that contact with the bare wood of the bench made no noise. The formalities involved in just passing one's bowls for rice and soup seemed insurmountable. The order was fixed, the bowls were specified, three fingers, the right hand, wipe before passing, on to the palm, gassho [Gesture pressing one's palms together, fingers upright, a hand's width from the face, expressing deep respect. This gesture is made frequently in Buddhist temples, often accompanied by a bow.], soup on the right, rice on the left, chopsticks point towards you, make an offering, seven grains of rice. Wait for the clackers. And they were off. Yes, it's Roshi at the front, Hogen coming up to his rear, Kindo bravely forging on. She was incredulous. They were guzzling their food with the frenzy of savages, yet making not a sound except for a stray chopstick accidentally grazing a tooth.

She chewed her rice thoroughly, methodically, yes, she told herself, even meditatively. She had expected them to eat as if seeking to become one with each grain, to exalt the physical exercise to a metaphysical one, dissolving subject and object with saliva, to chew the universe and swallow the cosmos.

Looking to Hogen for reassurance, she picked up her side plate with its little mound of brown slime. Greasy, oozy, it tasted as lethal as it looked. In the chilly gloom of the room where she could barely discern the mist of their breath, they were devouring it greedily. She had been faring reasonably well with her chopsticks up to that point. Perhaps it was an unconscious reaction to her conscious revulsion, but the viscous mess slid relentlessly round her plate, resisting every attempt to be scooped, speared, or even genteelly slid.

They were pouring water into the roshi's bowl. He was swabbing the bowl deftly with a limp yellow slice of some unidentifiable vegetable. From the corner of her eyes she could see them all variously filling their bowls, pouring, passing the hot water. Hogen was urging her to finish, yet still the mound escaped her, dripping and plopping through the sticks. Try the rice. That was gluier and by holding the bowl near her chin she could imitate them and shovel it in efficiently. They were wiping their bowls. She alone still had food at her place. Now they were wrapping the bowls. At least her rice was nearly gone. More clapping and clanging. She tried to stand when they sprang to their feet, holding their neatly wrapped bowls. Hogen pushed her back down. She felt like a dunce in the corner—mustn't cry. They were wiping the benches. She still hadn't finished.

"Good evening. Why don't you just pick it up and knock it back?" said a human voice, in a recognizable tongue. And now she really could have cried. "I'm Shonen, Go Roshi's son. You must be Annie. I'm enchanted." His smile crinkled behind the heavy frames of his oversized glasses. Uh, uh—she was bumbling and pumping his hand in how-do-you-do. His hand moved with his arm like a dead bough barely attached to its tree trunk. She must try to remember that the Japanese don't shake hands, but now the familiar pumping gesture, the human contact, and the easy smile lent her relief.

Patiently, he showed her how to eat every grain of rice, how to wash the oryoki by pouring the water from bowl to bowl. Then she should then drink it in order to waste nothing. Finally came the elaborate bowing and the folding involved in rewrapping the wretched things. He invited her to his room for tea—green tea and dried rice cakes. The latter looked and tasted like varnished cardboard, but she was grateful for the gesture. His room was tiny, scarcely bigger than her own hole, but bursting with books, manuscripts, and reams of practice calligraphy strewn in an arc around the desk. From the corners of the bookcases iron nails protruded at unexpected angles displaying wrinkled robes drooping in baggy folds.

He struck a match, then lit a stick of incense and a cigarette. Casually he stuck the incense in a brass bowl in front of a plastic Buddha, and reverently drew on his cigarette in a moment of appreciative silence. From outside came a voice, *"Shitsurei shimasu"* ["Excuse my rudeness"; "I beg your pardon."]. He jolted stiff upright and quenched the cigarette. "Hai." Hogen gently slid the door on its tracks, peeped slowly around its perimeter and grinned. "Yaa." Shonen threw the cigarette at him. With a loud laugh Hogen thanked him and lit it himself.

They began to chatter animatedly in Japanese. She heard her name mentioned often but was content just to lean against the bookshelf and observe. They looked comical. Two round bald heads nodding, living a fourteenth-century existence enveloped by the cloying clouds of HiLite King-size Filter-tip tobacco sticks. They reminded her of schoolboys puffing in the loo, the same innocence in the flagrant breaking of the rules. The conversation turned to her. They became giggly as they discussed her. This blue-eyed Scotswoman was to become a monk in a mountain temple of remote Northern Japan. Unbelievable!

It was only seven o'clock in the evening but to Annie it felt like midnight and still they all smiled. She smiled. She felt strained, her teeth clenched into a perpetual grin. "Please take a bath." All three nodded their heads and made polite noises. They led her to the bath. She wondered if everything was to be an ordeal. All the simple things that add some security to daily living seemed to have been uprooted—the strange ways of eating, of sleeping, of going to the toilet. Now even bathing was stripped of its familiarity. They found it hilarious to have to instruct a grown woman on how to take a bath.

They explained how a fire is lit under one huge bath that serves the entire community. Each individual then soaps and washes outside the tub from a little basin and when properly washed and rinsed, climbs in and lets the heat seep through knotted sinews. She tried to follow their instructions but that "soothing heat" singed her testing toes. She found it simply impossible to lower her body into the torrid liquid. Instead, she stood there, wet, freezing, covered with goosebumps. To hell with it. She quickly changed back into her clothes.

She cursed these uncivilized brutes as she groped her way back to her cell. There she dragged out the heavy, damp-smelling pads, her futons, and further piled up a heavy wad of assorted bedding. Strange—only one sheet. Already fully dressed, she added a woolly hat and scarf. Then, equally prepared for a Himalayan trek or a night's sleep, she lay down and hauled the bulk of the spreads over her body. She was on her back and wondered if she could even turn over under the weight. She stared at the void where the ceiling must be. In her stomach she felt a black hole as black as the void above her.

Did she have any idea of what she was undertaking here? Yet, gazing into that void, she felt that somehow her whole life had been leading up to this moment. It was no accident that she had stumbled upon a reference to this remote monastery. It was something that sooner or later she had to do. She must try. She must really throw herself into this. Still, she thought, what wouldn't she give right at this moment to be seated in front of an open fire with a wee dram of whisky in her hand.

Morning came quickly, insistent and cold. Bells were ringing. Vainly in her sleep she tried to dismiss them. Hogen was at the door, reading from a scrap of paper that said, "I show you get dressed." What was he to show her? She already met the "get dressed" requirement, having slept fully clothed. She opened the door wider. He was making squealing noises and obviously in a hurry. When she still couldn't understand, he started dragging her clothes off. Her first reflex was to belt him one but she reasoned that he'd hardly threaten her virtue at five o'clock in the morning in a bustling monastery. The sounds of washing and tooth brushing just outside gave further reassurance.

He pulled a parcel in from the corridor and shook out a kimono, vigorously gesturing that she should put it on. He showed her how the right side slipped under the left, then how to loop it up with various strings, seal it with a *majiku bando* ["magic band," borrowed English words for one kind of belt to tie up a kimono] and make sure not to let the lapels bag. This, he emphasized, was most important but it seemed to her just another of their ridiculous trivialities. Still she chuckled at the idea of a man dressing her so platonically, even maternally. As he patted the lapels flat on her chest it was apparently without consciousness that this was a woman's chest at all. Could there really be some corner on the earth where she might be free of her sex?

During her first few days her sense of time became completely disoriented. Each day seemed eternal and she always doubted whether she could survive until the next one. The year she had promised seemed unthinkable. Somehow she'd have to change that. Maybe, she thought, her aversion to the whole project was caused by the staggering number of fresh demands. While everything was new there was still a depressing absence of stimulation. Nothing really happened. She wanted out. That was all she knew. She was cold and bored and ravenously hungry. There were no heaters and it was December. She could never finish her meals on time so she opted for minute portions. No wonder she was hungry.

Today she was up at five A.M. to splash her face in the icy water of an outdoor basin, then wash by the light of the moon. Next came the *"ichi ni san shi"* [Literally, "one two three four," used to count movements in the morning calisthenics performed at some monasteries.] frenetic morning exercises, everyone roaring the count together. By half past six she found herself outdoors, sweeping the grounds. She stopped for a moment, fascinated by the raw red of her toes, like so many frozen sausages squelching round the thongs of the geta. Perched on those wooden platforms and in dawn's grey light, she could have been a geisha stepping down from her carriage after a night's work, not a gaijin with a bamboo twig stabbing listlessly at fallen leaves. She stared at her feet. "It's all wrong. I don't belong here."

"That's all wrong." She was startled to hear her thought echoed in curt Japanese accents. "Sweep like this." He demonstrated jerky little side whips with all the motion in the twig, the handle almost rigid. "There is a Zen way to sweep."

She muttered to herself. "I wonder if there is a Zen way to knock your arrogant block off."

A Zen way to sweep—this is humiliating, truly humiliating. Upstairs she had tried to dust and sweep the hondo. The first swipe of the duster had ripped a hole in the *shoji* screen [sliding paper door]. Then she had swept against the grain of the tatami, instead of up and down. She seemed to do everything wrong. Five days. Had she really been here only five eternal days? She said she'd stay a year. She questioned if it was humanly possible to endure a full week.

The daily routine varied between washing and sweeping inside and weeding and raking outside. It was a positive thrill to be allowed to spend one whole day sawing firewood but then she was back to sweeping and raking. Daily she cleaned the outbuilding altars and the bones room but they were never dirty. She had, after all, only cleaned them the day before. Every day she wiped away imaginary dust, dipping her hands in the icy water to scrub some candlestick that might in a few months more have become dingy. Oh, miserable existence and no one with whom even to share a laugh about the insanity of it all. Why? Why in the name of all that was sane and rational had she chosen to come to this godforsaken place and why was she staying on?

On her fifth day at the monastery they told her she would have her ceremony. Up to that time she had only seen Go Roshi at meals which were silent and stiff. He looked at his food. He ate his food. He bowed to them. They bowed to him. He went to his room where she could hear a television blaring.

What kind of man was he? She knew something of his story. He and his twin brother had been the eldest of a large farming family. His brother was destined to take over the farm and Roshi to become a priest. The family was very religious. When he was about eleven years old, his twin was accidentally shot. It was no one's fault, but Roshi, as the eldest son was then expected to inherit the farm and fulfill his filial duties. He protested that he still wanted to be a priest. They refused to let him go. He chopped off his finger to show his earnestness. They still refused, so he ran away from home, a terrible disgrace. He took to the roads, not yet even a teenager, wandering and chanting all the while, "Namu myo ho renge kyo." He roamed around the country questioning various Zen masters on the meaning of life and death. Finally he went to Daiko who said "When apples are ripe and falling from their branches, what will you do?"

"Gather them," said Roshi. Daiko gave him a basket and showed him to the orchard. He remained for thirty-five years.

The clock struck eight as he walked in. He walked over to the stacked benches, straightened one by about an inch, then came over to the waiting monks. That disturbed her. Surely he should be always collected and unaffected by such unimportant details as crooked benches. Strange. Is he really enlightened?

The lights were off. They sat in two rows. The shoji was open allowing harsh winter sunshine to stream across the passage and on to the benches. It lit Go Roshi's face. He was laughing and speaking animatedly. She couldn't understand the words so she just watched. The others sat formally. They didn't look at him. Eyes averted, they stared at the benches. Were they asleep or awake? They seemed to be having no communication with Roshi. He was gaily laughing and carrying on a monologue. Still they stared stonily at the grain in the wood. She couldn't help but smile. Perhaps her smile was inappropriate.

The story of his youth kept going around in her mind. The sunshine picked out each pore on his face, like a myriad of minuscule halos. As he laughed his heavily repaired teeth glinted golden. She thought of him at twelve years old, alone, on pilgrimage. It made this venture into Zen seem all the less probable for an ordinary person like herself. The little finger of his left hand was indeed a stub. But rather than indicating the strong religious conviction of a mere boy, could it not just as well have been the bad temper of a thwarted child, frightened and confused at the now real prospect of his own mortality? She preferred this version.

He mentioned her name several times during his talk. No one translated. She was slightly disconcerted but his continual smile reassured her that any *faux pas* she may have committed was not unforgivable. He stopped speaking, stared at her, laughed and addressed her in English. She was flabbergasted. She thought he knew no English. "Are you ready for your ceremony?"

"Ah-wh-ceremony, what ceremony?"

"You become priest ceremony."

She knew this would come sooner or later but she had thought later. "Well, er, um, I mean, well don't I have to know something, believe things?"

"No, the less you know and believe the better."

"Well, does it mean I can never leave?"

"No, leave when you please."

"But I mean, what do I promise?"

"I only ask that you request permission for outings."

"Really? Well, I suppose I'm ready then."

This was mystifying. A priest with no beliefs or commitments? Well, what was a priest anyway? Are they making an exception for her? It was extremely puzzling and not at all the Holy Orders and ordination of the Catholicism she had known in Glasgow. He clapped his hands in childish glee and dragged a huge cardboard box from behind the shoji. He unwrapped it slowly, with the precision and intentness of someone disassembling a bomb. He wound up the string and tucked it in his sleeve. Then he presented her with her robes and told her to try them on. His sense of delight was irresistible. To her it felt like Christmas and playing "dress-ups" all rolled into one. Swathed in the long kimono, swags of silk, barefooted, she floated back and forth the length of the corridor. She struck several model poses and Hogen instantly transformed himself into a Vogue photographer, focusing and clicking his imaginary camera to record the latest in temple fashions. The silent, empty corridors echoed with their hilarity.

Then Go Roshi went away for a few days and she felt miserable again. Misery seemed always to lurk a breath away. She felt so cut off. The lack of communication felt like a darkness around her, as if her entire world had sunk in on her, or her eyes were failing and the simple things she could take for granted had disappeared. The monks tried to talk to her, consulting their dictionaries. They said they felt comfortable with her, then conferred for the right words to tell her they were glad she had come to Shodoji. She felt a real affection for them. They were drawing her from some ancient place within herself, as if they had been her childhood playmates, her home before her home, and yet they seemed so totally foreign and unreachable. They treated her so kindly but could they possibly have conceived of who she was or the world from which she came? Nevertheless, she was here and so were they, and if their pasts and futures were also present, they were at least for the time being suspended.

Mochian came into the corridor carrying a tray. A serene smile played around his mouth. Putting down the tray, he prostrated himself on his knees. Bowing his forehead to the ground, slowly, reverently, he greeted her. Stunned, she nodded her head and mumbled. He grabbed her hand, pumping it vigorously, "Zank you, zank you." She wished she knew what she'd done. Instinctively she said, "Er, ah, you're welcome. Oh, thank you, mm, pleased to meet you." He was bowing again. Then he served everyone green tea. They all knelt on the bare brown boards. The day had turned grey and drizzly, looked as if it would turn to sleet. He was very pleased to offer her chocolate biscuits. It was obvious from his delight that they were procured for her benefit. Notwithstanding, the other monks dove into them, delighted with this unaccustomed extravagance compared with their usual frugal fare.

On the day scheduled for her ceremony, Shonen came to her room and told her to wear a white kimono. "And these socks—*tabi*. Ha, but your hair, no one has shaved your head yet. Hurry up." She gulped. Her thick dark hair had always been a source of pride for her. Still, she thought, I'll never have the chance to be bald again and I'm not that attached to just hair, so no problem.

"Okay? Shave your head okay?"

"Yes, fine. It's a nuisance anyway."

"Ah so, ah so. You not usual woman." That made her laugh and she found that she felt quite cheerful about it.

He began with the clippers. Her long locks looked so forlorn, so dead, strewn on the wood. They no longer seemed to have any connection to her. Sad. Now her head felt light. She clasped her hands to it. Naked. Bristling. It's as if a part of herself had been shorn from her, not a mere appendage. Shonen gathered the locks up, still in a hurry. She could only stare. So much for bravado. Shonen was hurrying her but paused for a long stare. "Ii ne, it suits you. Hee, hee, but you are not usual woman."

He doesn't know that she doesn't even feel like a woman any more. "What in God's name am I?"

"Please, fast, fast, fast. You now become a priest. In ceremony, repeat after me Japanese words."

"But, Shonen-san, what do they mean? I must know what I'm saying. This is so important."

"No, Miss Annie, words are not important. You cannot really make promise for you are not free. Do ceremony now and you begin life, where promise will naturally become itself. Come. Come. Never mind. Words are only words."

Well, then, why the hell do the ceremony, she thought. She could feel herself beginning to get angry. The Buddha is not a god but the place teems with statues and altars to him. And why all the formalities and petty regulations if one is supposed to become free? So much foolish ritual and bowing and—she was getting crosser and crosser. Her hand rubbed across her bald head. "I won't cry, I won't cry." She held back the tears and a small voice to whom she really didn't want to listen advised that she'd get nowhere by endless questioning and rejecting. This wise and unwelcome small voice admonished that the only way to understand this thing is not by analysis but by immersion. She reminded it that immersions have resulted in drownings.

Shonen hurried her into Hondo. The room smelled of straw mats and incense, a soothing smell. She breathed it deeply and felt calmed. She decided to avert her eyes from the gaudy altar, the huge vases of fake flowers: purple, red, orange. She could see no beauty in the statues. They were looming, grotesque with rows of candles and offerings. But all wrong. It felt like a pagan mockery of the Catholic churches of her childhood. She felt she had stumbled once again as an unwilling participant into the religious world she had left behind, but now as an accomplice to uglier, unconscious prejudices.

Shonen was signaling her to bow, to prostrate herself before the images. Somehow she managed. The ceremony seemed a blur. She remembered repeating in a whisper Shonen's cues. Cold drafts played upon her head. The roshi was waving in her face something that looked like a horse's tail and chanting. Everyone joined in, voices loud, the drum pounding, too primitive. They unnerved her. Their huge voices were booming with wild energy. Roshi gave her a paper with elaborate *kanji* [Chinese or Japanese characters] and intricate folding. The horsetail was waving again. The shouting finally ended. She felt faint. Now she was a Buddhist priest although no one would tell her what that was. They went downstairs for tea. Her new priestly name meant "mirror heart." Everyone said this was a good name. Still they all continued to call her Annie.

Mochian was smiling. "One moment pleez." He rooted through kimono sleeves and hidden pockets, chuckling to himself. "Pleez," he said and thrust a bar of chocolate into her hands. *"Omedeto gozaimasu,"* he bowed his head to the floor. Shonen translated this as "Congratulations" then continued, "You will make excellent priest. I very happy you do us the favor become this temple priest. We grateful. Thank you. Thank you. You give pure energy." This was embarrassing. She felt such a hypocrite. Well, it can't be helped.

The ceremony over, it was time for soji again. *Soji* is practically the first word she learned in Japanese and one she now wished she could forget. She went up to the third floor and climbed over the huge Buddha, dusting and polishing him. She wore five layers of undershirts and sweaters but still felt chilled into her very bones. The Buddha was not smiling, only enormous, awesome. She stared until she was too cold to stay longer.

She drew back the rice paper blinds from the window. It was starting to snow but the sun still made a bright square on the floor. She stood in it, vainly wriggling her toes to try to warm them. It felt good and the snow was beautiful, fluttering in the sun. But all this aesthetic appreciation wasn't getting the blasted soji done. She shuddered at the prospect of wringing the rag in icy water to wash the altars and floors.

Cleaning before breakfast was even worse. For this she began at one end of the corridor with a wet rag, hands on the cloth, hips high in the air, and ran down the passage with her weight on the wet cloth. It was effective but she was running in the smear of the water which instantly began to ice. Her feet froze and stuck as she ran. Each step felt like the sensation of ripping a bandage from a still raw cut. She asked herself if she could possibly put up with any more of this. Still, the thought kept throbbing in her mind. "I'm now a Buddhist priest."

She finished cleaning and hurried to put away buckets and dusters. Dashing into the first snow of the winter, a snowflake landed on her bald head. It pierced, then dripped, a totally new sensation, rather shocking. At first, she had no idea what it was. She had never before felt a snowflake melt on her bare scalp. It was a new sensation but not exactly the stimulation she craved. In fact, time had never seemed so heavy. Her imagination worked overtime trying to fill in the gaps left by lack of stimulation. She imagined hundreds of wonderful futures, retraced favorite memories, plotted out ways of coping with the present.

When this approach failed, she asked herself the question: "Why am I here?" She tried to avoid the question, forget the "why" and just be here. But then she'd ask, "Why am I here at all, not just in Shodoji, Japan, but here in this world, this century, why alive at all?" She knew that this game of playing diversionary tricks with her mind was an effort to avoid facing her misery. Yes, she was plain miserable. Now she'd gone and admitted it. MISERABLE. "I want out. OUT now. Calm down, Annie, don't admit it. Your mind is going in circles. No one to talk to, to confide in." But she knew that even if there had been such a person, the objective situation wouldn't be altered a bit. The place would still be frigid and with just as much detestable soji. She was forced to admit it wasn't purely the dismal situation that troubled her. It was her subjective relationship with it. "I must be strong. I must learn to stand by myself."

In her meditations during zazen she had counted her breaths from one to ten. When she lost count or her mind became distracted, she returned to one. She had yet to get as far as ten. Her record has been six breaths. It was frustrating. It's my mind, she thought, yet I can't quiet it to count as far as ten. She recalled the complex calculus problems her mind had fathomed at the university, the theories it had probed. The mind defies time and space by holding facts that no longer exist, facts from when she was young, from hundreds of years ago, events she never experienced, from places she'd been and hadn't been. It can hold them, more vividly than the present, affect them and be affected by them, can apply them, relate them, sift them, and arrive at new conclusions. This wonderful mind. But she couldn't count ten breaths. Simply incapable. She did breathe slowly. It took a while. Still, it couldn't take more than a minute. For one mere minute she could not still her mind. It flew off on a thousand fantasies. This might be forgivable, but why does it abandon its task to replay tired conversations or wonder if the black stuff at breakfast was seaweed or were her mother's favorite tulips white or yellow? It seemed to be mocking her.

She sat straight and stared at the sliding screen before her. One breath, two. Was that a cat she heard? She remembered that she liked cats. She remembered…and was gone. "This most intimate possession, belonging only to me, is not mine at all. It's downright annoying. Which is the mind? This incessant nonsense babbler? The prattler or the one struggling to shut it up, to drown it with numbers? But that's not right either. Shonen said it can't be forced. But if it won't stop spontaneously and can't be forced, it would seem to me to be a deadlock. Yet I think that's too rational an approach. Well, damn it. I am a rational being."

The next morning Annie went to her first dokusan. What could she say to Go Roshi? Shonen explained dokusan procedure to her. She should prostrate herself at the door, walk in, bow, more steps, another bow, up the aisle, prostration, slide forward, gassho, recite the koan. The exit is approximately a reverse process except for the position of the hands. When Hogen explained it to her it seemed clear. Now she stood at the door, Shonen behind her to translate. The Roshi wasn't looking at her, but into space, or perhaps she should say through space. His gaze did not seem to have an object but rather to slice. It was at once penetrating and vacant. His robes were patched purple silk. Across his knees he held a stick. She'd heard of masters beating their students and even a story of one getting his leg broken in dokusan. Here before her was the same dear man who had laughed with her, made her feel at home, but now he was frightening. He might do anything.

But her first dokusan turned out to be rather an anticlimax. Nothing had happened. He made the same innocent small talk anyone might make. When she went again the next day she expected to be calm. Yet standing at the door, her stomach felt sick. Behind him loomed the immense statue of his teacher. The lighting was from the base of the statue, giving it sinister shadows. Behind her stood his son ready to translate for them.

Again she bowed in all the wrong places, or at least felt that she had. This time he did not smile. A small hoarse voice, hers, spoke her koan. Why did she feel dwarfed by these presences? He's only human and a very kindly human—well, usually. Her temples were throbbing. Having said her koan, she waited. He paused an uncomfortably long time, cleared his throat. "You must work now on muji koan. Become one with muji. Never let go of muji. Throw away your head. Stop reading. Don't concern yourself with the meaning of muji, become muji. Let it fill you like a great piston pounding up and down in your belly until you feel that you'll explode." She wanted to ask what muji was but had no voice and anyway, she knew she was not to be concerned with the meaning.

"But if I don't know what it is, how can I lose myself in it?"

"Never leave it, practice this koan when you clean, when you eat, when you go to the toilet. You never know when or where satori may strike you."

This was puzzling. He explained a bit more but nothing stuck in her mind except "I don't understand. He's beaming, he's finished."

"*Gambatte kudasai.*" ["Good luck." / "Please do your best." / "Don't give up."]

She returned his smile, feebly, not knowing what she should be doing. He rang the little brass bell to dismiss her.

Outside the door she pounced on Shonen. "What IS muji?"

"Nothing."

"What?"

"I'll explain later, now it's time for sutra service."

With gongs and drums pounding, the monks' voices chanted the sutras. Her mind pounded in matching turmoil. Did he mean to become muji? Become nothing? Her body was quite solid and material, but that was a contradiction in terms.

After breakfast Shonen called her into his room. Now it seemed to her to have a cozy homeliness about it. The altar needed dusting and fresh flowers. A Bank of Tokyo calendar was peeling off the walls. No windows. His long robes still hung at odd angles about the room. He was smiling and peeling an apple. "It's puzzling, isn't it? Here, *dōzo* [help yourself], this Nagano-ken apple. Most delicious. I must tell you first that your koan originated with a famous monk named Joshu. One day a young monk asked Joshu, 'Does a dog have Buddha nature?' Joshu answered, 'Mu.' Mu is a negative answer. It means no, nothing, nothingness. But in Buddhism everything has Buddha nature so how can Joshu say 'mu'? You live in world of things, phenomenal world where everything appears separate. I am here, you are there, apple is there. There is no connection. At the same time, there is essential world. There is no thing. No separate thing."

"I don't understand."

"Everything is atoms, yes? Atoms are particles. Now scientists discover these act both like wave and particle." This rings a vague bell for Annie. "Think particle has decided place, size, time. How can it be both? How infinite and finite? This is impossible. Impossible to our minds because our minds can only think in our concepts. Our concepts come through our language from our experience. Our senses say apple and Shonen and Annie are separate. This is practical. This is functional. This works so we say it is truth. Science of Newton worked so everyone said it was true. Newton's science was science of separate things, of finite molecules and atoms. You understand?"

"I'm listening. Go on."

"Newton's science still very useful. When you build car or oven, you want Newton science. But it is not whole truth. In everyday world we not experience whole reality. So no understanding, and we become very attached to finite things. But for twenty-five hundred years Buddhism has taught this world what modern science now realizes. How? No special tools, computer, science buildings. Through zazen many people experience for themselves, in own body, this reality."

By now Shonen was excited, passionate. She didn't think this was in him. "Muji reality and separate. Shonen, Annie, apple reality are also not separate. Like front and back of cloth. The threads are the same, the appearance is different. But even when scientist knows this, he is not enlightened. Why? He only know with his head. No experience. Not know with whole body, with every cell. So he still not free. Poor scientist. He need so many experience tools to understand, and even then not liberated. But you can understand, Miss Annie. You need no scientific building, only patience to sit and sit and sit. Many people have kensho early, sometimes after only a few weeks, but then must train a long time so understanding goes into cells."

She asked Shonen to explain what kensho is. "Kensho is first see essential world, of yourself, you Miss Annie. First time you see yourself. For some people this is very deep and at once understanding everything. Most people this is shallow, the beginning. You work on muji koan until kensho, then train with other koans."

"Shonen, when did you have kensho?"

"Not yet, Miss Annie. I try very hard but still muji is my koan. Many young priests come and have kensho quickly, but I am patient. Last month my father give sesshin and man, fifty-one years with muji koan, have kensho. My father crying. This man, so pure heart, so beautiful kensho."

She felt discouraged—fifty-one years. She munched her apple. "But you understand so well, Shonen."

"That my problem. I'm like scientists. My father say, 'You understand with head, now with your belly.'"

The smell of incense drifted towards her, her mind drifting with it. It was only eight in the evening but she was nodding off. She would have liked to talk longer with Shonen but decided to take a quick nap before it was time to work again. Nothingness. Hmmm. She repeated in her mind. "Nothingness, nothingness." "Well, Shonen, maybe your cells don't know what you're talking about, but you've helped me. Thanks." Shonen bowed, then waved.

Back in her room she dropped heavily on her futon. She was trying to puzzle the whole thing out but dropped into a deep slumber. "Miss Annie, Miss Annie," Hogen was calling her. "Soji, soji." She felt she had slept only ten minutes but saw that it was closer to two hours. This is crazy. There must be some more civilized, more human way of doing this. Are these men all masochists? She grabbed her duster and scampered off.

The cold grew more bitter as the days grew shorter. Kindo had given her a bunch of flowers. The water in the vase froze and broke it. She washed out her underthings but they froze before they could dry. She was used to winter but had always observed it through the window of her centrally heated home, without any real contact with the season's rigors, with a fur coat, an efficient subway system, and no inclination to outdoor sports. Idly she wondered if the itchy spots on her feet could be frostbite. She thought, "I shouldn't let my mind drift like this. Nothing, nothingness, mu." Should she be hypnotizing herself? The sheer drudgery of the work would be enough to hypnotize anyone.

The monthly zenkai began. For this event, people from the area, and the more devoted practitioners from a distance, assembled for one day and two nights of extra meditation, dokusan, and talks by the roshi. Hogen instructed her in the appropriate clothing to wear. He liked to fuss about her, a real mother hen. Now he made sure her collars all overlapped properly, straightened and tugged everything into place, then stepped back a moment to admire.

She went to dokusan again. Go Roshi said she was to come alone. They struggled in his primitive English. He asked, "What do you make of muji?"

"Your son explained to me many things about muji and Buddhism and enlightenment, but frankly I can't make anything of it. I repeat 'nothingness' whenever I can remember to but don't see what it's all about." She didn't add: but did wonder how such monotonous reiteration could lead to any enlightenment at all.

"Hmph, my son doesn't know a thing about Buddhism." That astonished her. "Your approach is incorrect. You must use the Japanese syllable 'mu,' never mind the meaning, only concentrate, pour your entire being into it. When you scrub the floors..." He startled her by jumping up, puffing and panting a pantomime floor wash, heartily wringing his rag and scrubbing with an energy that left her feeling limp. "That is muji, when you wash your face." Miming again he splashed water, then jumped back in mock horror. "Ah, it's freezing. *Brr, brr.* That's muji. Oh, today I'm exhausted." He stretched. "Ah, a nice snooze." He flipped on his cushion and snored outrageously. "That's muji. Do you understand?"

"I don't know."

"Good. That's best and 'don't know mind' is best. Hold on to 'don't know mind' and fight with all your might." *Ding a ring ding.* He shook the little hand bell. She was dismissed.

"Hold on to 'don't know mind,'" he had said. Yet apparently that's not the same 'don't know' as Shonen's. He said his son didn't know a thing about Buddhism. That's puzzling, too. Shonen was obviously very learned in Buddhist matters. The whole business baffled her. Why can't it all just be straightforward and logical?

She went back into the meditation hall. She loved its smell. Tonight, for zenkai, they were using little oil burners. The tatami felt warm, almost alive beneath her feet. The hall was filled to capacity. She was pleased with the sight. It was more encouraging than the usual handful of monks, huddled, half-freezing in the semi-gloom. The people gave her energy, and the roshi's words were fuel. She stared at the shoji screen before her. *Mu, mu, mu.* The patterns of the shoji began to dance in an odd way. Her eyes were unfocused, though concentrated. The effort made the shoji seem to shine. Her breath came slower and slower. *Mu, mu.* She felt as if she was at the bottom of a clear pool. Sounds were muffled, words and sentences floating on the surface. She was at the very bottom, looking up a great slow distance at the light. *Mu, mu, mu.* It came from the pit of her belly. A tangible peace was settling through her body, a vast stillness, a hollow, booming mu. *Bong. Kinhin.* ["Kinhin" is slow walking in a meditative state between sitting periods.] They walked in silence twice around the room and were seated again.

After zazen they had ookyo. Usually she found ookyo loud, even unpleasant, but this time she was very moved. She watched Hogen's pudgy little face. He was chanting with his whole heart. His eyes kept puckering. They were all totally wrapped up in this. Although the incense, the words, the costumes were still completely foreign to her, her eyes slid fondly across each ardent face. She felt she might cry but didn't.

Afterwards, they had tea. Forty-five people knelt in lines behind their benches. One by one each person stood to give a short self-introduction. One elderly man with gold teeth and thick glasses spoke too long. He drummed his fingers and laughed at his own jokes. No one else laughed. Shonen translated for her. The people clapped. The golden-toothed finger-drummer asked if it's true that the foreign lady would really do takuhatsu. Shonen asked her. "Tell me again what takuhatsu is. I've forgotten."

"Miss Annie," he whispered back. "You must learn this word. *Takahatsu* is begging."

She was indignant. "Of course I'll go." Did he think because she was a woman or a foreigner that she wouldn't?

"Ah so desu ka." He said prolonging the syllables meaningfully. The introductions continued around the room. She recovered from her outrage and began to wonder just what this begging could involve that her decision to do it produced such obvious awe in the assembly.

Zenkai finished and a handsome, elderly man signaled her to follow him. Again it was that strange gesture that looked more like "go away," but his eyes were a friendly "pleezu come zis way." She did. He, Shonen, a plumber, and a skinny, awkward computer programmer blessed her ears and her tongue. It was a small bare room she hadn't seen before. Inevitably, they were smoking. They smiled and said their names, which she immediately forgot.

The skinny one pounced first. "Why are you here?"

"He signaled me to come," she said, mischievously.

"No, no, not here, HERE, why are you training?"

She was prepared. She knew sooner or later she'd have to answer this. "I intend to become enlightened."

"Hmmm." He returned to the attack. "Who are you?"

She wondered if she had to put up with an existential cross examination? Who can answer such a question? This scrawny little man was beginning to annoy her. He was putting on probing Zen-master airs. "Do you mean what am I called?" she replied, her voice innocent, her intention insolent.

He paused, unsure of himself, feeling for a trap and took the coward's way out. "Yes."

"I'm Annie Shaw." She smiled. She had won.

The handsome man flashed the computer operator a look that clearly said, "Don't be a pest." Then he made pleasant, inconsequential conversation about her family and her journey. She warmed to him at once. He spoke softly but firmly. When he flicked his ash he'd rest a moment, watch it, and resume what he was saying. It gave an unhurried flow, almost melodic to his manner. He took a long pull on the cigarette. Slowly, with complete attention and a revolving motion, he stubbed it out. He exhaled a long steady stream of smoke. "Miss Annie, do you know you are Buddha?" he said.

"Er, ah, I beg your pardon?"

"You are Buddha."

"Do you mean some kind of reincarnation?"

"No, I do not."

"Well, Buddha died some two thousand years ago, didn't he?" She recalled Shonen mentioning that figure.

"No, the Buddha is alive and before my very eyes. Miss Annie, you are Buddha."

She was flattered but a bit embarrassed. "No, really, I'm just plain Annie Shaw from Glasgow. I can't even sit cross-legged properly."

"Plain Miss Annie Shaw even with weak legs is Buddha. You must know that. You must realize that in your every moment, and every movement, you and Buddha are not different. You have nothing to seek. You are living Buddha. You have no need to search, but you do not know that. You must take my word for it, but you will search in vain, search frustrated until you realize beyond any doubts or questions that you are Buddha completely and that you have never been anything but that."

This was heady stuff. She'd have to think about it. Meanwhile he and the plumber told of how they had reached enlightenment. Her interrogator, the computer-kid, had not yet experienced kensho. She wasn't surprised and felt slightly smug. "I'll show you, you wee ninny. You've read too many Zen stories. You have the banter but not the batteries."

They told other enlightenment stories, remembering this or that character, laughing. They spoke of the monk who was carrying a basin of hot water with great concentration. He bumped into a pole and came to an awakening. Then there was the one who was drinking his soup, saw a potato and his world fell apart. He cried out in the silence of the meal. Another one stared at the sky all night, but believing it was only half an hour, met the dawn with tears. When the roshi came out of his room to wash, the monk was prostrating himself outside the door. He'd been there for an hour, weeping in gratitude. Many stories were not so dramatic. Most people were doing sesshin and got kensho in the roshi's room.

She went to her room extremely excited. Becoming enlightened needn't be a matter of decades in a mountain cave. It could be hers soon. What had he said—that she'd realize she had never been anything but Buddha—the idea was intoxicating. His voice was so authoritative, his manner compelling. That night when she fell asleep her dreams were full of mu.

Next day the roshi suggested that she should buy thicker underwear before takahatsu. He gave Bodhin money and asked him to accompany her to the village. She didn't particularly like him. He was the one who, at the beginning, had corrected her leaf-sweeping. Bodhin had constantly picked on a new young monk, harshly pointing out his mistakes, making a fool of him before the others. She had cringed for him. Often she made the same mistakes but perhaps out of mercy or because correcting her in English was too laborious, usually nothing was said to her. With the young lad he was relentless. Bodhin interrupted meals, services, zazen with a deafening shout, chastising the youth. It seemed cruel when there were so many minute details to remember, none of which were taught systematically. Anyway, they were to go to the village together.

This was the first time she had left the monastery since she arrived. It crossed her mind to make a dash for it and escape now while she had the opportunity. She knew other monks had "leaped over the wall." Could she just disappear, too? Did Bodhin guess what she was thinking? On his lips played a faint enigmatic smile.

The village streets were charming, small, higgledy-piggledy, like village streets in the Highlands. The shops displayed their wares out front in colorful stalls. Everyone seemed to know everyone and, in spite of the bitter weather, chatted comfortably. Occasionally they bowed to Bodhin and

Annie. Bodhin reverently returned the greetings. From the lampposts on every street hung bright plastic and tin decorations in the shape of colored snowflakes. In the afternoon sunlight they looked gay and festive. Bodhin said that they always hung there, different ones depending on the season. She liked them. They were garish but gave every day an air of holiday. Some people stared at her curiously. One shopkeeper asked Bodhin if she was a boy or a girl.

It was a country village but bustling with life. Then they went into a shop where "Jingle Bells" was playing and her heart missed a beat. The air had the crisp tingle of Christmas, even its expectant atmosphere. But this was Japan, Buddhaland, far away from Santa Claus and holly and mistletoe, far from her father's hot punch and her mother's plum pudding.

The next day would be Christmas Eve. She knew she must be strong. *Mu, mu.* It had no appeal, couldn't distract her. She sighed. With twilight came the first snowflakes. Gradually lights flickered on throughout the village. They walked back slowly, silently. She hunched her shoulders but a war of indecision was being waged within her.

They returned just in time for dinner, some kind of seaweed roll, not too bad. After the final clapper sounded, Annie was startled to see Mochian enter the room carrying a tray of soft drinks and a single bottle of champagne. The champagne was meant to be her Christmas celebration. Together the monks began singing "I'm Dreaming of a White Christmas." They all huddled around low benches, looking excited and blowing puffs of icy breath. Mochian opened the bottle. It was only the size of a beer bottle, just a sweet and swift sip for everyone. The tiny taste was merely tantalizing. She would have loved more.

Then the entertainment began. Mochian stood up slowly, breathed deeply, and from the pit of his belly poured forth his song. There was deep melancholy in it, as if the mountains were mourning beside a churning sea. It became wild, tempestuous. He seemed to sing with emotion that was hardly human, rapt, apparently unaware of the watching band, breathless. When he had heaved the last strains from deep in his gut, they all clapped uproariously, almost relieved that his suffering was over. Mochian smiled his usual boyish smile, knelt down at his place, and poured the last drop of his champagne into Annie's empty cup. Her eyes were watering and she could scarcely tear them away from him long enough to ask Shonen, "What on earth was that about?"

"Frogs in a rice paddy at dawn," he said.

"What? It can't be! Are they all committing mass suicide or something?"

He looked at her, puzzled. "No, Miss Annie, no mass, no suicide, just frogs."

"But one can't put that much feeling into just frogs."

"Well, I think Mochian-san likes frogs, also sunrises."

Hogen was next. He gently crooned "Silent Night, Holy Night." The others joined in timidly, Annie croaking along, too. "Round yon virgin, mother and child." Hogen's face was cherubic. "Pleez, Miss Annie, not homeshikuness." But she to her surprise felt at home, a strange home certainly, but the peace of a real home. When it was her turn she sang "God Rest Ye Merry, Gentlemen." She guessed they might be familiar with it and sure enough, they beamed in recognition of her good wish. Soon it was eight o'clock, time to break up the party, and she was struck by its absurdity. This merry band of monks, squatting on straw mats around a bench, hunched against the inescapable cold with this Western woman—it was such an unlikely combination. Yet she knew that in this little Buddhist temple in the snowy mountains of Japan, the Christmas spirit was more genuine than any she had experienced in recent years. Not once until she lay on her futon did homesickness overwhelm her. Then her peace and pleasure crumpled. It was, after all, Christmas Eve.

When she woke in the morning, her quilt was frozen from her condensed breath. For a moment she had no idea where she was. She didn't want to know. She reversed the quilt and hugged her knees to her chin. It was five minutes to five, pitch black and bitter cold. Go on, she thought, have yourself a merry little Christmas Day.

No one in the monastery seemed to realize that Christmas itself is the most important day of the year for Westerners. At Shodoji it was a just day like any other. Soji as usual. Her psyche was prepared to brood but before she could bemoan her condition sufficiently to summon a full-fledged depression, Wakuan bustled in, interrupting her languid dusting of Kannon-sama. "Miss Annie, Miss Annie, vely solly, vely solly, have work for you. Come thees way, pleez."

Her mother always claimed that a change is as good as a rest and with little likelihood of the latter, the former did seem appealing. He led her to a storeroom filled with bundles of dried beans still on their stalks. "Vely solly, now everyone vely vely busy. Everyone make daihannya." This was true. They had spent the past week folding sheets of paper in intricate fan-like patterns, writing on them, then binding them with red paper bands. These daihannyas were amulets sent each New Year to the temple's supporters. She had admired their fine, precise concentration in the folding, then the bold sweeping strokes of calligraphy. They worked all day and late at night after she retired.

"These beans we need by New Year. Will you pleez do? Take off all skins." She felt like the lazy daughter in the tale of Rumpelstiltskin—presented with a room full of straw to be turned to gold and commanded to start spinning. He might as well have asked her to turn the beans to gold. How on earth could she shell them all in a week? "Vely solly." Ah, sure, happy Christmas to you, too, she thought. All of a sudden the dusting didn't look so bad anymore. He showed her the bags and bowls and even gave her a cushion.

Then he slid the door shut. She heard his feet pattering off on the bare planks and then silence. The depression that had been threatening all day hit unbidden. In the feeble light she stared at those mounds of gnarled bean stalks. She screamed and hurled herself on them, weeping and weeping from her guts. All she'd held in, all the "be strong's" and "it's okay, you can do it's" were ripped away in the roaring torrent of her tears. She cried and cried and cried. No one even heard. The gong sounded for lunch. She didn't want to go but had to go. It was Christmas dinner, stringy noodles in hot water and soy sauce soup. Shonen asked cheerfully how it was going. She wanted to spit but was afraid she'd sputter so pretended not to hear and hurried out.

She went to her room and tried to rest but could only think of the beans, so she went back downstairs. There was a musty smell in the room. She began by stripping the beans still in their shells from the stalks and throwing them into boxes. Six o'clock rang for the evening meal. They ate silently as usual. Shonen didn't risk asking her how it was going. She returned to her prison. Outside it was murky, but in that dank, windowless cell it was just the same as it had been at ten in the morning. She worked and worked until her body was limp. She dragged herself back to her room. It was midnight, five hours after her usual bedtime. Her hands were filthy. She didn't wash them or her face or teeth. She took off her outer robe and fell into her futon.

Again it was five A.M. After breakfast there was no break, straight down to the beans. After lunch—the beans. For dinner they had beans. She thought she'd puke but instead returned to the beans. Four hours' sleep, still no bath. The others were working similar hours with the daihannyas, but it didn't seem to take the same toll. None of them had the huge dark circles that sagged below her eyes. They were still human, chatting and joking among themselves. She grew grouchier and grumpier, more and more resentful. Why was she stuck with this job? This was being irrational, of course. The others were laboring just as hard—but beans, dirty beans, in that dark hole, alone. Her fingers, unused to the friction, were blistering. She tried keeping her mind on her koan, "mu, mu," over and over again, tried just to focus there. At times it was soothing, more usually infuriating.

It was the fourth day of the beans. She was progressing but couldn't possibly be finished in time. During those four days she'd barely exchanged a word with anyone, just huffily snapped at Shonen. Anyway, they were all busy. The tiredness gnawed the back of her eyeballs. Her fingers and wrists ached. She hated the others for working hard with such equanimity. That night she looked at the pile, contemplating "accidentally" setting fire to it. Instead she decided to give herself a bit of a treat, have an early night and quit at ten-thirty.

At 10:07 she heard a scuffling sound outside the door. Rats? But no, it was Mochian, carrying a tin tray, "Miss Annie sleepy?" The question was such a grossly inadequate estimation of her condition that she had to laugh. The laugh was too loud, too long; it was a laugh of semi-hysteria but a great relief. Mochian cocked his head to the side and looked a little puzzled but smiled pleasantly and offered her a steaming mug of hot chocolate. It was frothy and sweet. She drank it very slowly without really looking at him or talking, but each sip felt like a long sigh. As she finished she became aware that he had been staring at her. He knelt patiently with the battered aluminum tray, waiting for her to finish. He took her empty cup and scampered away. About five minutes later he reappeared, this time with a mug of coffee, a cucumber sandwich, and a plate of bean paste cakes. Again, from his knees he humbly offered them to her. He knew so little English and yet understood so well that she needed him. This time she wolfed the food down. The bread was dirty from her irretrievably filthy fingers. As she gorged on the bean paste cakes, Mochian started stripping beans. Soon he was working with the same rapt concentration she had seen when he removed chaff from the rice. He seemed unaware of her or anything else. There may be advantages to simple-mindedness, she thought. Annie, you're a bitch. Stop it.

She got back to work, too, energized. 10:30 slipped by, 11 o'clock, 11:15; 11:20. He showed no signs of tiring. She was beginning to feel irritated again. If she didn't keep at it as long as he, she'd feel guilty. But she really wanted to sleep. 11:30, 11:35. She was grateful, but enough is enough. She tried to tell him—okay, you can stop now. He just smiled and nodded. Finally at 12:10 she could stand it no longer and said good-night. He smiled and nodded and said, "good night." Crazy masochists!

The next morning at five he was, as usual, busy in the kitchen. After breakfast she returned to her dungeon. He had managed two-and-a-half boxes of beans. How could he? He mustn't have slept at all. The fifth night he brought her refreshments and disappeared. Shortly afterward she went to bed. In the morning three more boxes had been mysteriously shelled. Mochian, a.k.a. Rumpelstiltskin. Her resentment melted into shame.

On the sixth night he brought her coffee and *miso dango* [kind of rice dumpling made with miso paste]. He began to work. She was determined to keep up with him. As the hour grew later the cold became more intense. He wrapped her in a bright green blanket. She was bleary-eyed but now her heart was in it. Like the disciples at Gethsemane, however, the flesh was weak. She dozed on a box of beans and awakened at four o'clock with a pain in her neck, draped over the bean box and chilled to the bone. Mochian may not even have noticed. He was still working with the same speed and concentration. Finally completion of the task in time looked feasible. On the seventh day at 4:15 they finished. There was a momentous quality about the event. She should have been elated but she only wanted to collapse, take a bath, and cross the whole week out of her mind.

The following day was New Year's Eve, a day that means as much in Japan as Christmas does in the West. For many Japanese it is the occasion for making an annual pilgrimage to a temple, either Buddhist or Shinto. This is usually followed, at least for the men, by a heavy drinking session. Shonen warned her that she should catch a nap after the evening meal. She needed no persuasion. At 11:30 he woke her and told her to put on her ceremonial robes. They went down to the main doorway. Already people were beginning to gather, mostly country people with children whose eyes sparkled with excitement, bundled up warmly. Some little ones were drooping with sleep, strapped to a bent mother's back. The doors were wide open, as always.

The visitors helped themselves to big bowls of sweet black beans. These looked sickeningly familiar. The temple bell, housed at the top of a stone tower under a wooden roof, would begin to ring at midnight. Half a dozen people could easily have stood inside this bell. It is rung by means of a thick wooden beam suspended by chains and rammed into its side. At midnight it boomed into the darkness, across the snow-covered village, echoing off the mountains. Slowly, sonorously it sounded again, then again, one hundred and eight times.

Inu was the bell ringer. She could just imagine how cold his bare head must be. The other monks were inside but with the door open they weren't much warmer. They did the required chants and took turns making prostrations. Then they trailed around the temple offering incense before a multitude of small altars she'd never noticed before.

These were tucked away on little shelves in corners—a smiling bodhi-sattva, a menacing guardian deity, each with a couple of flowers, a candle, and an incense holder. The rituals were becoming familiar to her, but it was the breakfast that surprised her.

Saké the first thing in the morning, before even a bowl of rice! The meal was a feast. In front of each monk were five little plates of mysterious Japanese delicacies. She recognized carrots and fish but nothing else. Even the staples, rice and soup, were special. The rice was pink, mixed with adzuki beans and topped with sesame. The clear soup had carrot flowerets floating prettily in it, as well as ornamental mushrooms, pink whirligig circles. In the middle was a white gluey lump called *omochi*, a kind of rice cake associated with prosperity, celebration, and a Happy New Year.

PHOTOGRAPH TAKEN IN APRIL 1980.

CREAKING TO THE POST OFFICE
ON MY RUSTY BIKE
I SAW ONE PURPLE IRIS
WILD IN THE WET GREEN
OF THE RICE FIELD.
I WANTED TO SEND IT TO YOU.
I CAN ONLY TELL YOU
IT WAS THERE.
—MAURA O'HALLORAN

Epilogue

Statement by Maura's brother Scott

In October of 1982, Maura finally set out to return to the West. Before going to Ireland, however, she planned to tour for two months in southeast Asia, then spend Christmas with her family in Maine. The temple people didn't want her to leave, but the fact that I was due back in school by mid-October gave a good reason for our early October departure from Japan.

On the flight from Tokyo to Bangkok, we met a charming Hong Kong woman who invited us to stay in her apartment in that city for a few days. So we explored Hong Kong and then took an overnight trip to Macao. Hotel rooms were too expensive there, so we spent the night on a huge rock that jutted out from a wall in Macao. We caught up on our sleep the next day on a bus trip through the Chinese countryside, then back to Hong Kong.

Next we flew to Bangkok where we stayed several days at a guest house owned by the Devahastin family, Thai friends whom we had known in Dublin. Here Maura arranged the itinerary for her Asian journey, which was to start with a bus trip to the ancient capital of Thailand in the north, Chiang Mai. She was one of the last passengers to board the bus for the overnight trip so she sat at the front near the driver. When he fell asleep near dawn the bus went off the road killing Maura, the driver, and two other passengers. Although her passport and journal were stolen with her luggage, the police were able to identify her by means of a ticket stub they found in the pocket-like sleeve of her monk's robe. On October 23rd, I received the phone call from the U.S. State Department informing us of the accident. The consul at Chiang Mai arranged for the return of her remains after the cremation at Lapsang.

Maura's ashes are interred beside her father and mother's in Mt. Hope Cemetery in Lewiston, Maine.

Letter of condolence from Tetsugyu Ban to the O'Halloran family

On December 8th, 1979, Maura O'Halloran joined Toshoji Doairyo, and we had a Tokudo Ceremony on December 10th. Her Tokudo name was Daigo Soshin Hikyuni. She began her vigorous training from that day.

On January 5th, 1980, at 6:30 A.M., she left Ueno Station to the Kannonji in Yahabacho, Iwate-ken, with Sato Jiko and Dote Tessen. For thirty days, from January 6th, she trained in strict "Kan-Shugyo" (training in the freezing cold). It was -20°C weather in Morioka where she had her training. She returned to Toshoji on February 6th.

When I was ten, I had my Tokudo Ceremony at Fukuzo-ji in Johoji, Iwateken. My master Fuchizawa Chiaki said, "Zen monks must work 20 hours, and 3 hours for sleep every day." Maura did exactly that.

Our grand master Dogen went to China and to the Tendo mountain for one thousand days, working hard all day, he sat for meditation at night. He slept two or three hours in the sitting position. Maura did the same. She was the modern Dogen.

There was a spring training at Kannonji from May 2nd for five days. Maura reached her enlightenment on the first day. She went in for meditations twice, three times a day, and solved all three thousand koans. We had her Hishinsai (graduation ceremony) on August 7th, 1982.

She requested to become a Tenzo for the fall training, starting from October 1st. Her wish was granted. She completed her circle and left Narita airport on October 9th.

I received an international telegram on October 25th, 8:00 P.M., which said Maura had died in an accident in Thailand on the 22nd...

She had achieved what took the Shakuson [Shakyamuni Buddha] 80 years in twenty-seven years. She was able to graduate Dogen's thousand-day training. Then she left this life immediately to start the salvation of the masses in the next life! Has anyone known such a courageously hardworking Buddha as Maura? I cannot possibly express my astonishment.

—Ban Tetsugyu

October 27, 1982, 11:00 P.M. as I watch the eleventh day moon.

Inscription on a statue dedicated to Maura at Kannonji Temple

Maura Kannon (A brief history)
Miss Maura O'Halloran from Ireland.

On the 10th of October in the 54th year of Showa [1979], at Toshoji Temple she became a nun and completed 1,000 days of continuous Zen practice at Toshoji and Kannonji temples. Her daily practice included three hours of sleeping in the zazen position and twenty hours of devotion to her studies in order to attain salvation not only for herself but also for all people.

On the 7th of August in the 57th year of Showa [1982], she was conferred an authorized certificate of "Enlightenment Achieved."

On the 22nd of October, on her way back to Ireland, at Chiang Mai, Thailand, by some traffic accident her life ended at the age of twenty-seven.

She is given the posthumous name of "Great Enlightened Lady, of the same heart and mind as the Great Teacher Buddha." Miss Maura has been a real incarnation of Kannon Bosatsu to be loved and respected forever.

We dedicate the Maura Kannon Statue here to her extraordinary memory.

Nirvana Day [February 15th] in the 58th year of Showa [1983], by Tetsugyu So-in, founder of Kannonji Temple.

—translated by Shiro Tachibana

Account of Maura's last days in a letter of condolence from the Devahastin family, Thai friends

October 1982

Dear Mrs. O'Halloran and family,

It is with deep shock and sorrow that I write to you about Maire. Please forgive me for not writing sooner, however I found it difficult to begin this letter knowing that you all must feel very sad at this moment. I can say we were all overcome with sadness not just because of the suddenness of her death but because Maire was such a good person, so selfless and pure. We were all overcome by her presence even though she seemed so humble about what she had accomplished; it was quite obvious she had reached a very pure state of existence. Many times Scott would say, "Maire always brings out the best in people." She talked about many things while she was here—about her worry over the fact that you did not like her doing what she did because you feared perhaps in the next life you may not meet. This was her only misgiving. However, now that I have lived in a Buddhist country I feel that Buddhism is not so much a religion but more a philosophy. It tends to fit in with what you believe. Seeing Maire I can only feel confident that if there is a heaven, then surely she is there.

We went to a lot of temples and we did some shopping. Quite by coincidence, Maire's best friend Nina also arrived at the same time. We had a lovely day at the Emerald Buddha Temple, the largest in Thailand. Maire was so taken by it that she returned the next day and spent all day there. At night we chatted mostly. Maire talked about her travels in South America. She said to Fiat that she felt she had a good, full life, and she did not fear death. Every day—I'm not quite sure how often per day—Maire meditated. On Wednesday, Scott, Maire, Sida, and myself went to see the Royal barge procession. Later Maire saw Scott off at the airport [her brother Scott had to return to the U.S. to finish his senior year in high school]. She returned at about 12 o'clock at night. The next day she spent her time shopping. In fact, Maire gave us a beautiful Chinese teapot. On that night (Thursday, the 21st) Maire asked Fiat if she could pray over a relic of the Buddha. This relic has been handed down to Fiat's mother. Maire spent over an hour praying. During her prayer she sang; also she used a bell. After this we had supper. Maire doesn't eat meat, so I made her asparagus soup and she had fried vegetables and rice. During her time here, Maire seemed very happy. Fiat tried to persuade her to wait until the next morning, but she had made up her mind. She left about 7:45. We thought she was taking an ordinary bus, but she decided to take an air-conditioned bus. This bus left Bangkok at 8:30. P.M.

We received your telegram [regarding her death] on Sunday morning. On Monday we phoned the [American] embassy here in Bangkok; however, we finally had to contact Chiang Mai.

It takes about 12 hours to get to Chang Mai (northern Thailand). Maire was the last person on the bus. In fact, she arrived late, so they did not take her name. Maire sat at the top of the bus next to the door. At about 6:30 A.M. on Oct. 22nd the driver fell asleep, and the bus went off the road. Maire died instantly, along with three others...

Fiat and I have both performed Buddhist rites for Maire. We have given food to six monks. They believe all the goodness will go to the person you think of. This Friday, 5th Nov., I will attend a Mass for Maire. I am sending a Mass card with this letter.

Maire talked a lot about your visit to Japan, Ruth, how you found it very difficult to adjust to temple life, and how good you were and what a good sport. She enjoyed Scott's visit and her time in Japan.

I know that you must feel sad that Maire departed so far from home, but I assure you she was among friends; we felt her more like a sister.

Please let us know if there is anything we can do here.

God Bless to you all at this time,
Fiat, Finola, and family [Devahastin]

Maura's "Machu Picchu" letter*

Dear Nana and Mum,

...[We went] for a five-day hike to Machu Picchu. It's through the mountains, far from even any villages, and all along are scattered Inca ruins. I bought a new pair of runners for the occasion.

...So anyway, pretty tired, we caught the train to where the walk starts. There must have been a sale on chickens 'cos there were hens in bags, hens strutting around, a woman holding an apron of baby chicks through the whole journey. We were some of the last on. It was so crowded I spent the whole journey standing on one foot on my rucksack. We were going 2nd class. I had to smile when we were stopped in a station opposite a "tourist class train". In the carriage was a tour of Japanese sitting at their tables all with their white cardboard packed lunches in front of them. They whipped out their expensive cameras and photographed us away. First class may be more comfortable but it didn't look like much fun.

We started the hike and I think it must rank as one of the most wonderful experiences of my life. First we had to cross the river. Of course the bridge was down, so they whooshed us across on a kind of cable thing—great fun. Then we started to climb. It was like desert scenery, lots of cactus with fantasy blooms. We went through a eucalyptus forest and climbed up into the open. The rainy season is starting now and that afternoon it rained just as we came to a straw roof shelter. We huddled underneath with 2 fascinated Indian kids. The raindrops caught on the straws and hung like dewy prisms. In front of us the mountains were huge. They're called fold-mountains and really do go in folds. They were all the one colour and seemed to be velvet ripples except the top which looked as if someone had gone crazy with a chisel. A huge

---

*As this edition of *Pure Heart, Enlightened Mind* was being prepared for printing, a letter from Maura's South American travels, along with the two undated poems that appear in Appendix I, was found. The letter, appearing in an edited version here, is exemplary of Maura's sharp documentary skills. More notably, it allows us to glimpse her elevated attitude about the idea of her own death.

double rainbow came out and framed the tiny five-hut village below. It was the first time I'd ever been above a rainbow.

After the rain we kept walking and everything glistened wet in the sun. That night we built a fire and had a big communal soup. Next morning we started to climb again and passed through an enchanted forest. The trees didn't seem to have a bark only a shiny surface that twisted and gnarled gracefully. All around were ferns, mosses and lichens. From the trees hung lacy beards and the sun shone through all the greens making them irridescent. We picnicked by a stream in a clearing. Here we kept climbing to the 'first pass' or summit of over 12,000 feet. It started to drizzle but we all had raincoats so no one cared. When we got to the top I threw down my rucksack and even after all that climbing, started running around and dancing like a loonie. The view was gorgeous. In the distance the mountains merged and melted with the mist in shades of grey. Now, you think of grey as a non-colour, but this seemed really vivid and with the sunlight playing in places, it became silver. But then the elements chose to reflect our moods. They went crazy. The sun came out, the wind came up, it started hailing and down below burst another rainbow.

There were so many beautiful scenes. If I saw them in a painting I wouldn't like them. I'd find them too contrived, too perfect. Two mountains would sweep down to frame a third and all the rocks would form striations emphasising the downward motion. Or as some clouds would sit cupped in a hollow a band of sparkling snow would provide just the right accent to their nebulousness.

After the summit we went down. Evening was approaching and the mountains were a jagged indigo. I sat high on a rock entranced at the spectacle. The mountains were surrounded by clouds so you could see no ground. The clouds were swirling and climbed the mountainsides only to fall back in curls. It kept rapidly changing—-the whispy white and the strong dark blue. You felt someone must have been here and that was when it was decided that heaven was in the clouds. As I sat there it literally brought tears to my eyes, which no scenery has ever done before.

We saw so many magnificent sights that sometimes it got to be a bit much. Each bend you would come around you find yourself whispering "this is the most beautiful thing I have seen in my life" 'til the phrase lost meaning and there were no more words. There were lakes, and ruins, fields and feathery pampas grass and jungle. The jungle was exciting. It was really lush, full of bamboo, umbrella trees, philodendrums, vines hanging from the trees, exotic flowers and birds screeching to each other. The path was hot mud and we took it barefoot. Most nights we slept by old Inca ruins, in caves or staw cabanas (except the last night). One ruin was the so-called City above the Clouds and it really was.

It was our last full day of walking. A snake crossed the path and some-one killed it. One of the girls, Cassandra-like, said "that's a bad omen." We all pooeyed but it made us feel a bit uneasy. We drifted on, admir-ing the snowy peaks all around. We were getting near Macchu Picchu at this stage and got to the construction site for a new fancy hotel. An arrow directed across the site. It was Saturday so no workers were around to warn us otherwise. The crossing looked like a fairly sheer rock face with a 12,000 foot drop below. Reeny and I were together and thought it looked mad yet the arrow pointed that way and we could see our friends on the other side. We reckoned it must just look worse from the side. On the contrary, it was a lot worse than it looked. We were about half way out, clinging to 2"–3" juttings of rock when our friends turned around, screamed that it was impossible and told us to go back. Apparently it was a series of freak circumstances. Normally there was a plank and a cable there that had come down. The workers put up a barricade but some Italians had taken it down. There had been a load of sand there which made the thing crossable, but as the others had crossed it fell. So there we hung. We had gotten to the stage where it was impossible to go back and impossible to go forward. Reeny was in a worse position than me as she was in the dirt, I at least clung on to solid rock. I will never forget seeing her slide as the whole surface went with her. I was sure she was gone. At that stage I was really scared, the view of the Urubamba river thousands of feet below is frozen in my memory. But do you remember I told you about a guy in Canada who could supposedly see my aura? He said I had a white spirit with me and wasn't just lucky, but blessed. Well, I felt it there. For days we had seen no-one but our group, and suddenly a bunch of French arrived from nowhere, one of which was a soldier. He was on Reeny's side and went out for her. They had to go up a hill, around and down another diffi-cult path to get to me. Meanwhile the leg all my weight was on was get-ting tireder and tireder. Finally he reached me. He took off my rucksack. But then we had to climb and climb the rockface. It was an arduous ascent—three times rock came away in my hand as I tried to pull myself up. It is strange though to see how the mind works. Everything became so unreal that I started joking with the guy in French. I remember one stage I was completely stuck. I was on my left knee with nowhere to put my left foot so that I could shift my weight. I looked down and thought—I could die now. Well, if I am going to go, I am going to go. Then instead of my life flashing, or a last confession, all I could think was how beautiful were the patterns in the rock and how I had never really noticed them before.

Anyway, as you can see, that courageous guy got me to safety. What a relief. But one really good thing came out of it for me. I don't think I will ever be afraid of dying again. Death and I looked in the eye and now I think when my time comes I can go peacefully.

Next day Macchu Picchu looked beautiful in the stark early morning light. We descended almost reverently, the first ones there. It was com-pletely different from being there before with all the tourists. Like so much of the journey, one felt a real sense of godliness. It is the only way to describe that feeling of awe, of power and creation so much greater than yourself. One guy jokingly asked me was it worth it. And you know, it really was (though I really could skip the last part the next time).

Much love and kisses,

Màire

Publisher's Afterword

In 2005, we at Wisdom got an offer to meet with Maura O'Halloran's family about the publication of an expanded volume of *Pure Heart, Enlightened Mind*. We jumped at the chance. A handful of us drove North to Maine, to talk about Maura, and the future of her one-of-a-kind book, with Ruth O'Halloran and her daughters Beth and Kate. Ruth was very close to her death at the time, yet she insisted on meeting the prospective publishers of the new edition, and securing its release, as a last, dying wish.

Our three hosts clearly understood what the book could and should be. But most notable was their loving appreciation for each other, which seemed almost tangible. Ruth had clearly raised up an impressive group of strong, artistic, charismatic women, and had served as a fine role model for them too. But had they all become even more close-knit in response to the loss of Maura?

There's no way to answer such questions, of course, but having just finished reading this book, you know: Maura's words—her very life—had a unique way of reaching into people.

As we've seen, Maura was regarded as a kind of saint in Japan, but she has since achieved a sort of casual, honorary (albeit wholly unofficial) sainthood by some Westerners as well. As Robert Ellsberg writes in his book *All Saints: Daily Reflections on Saints, Prophets, and Witnesses From Our Time*:

In a Buddhist monastery in northern Japan there is a statue of a young Irish-American woman whose memory is revered by many pilgrims. How a Catholic woman came to be honored as a Buddhist saint is an interesting story of "interreligious dialogue." But it also says something about the convergent paths of holiness and their capacity to meet in a spirit of compassionate awareness. [...] Her short road to holiness in a Zen monastery has been compared to the compressed career of Thérèse of Lisieux, the French nun who set out as a child to become a saint. Both young women, having accomplished their spiritual business in this world, promptly departed.

Writer Garth Stanton furthered the idea of Maura as religious inspiration to Buddhists and Christians alike to his peers in Bulletin 66 of *Monastic Interreligious Dialogue*:

Can we not say, in truth, that Maura O'Halloran, formed by the Word, brought that Word, the essence of God, which is Love (1 John 4:8) in silence to the People of the Silence so that they could comprehend it? And comprehend it they did—the statue at Kannonji Temple honoring Maura as a Bodhisattva (a Buddhist saint) attests to that!

If some readers (Christian, Buddhist, or otherwise) are given to thinking of Maura as a saintly guide, it's no doubt because she had—*has?*—such humanity; we can see in her life our best selves, and the way we struggle to let our best selves flourish, in them.

"MAURA SOSHIN O'HALLORAN."
ICON PAINTED BY FR. WILLIAM MCNICHOLS.

As Sumi Loundon, anthologist of many "voices of young Buddhists," writes in a full-page appreciation of *Pure Heart, Enlightened Mind* as "Dharma Classic" in the premiere issue of the Buddhist magazine, *Buddhadharma* in the Fall of 2002:

Some of the most important lessons I've learned from Buddhism haven't come from His Holiness the Dalai Lama or Thich Nhat

Hanh. Rather, they came through reading the personal reflections of the late Maura O'Halloran. [...] Maura's experience spoke to me not only as a woman but as a Westerner. In her simple, down-to-earth way, she describes the lived Zen experience that is much more *human* that it is Eastern or Western. [...] For me, Maura's book is a gift, offering guidance and inspiration. Reading about her life, I'm able to reflect more clearly on my own experience, and to glimpse what I do not yet know or understand.

Readers outside the Buddhist and Christian worlds had taken notice of Maura, too. The book itself was hailed as a "fine legacy" by *Publishers Weekly*, and "a fascinating portrait of an apprentice sage," and "grand adventure" by the *New York Times Book Review*.

While *Pure Heart, Enlightened Mind* has already been translated and published in German, Italian, and French (with new foreign editions sure to come in those and other languages), Maura's legacy seems to be growing beyond the confines of the printed word. In 2002, director Alan Gilsenan, in association with Yellow Asylum Films, released *Maura's Story* ("the story of a young Irish-American woman who became a Buddhist saint"), an extremely well-received documentary for Ireland's national station, RTE. A song for Maura is also to be featured on upcoming album by the popular Irish band, Kila.

Perhaps the most evocative and succinct tribute to Maura also comes to us from the world of popular music. In "Soshin," from his 2001 album *Between the Mountain and the Moon*, singer-songwriter Luka Bloom shares not only Maura's story, but also the way it has moved him, and each person he's told it to:

> The snow begins across the mountains
> Covers the rice fields
> Down below a woman awakens
> Her breath is frozen in the early morning
> Out on the freezing streets
> With bell and bowl she goes

People come to see the face
People come to feel the light
Of an Irish girl

Everything in the world is new
Everybody I tell wants to know you
Soshin ... Soshin ...

She washes noodles by the open window
Wet and soft between her fingers
The air of spring blows on her face
And the moment is eternal
Maura sits in the dark womb-like stillness
She's thinking "How can I die or cease to be?
I am eternal, I am Roshi!"

Everything in the world is new
Everybody I tell wants to know you
Soshin ... Soshin ...

She may not change a blade of grass
Nor light the flame for souls to see
But in this silent Easter morning
She has found a friend in me

An Irish girl

We can't know in what ways Maura's memory will continue to influence readers, but it seems safe to say that she will be "finding new friends" for a long time to come. We hope you consider yourself one of them.

Glossary

atama   head

Ah, so desu ka?   "Ah, really?" / "Is that so?"

banka   Service with chanting, usually in late afternoon

bansan   Evening sutras, chanted after evening zazen or during banka

benkyoo-kai   study group

Bikkuri shita.   "You surprised me."

bodhisattva   A Buddhist enlightened being committed to helping all beings awaken. The term is generally used for any helpful, kind person, but also refers to great archetypal, venerated figures like Jizo or Kannon.

bonpu   the mundane unenlightened state of delusion

buppan   small rice offerings placed before Buddha statues

Busshari-to   Hall of Buddha Relics, where relics of the cremated are enshrined, usually including family ancestors of the congregation

chawan   bean soup

chincho   Literally, "How valuable." More informally, "Thank you for your answer" or "Take care of yourself," called out by the questioner after the response during a mondo ceremony.

chokka (ino)   morning service [same as *choka*]

chonan   eldest son

chosan   morning teaching at which Roshi discusses important matters

Dai hi shin darani   Great Heart of Compassion Dharani; an incantation chanted daily, usually at evening service

dai-genkan   "Great," main entrance hall to the temple

daigo   great enlightenment

daikan   the great cold of the winter

daikon   Japanese radish

Dame "That's wrong."

dameda "no good"

Denpo-shiki Dharma transmission ceremony

Do itashimashite. "You're welcome."

dojo Zen practice place

dokusan interview with Roshi about one's practice

doshi priest officiating at services

dōzo "Here you are." / "Help yourself." / "Enjoy."

Eiheiji one of two headquarter temples of the Soto Zen sect, established by the Founder Eihei Dogen

Fukudoji Happiness Hall Temple

gaijin foreigner

gaijin ookyo foreigners' sutras

Gambatte kudasai. "Good luck." / "Please do your best." / "Don't give up."

gassho Gesture pressing one's palms together, fingers upright, a hand's width from the face, expressing deep respect. This gesture is made frequently in Buddhist temples, often accompanied by a bow.

genmai brown rice

geta wooden platform sandals

Gidaji name of a temple

goeika music Japanese Buddhist music with hand bells and small metal gongs, with short poems of praise sung, commonly performed along with important Buddhist ceremonies. The poems often relate sufferings and pleasures of ordinary life. The goeika performer's heart should be free of distractions and attachments.

goma ground sesame

goma sembei sesame seeds

Gomen kudasai. Instead of knocking at the door, this phrase is called out.

Gomen nasai, ne. "Sorry." (in polite form)

gyo a particular practice, short for *shugyo*

hai yes

hara abdomen / root of energy and emotion

hara-kiri   ritual suicide by disembowelment

hiragana   phonetic Japanese syllabary letters

hondo   hall for teaching and chanting

Honto?   "Really?"/"Is that true?"

ichi ni san shi   Literally, "one two three four," used to count movements in the morning calisthenics performed at some monasteries.

Ii yo.   "Yes, definitely."

Ii yo, nandemo ii yo!   "It's OK! Anything's OK!"

Ii, ne, ii, ii.   "That's good, isn't it? Good, good."

Inaku nara (day)   the day the Buddha left this world, Parinirvana

Ino   Sometimes the priest in charge of the monks, and of all ceremonies. Also used for the leader of service, who calls out the names of chants.

Inochi o suteru   to abandon my very life

insatsu   printing

Iranai.   "I don't need it."

Isshi, konna ishi?   "Stone, this stone?"

isshoken mei   with all one's heart and soul

Itai, itai.   "That hurts." / "It stings, it stings." / "Bitter, bitter."

Jizo-sama's room   The hall dedicated to Jizo Bodhisattva, with an enshrined image. Jizo (Earth Storehouse) especially looks after deceased children and prisoners, along with all those roaming in the afterlife and any people in hellish situations.

jonin   meal-server for meals eaten formally in the meditation hall

jushoku   head priest of a temple

kanji   Chinese character

Kannonji   Roshi's temple in Iwate Prefecture

Kannon-sama   Kannon, the much beloved Bodhisattva of Compassion, who hears and attends to the cries of the world.

kanshugyo   practice in the cold

Kanzeon, namubutsu, yobutsu in...   beginning of the short Kannon Sutra for Protecting Life

katakana   Japanese phonetic script used for foreign words

kensho   flash of enlightenment; experience of "seeing [Buddha] nature"

Kensho shita. "You have realized your Buddha nature."

kiku chrysanthemums

kinhin slow walking in a meditative state between sitting periods

koans Traditional Zen teaching stories, sometimes paradoxical, that are studied in various ways according to the teacher, sometimes during zazen

komugi wheat

kotatsu quilt-covered heated table

kyosoku keisaku-stick used to compassionately strike sitters who might be sleeping or losing concentration

lotus Cross-legged sitting position: full lotus has both legs up on opposite thighs, half-lotus has one leg up.

majiku bando "magic band," borrowed English words for one kind of belt to tie up a kimono

makyo distorted perceptions occurring in zazen

mamemaki bean throwing

macha powdered green tea used in the tea ceremony

Mora-san desu ka? "Are you Maura-san?"

Mora-san go kensho itashimashite. "Maura has seen her Buddha nature."

miso dango kind of rice dumpling made with miso paste

mochi type of pounded rice dumpling or cake

momi chaff

mondo "Dharma combat" ceremony with Zen questions and responses. In Japanese Soto, this ceremony is usually directed not to the abbot, but to the *shuso* or head monk at the end of a practice period.

mozo something that distracts; extraneous thoughts

mu Literally "not," from the renowned koan in which the master answers "mu" to the question of whether a dog has Buddha nature. In many lineages, this is the first or primary koan engaged by Zen students.

Mu-dō? "How is your mu?"

muji the Chinese character for mu; or the koan of mu

Mumonkan *The Gateless Gate,* one of the primary collections of koans

Namu ki e butsu. "I take refuge in Buddha."

Namu myo ho renge kyo "Homage to the Lotus Sutra," chanted as its main practice by the Nichiren sect

Namu san ze sho bu(tsu) "Homage to the buddhas of the Three Worlds"

narikiteru totally being

nemaki nightgown

nirvana liberation from all suffering

obento lunch in a lacquer box with various compartments

obon Summer Buddhist festival for summoning forth restless spirits, and also the remembrance of deceased ancestors or loved ones, in order to nourish and appease them.

obosan ordained priest or monk follower of Buddha

o-genkan entrance where footgear is left

Ohayo gozaimasu "Good morning."

ohigan spring equinox

oishii tasty

ojisan uncle

okusan lady, or wife

Okōchan Mum

okashii strange, or funny; can also mean "cake"

okesa outermost patched robe of the fully ordained priest

O-mairi ni kimashita? "Have you come to visit the shrine?"

Omedeto gozaimasu "Congratulations."

omochi pounded rice cake or dumplings

onnagata female impersonator

onsen hot springs

ookyo sutras

oryoki nestled eating bowls wrapped in cloths for meals in the meditation hall

oryoki wrappers eating bowl wrapping cloths

Oto sasanaide. "Don't make noise."

rakusu bib-like abbreviated monk's robes, also worn by lay ordained [non-monastic] people ramen   Chinese noodles

renshu   "practice" or "exercise," as in practicing music, or a foreign language

Rinzai   one of two main Japanese Zen Buddhist sects, along with Soto

risshin   success

roca   hallway

romaji   English characters

rusuban   caretaker

Saikō!   "The best!"

Sakusha wa [Sakusha wa]   "Oh Teacher," shouted at the beginning of questioning during a mondo ceremony

Sama   an honorific title of high respect

samadhi   intense, effortless concentration; state of complete awareness, not a constant state

Samugi   work outfit

sangha   community; congregation; originally the order of monks and nuns

satori   enlightenment experience

senbei   rice cracker

sensei   common word for teacher

sesshin   week of intensive zazen

sesshin toki   time for intensive zazen

Shiku Seigan Mon   Four Bodhisattva Vows: to awaken all beings, to end all delusions, to master all teachings, and to accomplish the Buddha Way

shin, jin, tome   past, present, future

Shitsurei shimasu.   "Excuse my rudeness"/"I beg your pardon."

Shobogenzo   an important collection of writings by Dogen, the founder of Japan's Soto Zen sect

shoji screen   sliding paper door

shosan   ceremony where all students present questions in front of the assembly

Showa 55   1979–80, 55th year of reign of Showa emperor, Hirohito

soba   buckwheat noodles

soji   temple cleaning

Sojiji   one of the two headquarters temples of the Soto sect with Eiheiji

Soto   one of the two main Japanese Zen Buddhist sects, within which Maura was training

subarashii   splendid

sukiyaki   one-pot dish

sumi-e   ink brush painting

sushoku   head priest

sutras   the teachings of the Buddha, chanted in temple services

tabi   white socks with a split between the big toe and the others

tada   "just," "only"

takuhatsu   formal Zen begging rounds

tamago   egg

tamago saké   egg saké

Tanoshi tanjoobi da to ii desu ga.   "Enjoy your birthday."

tatami   rush-covered mats used as flooring that are usually three feet wide and six feet long

teisho   formal Dharma talk

Ten ni mo chi mo tada ware hitori.   "In heaven and earth there is but I, myself." Statement attributed in legend to the baby Buddha Shakymuni.

tenjin   a refreshment after takuhatsu

tenzo   chief cook of a monastery, a highly respected position

Tetsugyushi   Go Roshi's book

u   something; existence

ue   upper levels; above

umeboshi   pickled plum

unsui   monk undergoing Zen training

Wakaranai.   "I don't understand."

Wakaru?   "Do you understand?"

yakuba   ward office

yasashii hito   gentle people

Yuck, iranai.   "I don't need it." / "I don't want it."

zazen   sitting meditation

zazenkai   a gathering for zazen

zendo   meditation hall

zenkai   Zen meeting or class

zenpan   chin rest

zenzen wakaranai   "You don't understand at all."

About Wisdom

Wisdom Publications, a nonprofit publisher, is dedicated to making available authentic works relating to Buddhism for the benefit of all. We publish books by ancient and modern masters in all traditions of Buddhism, translations of important texts, and original scholarship. Additionally, we offer books that explore East-West themes unfolding as traditional Buddhism encounters our modern culture in all its aspects. Our titles are published with the appreciation of Buddhism as a living philosophy, and with the special commitment to preserve and transmit important works from Buddhism's many traditions.

To learn more about Wisdom, or to browse books online, visit our website at www.wisdompubs.org.

You may request a copy of our catalog online or by writing to this address:

Wisdom Publications
199 Elm Street
Somerville, Massachusetts 02144 USA
Telephone: 617-776-7416
Fax: 617-776-7841
Email: info@wisdompubs.org
www.wisdompubs.org

The Wisdom Trust

As a nonprofit publisher, Wisdom is dedicated to the publication of Dharma books for the benefit of all sentient beings and dependent upon the kindness and generosity of sponsors in order to do so. If you would like to make a donation to Wisdom, you may do so through our website or our Somerville office. If you would like to help sponsor the publication of a book, please write or email us at the address above.

Thank you.

Wisdom is a nonprofit, charitable 501(c)(3) organization affiliated with the Foundation for the Preservation of the Mahayana Tradition (FPMT).

Publisher's Acknowledgement

The publisher gratefully acknowledges the generous help of the Hershey Family Foundation in sponsoring the printing of this book.